PREVIOUS BOOKS BY MARGO MCLOONE-BASTA AND ALICE SIEGEL

*Tom Seaver's Baseball Card Book*
*The Kids' Book of Lists*
*It's a Girl's Game Too*
*Sports Cards Collecting, Trading and Playing*
*The Herb and Spice Book for Kids*

# The Kids' WORLD ALMANAC

## OF RECORDS AND FACTS

**MARGO MCLOONE-BASTA AND ALICE SIEGEL**

**Illustrated by Richard Rosenblum**

**WORLD ALMANAC PUBLICATIONS**
New York, N.Y.

Book design: Helene Berinsky
Illustrations: Richard Rosenblum

First published in 1985

Distributed in the United States by Ballantine Books, a division of
Random House, Inc.

Library of Congress Catalog Card Number 85-50996

Newspaper Enterprise Association ISBN 0-911818-65-0
Ballantine Books ISBN 0-345-32660-1

Printed in the United States of America

World Almanac Publications
Newspaper Enterprise Association
A division of United Media Enterprises
A Scripps Howard company
200 Park Avenue
New York, New York 10166

10 9 8 7 6 5 4 3 2 1

For Jane Flatt, the inspiration
for this book and . . .
For our beloved parents . . .

# Contents

## ACKNOWLEDGMENTS

Our thanks to the many people in libraries, foundations, museums and organizations throughout the world who gave us their help. Special thanks to the following who provided particular help or inspiration. Our gratitude to Anna Basta, Douglas Basta, Vicky Beal, Daril Bentley, Nancy Bumpus, Miriam Chaikin, John F. Curtin, Carol De-Matteo, Debby Felder, Rob Fitz, June Foley, Mark Hoffman, Mike Madrid, Tom McGuire, Annie McLoone, Trish O'Connor, Leah Olivier, Laura Shucart, George Siegel, and Elyse Strongin.

# Amusement Centers

Every kid loves to have fun at an amusement park. The attractions of twelve notable amusement centers in the United States can be found here—including the world's smallest amusement center and a park with the world's largest manmade "ocean."

## THE FIRST U.S. AMUSEMENT PARK

Jones Woods in New York City was the first amusement park in America. It was built in the 1800s on 153 acres of wooded land on Manhattan island between 70th and 73rd Street near the East River. Bowling, billiards, shooting galleries, donkey rides, swings, and merry-go-rounds were among its attractions. In the 1860s Jones Woods closed because the land was needed for apartments and stores.

## AN AMUSEMENT PARK WITH A MUSIC THEME

Opryland in Nashville, Tennessee, is known as the "Home of American Music." Visitors are entertained by dozens of live music shows which play simultaneously. The shows range from bluegrass to rock 'n' roll. A highlight of this amusement center is a visit to the world famous Grand Old Opry house where countless American musicians have performed.

## AN AMUSEMENT CENTER WITH AN AMERICAN MOVIES THEME

Universal City in California features a Universal Studio tour which offers a behind-the-scenes look at moviemaking. A tram ride takes visitors through outdoor sets which are used for movie and television scenes. A special feature of this tour is a ride through the special effects area where frightening situations such as bridge collapses and runaway train rides are re-created.

## THE FIRST AMUSEMENT PARK TO HAVE A REGIONAL THEME

Six Flags Over Texas in Arlington, Texas, was the first park in the U.S. to combine a historical theme with amusement. The park is divided into six areas, each featuring as its theme one of the six flags that have flown over Texas. They are the flags of France, Spain, Mexico, and Texas, the Confederate flag, and the U.S. Stars and Stripes.

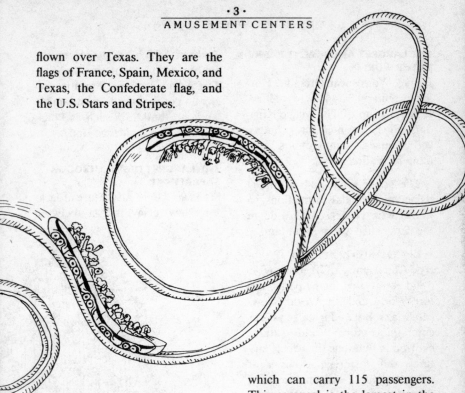

## AN AMUSEMENT CENTER IN MINIATURE

Roadside America in Shartlesville, Pennsylvania, has been called the world's greatest miniature land. It is a masterpiece of the American countryside which shows how people lived and worked during the past 200 years. There is also the continual movement of tiny trains, trolleys, and aircraft in this miniature America.

## THE AMUSEMENT PARK WITH THE LARGEST CAROUSEL

Marriott's Great America in Santa Clara, California, has a double-decker carousel 10 stories high which can carry 115 passengers. This carousel is the largest in the world and is called Columbia. It is adorned with horses, camels, giraffes, lions, tigers, ostriches, pigs, and Roman-type chariots. The theme of this 200-acre park is North American history.

## THE FIRST SEA LIFE AMUSEMENT CENTER IN THE U.S.

Hanna-Barbera's Marineland of the Pacific is the oldest sea life park and has the world's largest collection of marine fish and mammals. Located in Rancho Palos Verdes, California, it features a new animal care center where visitors can see how sick, injured, and found animals are cared for.

## THE LARGEST AMUSEMENT PARK IN THE WORLD

Disney World near Orlando, Florida, is built on 27,443 acres of land. It is made up of The Magic Kingdom, EPCOT center, resort hotels, golf courses, campgrounds, and other recreation areas.

The Magic Kingdom has, among its many popular attractions, a multimedia roller coaster ride in the dark called Space Mountain.

EPCOT (Experimental Prototype Community of Tomorrow) is divided into two theme parks: Future World and the World Showcase Plaza. Both educate as well as entertain. Future World features enormous buildings in which cultural and historical exhibits of transportation, communication, and land are displayed. Of special interest is the 3-D movie, *Magic Journey,* which is shown in the Journey Into Imagination building. The World Showcase Plaza is a re-creation of the worlds most famous landmark buildings such as Philadelphia's Independence Hall.

## THE LARGEST DRIVE-THROUGH SAFARI PARK

Six Flags' Great Adventure in Jackson, New Jersey, halfway between

Philadelphia and New York City, is located on 450 acres of land. More than 2,000 exotic animals such as tigers, panthers, and wallabies can be viewed from your car window as you drive through. No other park outside Africa has the number and variety of animals that can be seen here. There is also an entertainment center on the grounds which features 60 different attractions.

### THE AMUSEMENT PART WITH THE WORLD'S LARGEST MANMADE OCEAN
Big Surf, with its manmade ocean, is right in the middle of the Arizona desert. Located near Phoenix, Arizona, this park boasts the world's largest manmade ocean. The "ocean" covers 2½ acres, has 5-foot-high waves, and is surrounded by a beach dotted with palm trees. Among the activities enjoyed here are swimming, body surfing, and raft riding. There is also a 300-foot-long "surf slide."

### THE AMUSEMENT PARK WITH THE LONGEST WOODEN ROLLER COASTER
At the Six Flags Over Georgia amusement center in Atlanta, Georgia, you can ride the world's largest and tallest wooden roller coaster. It is called the Scream Machine and stands 105 feet in the air. The cars travel 57 miles an hour in a roller coaster journey that takes about 1½ minutes to complete.

# Animals the World Over

An animal must be able to move, obtain food and oxygen, get rid of unwanted waste, make a place for itself in its environment, and reproduce to make a next generation.

Almost every part of the earth is inhabited by animal life. There are over a billion different varieties (species) of animals. To make it easier to study

animals, scientists have divided them into groups. The two main groups are: animals with backbones and animals without backbones. A backbone is made up of small bones called vertebrae. Animals with backbones are called vertebrates. Animals without backbones are called invertebrates. The vertebrates make up about 90 percent of all the animals in the world and are more complicated animals because they have nervous systems.

The following is a partial list of vertebrates and invertebrates.

# VERTEBRATES

| Species | Main Characteristics |
|---|---|
| **FISH**<br>Eel, flounder, perches, seahorses, sharks, tuna | Covered with scales, bony plates, or skin; live in water; breathe with gills; swim with fins (except for eels which use body muscles); cold-blooded. |
| **AMPHIBIANS**<br>Frogs, newts, salamanders, toads | Covered with moist skin, not scales; live in water and breathe with gills as a baby; adults have lungs and live on land; cold-blooded. |
| **REPTILES**<br>Crocodiles, lizards, snakes, turtles | Covered with dry scales or bony plates; lay eggs; cold-blooded (body temperature changes according to weather). |
| **BIRDS**<br>Chickens, peacocks, penguins, sparrows, swans, turkeys | Feathers; ability to fly, except for the following 8 non-flying birds:<br>cassowary    ostrich<br>cormorant   penguin<br>emu         rail<br>kiwi        rhea |
| **MAMMALS**<br>Bats, cattle, cats, dogs, horses, monkeys, whales | Body hair; warm-blooded (constant body temperature whether in a warm or cold place); young fed milk from mother's mammary glands. |

# INVERTEBRATES

| Species | Main Characteristics |
|---|---|
| **PROTOZOA**<br>(The simplest form of all animal life) | Single celled; invisible to the naked eye; live chiefly in water or on other animal bodies as a parasite. |
| **SPONGES***<br>Spongia mollissima (common bath sponge), sycon | They are usually sedentary and move very little; live in water. |
| **COELENTERATES**<br>Corals, jelly fish, sea anemones | Bodies have large central cavity called coelenteron; live in water. |
| **ECHINODERMS**<br>Starfish, sea corals | Bodies are star shaped with five points and have spiny skin; live in water. |
| **WORMS**<br>**Flatworms:** flukes, tapeworms | All have long narrow bodies. Body is flat; move by creeping; live in water, on land, and on other animal bodies. |
| **Roundworms:** hookworms, trichinia | Body is spindle-like and whitish in color; move by whiplike contortions; live in water, on land and on other animal bodies. |
| **Jointed worms:** angleworms, earthworms, leeches | Body is made up of a row of rings; move by creeping; live in water and in soil. |
| **Rotifers:** conchilus, philodina | Body has two circles of hairlike bristles. In motion they look like wheels. Microscopic but may be seen with the naked eye; live in water and on animal bodies. |
| **MOLLUSKS**<br>Clams, oysters, slugs, snails | Body is soft, usually enclosed in a hard limy shell; live in water and on land. |

*An animal that looks like a plant

| *Species* | *Main Characteristics* |
|---|---|
| **ARTHROPODS** | Segmented body; body skeleton is on the outside. |
| **Crustaceans:** barnacles, crabs, crayfish, lobster, shrimp | Have pairs of jointed legs; most live in water and breathe with gills. |
| **Myriopods:** centipedes, millipedes | Have 15 pairs or more of jointed legs; live on land. |
| **Arachnids:** mites, scorpions, spiders, ticks | Have 4 pairs of jointed legs, 2 body parts; most live on land. |
| **INSECTS·** <br> Ants, bees, beetles, bugs, butterflies, silkworms | Have 3 pairs of jointed legs, 3 body parts; live most places on earth. |

*·More species than all other animals (and plants) combined*

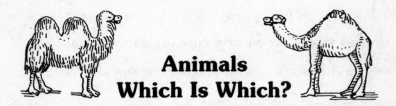

# Animals
# Which Is Which?

**ALLIGATORS AND CROCODILES**
The major difference between alligators and crocodiles is the snout. The crocodile has a long, tapered snout, which narrows sharply from the eyes to the end of its nose. The alligator's snout is rounded. It is almost as broad at the end of the nose as at the eyes.

**CAMELS, ONE AND TWO-HUMPED**
The one-humped camel is known as a dromedary. The dromedary, because of its long legs, is taller. It is native to India and North Africa. The two-humped camel is a Bactrian and lives in China, Turkey, and Mongolia.

**ELEPHANTS, AFRICAN AND ASIAN**
The most obvious difference between Asian and African elephants is size. African elephants are much larger than Asian elephants. Also, African elephants have enormous floppy ears. The Asian elephant has a strongly

arched back and four toenails on each of its hind feet. The African elephant's back is not arched and it has three toenails on each of its hind feet.

## FROGS AND TOADS
Frogs have moist, smooth skin, and are great jumpers. Toads have dry, rough skin. They move around by clumsy, short hops.

## INSECTS AND BUGS
A bug is one kind of insect. It has features that set it apart from other insects. A bug's front pair of wings is larger than the back pair and the sucking mouth parts arise from the front of the head. Other insects that are similar to bugs have large front wings and sucking mouth parts that arise from the back of the head.

## MONKEYS—OLD WORLD AND NEW WORLD
The two types of monkeys are Old World (Asia and Africa) and New World (South America and Central America). The difference between these two types is the tail. The New World monkeys have grasping (holding) tails; Old World monkeys do not.

## PANTHERS, PUMAS, CATAMOUNTS, COUGARS, MOUNTAIN LIONS, AND BEARCATS
These are all names for the same animal; a large brown cat.

## RHINOCEROS—AFRICAN AND INDIAN
The Indian Rhinoceros has one horn; the African Rhinoceros has two horns.

## SKUNKS AND POLECATS
The American skunk has a white stripe down its back. The European polecat, its cousin, does not have a stripe.

## TURTLES, TORTOISES, AND TERRAPINS
All of these reptiles can be called turtles in a general sense. Turtles that live on land all the time are called tortoises. Fresh water turtles that are edible are called terrapins. All other fresh and salt water species are called turtles.

# Animal Names
## GROUP, MALE, FEMALE

| Animal | Group | Male | Female | Baby |
|---|---|---|---|---|
| Ass | (Not known) | Jack | Jenny | Foal |
| Bear | Sloth | Boar | Sow | Cub |
| Cat | Clutter | Tom | Queen | Kitten |
| Cattle | Drove | Bull | Cow | Calf |
| Chicken | Brood | Rooster | Hen | Chicken |
| Deer | Herd | Buck | Doe | Fawn |
| Donkey | Pace | Jackass | Jenny | Foal |
| Dog | Kennel | Dog | Bitch | Pup |
| Duck | Brace | Drake | Duck | Duckling |
| Elephant | Herd | Bull | Cow | Calf |
| Fox | Leash | Dog | Vixen | Cub |
| Goose | Gaggle | Gander | Goose | Gosling |
| Giraffe | Herd | Bull | Cow | Calf |
| Horse | Team | Stallion | Mare | Foal |
| Kangaroo | Troop /Herd/Mob | Buck | Doe | Joey |
| Lion | Pride | Lion | Lioness | Cub |
| Nightingale | Watch | (Adult) | (Adult) | Nestling |
| Pig | Litter | Boar | Sow | Piglet |
| Quail | Bevy | (Adult) | (Adult) | Chick |
| Rabbit | Nest | Buck | Doe | Bunny |
| Seal | Trip | Bull | Cow | Whelp |
| Sheep | Block | Ram | Ewe | Lamb |
| Swan | Flock | Cob | Pen | Cygnet |
| Tiger | (Not known) | Tiger | Tigress | Cub |
| Turkey | Flock | Tom | Hen | Poult |
| Whale | Pod | Bull | Cow | Calf |
| Wolf | Pack | Dog | Bitch | Pup |
| Zebra | Herd | Stallion | Mare | Colt |

## SCIENTIFIC NAMES

Scientists have given animals official names. These names differ from the animal's common name. Below is a list of descriptive English words based on the animal's scientific name.

| | | | |
|---|---|---|---|
| **apian** | like a bee | **leonine** | like a lion |
| **avian** | like a bird | **lupine** | like a wolf |
| **bovine** | like a cow | **ovine** | like a sheep |
| **canine** | like a dog | **simian** | like an ape |
| **equinine** | like a horse | **taurine** | like a bull |
| **feline** | like a cat | **ursine** | like a bear |

# Animal Champions

### Fastest

| | | |
|---|---|---|
| Bird | **Indian Swift** | 200 miles per hour |
| Land animal | **Cheetah** | 70 miles per hour |
| Ocean swimmer | **Sailfish** | 68 miles per hour |

## Slowest

| | | |
|---|---|---|
| Fish (marine) | **Sea Horse** | 10½ inches per minute |
| Animal | **Snail** | 2 to 3 ft. per minute |
| Mammal | **Three-toed Sloth** | 6 to 8 ft. per minute |
| Reptile | **Tortoise** | 15 ft. per minute |

## Largest

| | | | |
|---|---|---|---|
| Animal (living or extinct) | **Blue Whale** | 100 ft. long, | 150 tons |
| Fish | **Whale Shark** | 45 ft. long, | 13 tons |
| Land animal | **African Bull Elephant** | 10 ft. tall, | 6 tons |
| Reptile | **Saltwater Crocodile** | 16 ft. long, | 1,150 pounds |
| Freshwater fish | **Pirarucu** | 15 ft. long, | 500 pounds |
| African cat | **Lion** | 10 ft. long, | 500 pounds |
| Bird | **Ostrich** | 8 ft. tall, | 300 pounds |
| Lizard | **Komodo Dragon** | 10 ft. long, | 200 pounds |
| Rodent | **Waterhog (Capybara)** | 4 ft. long, | 150 pounds |
| Amphibian | **Giant Salamander** | 5 ft. long, | 100 pounds |
| Flying Bird | **Condor** | 15 ft. (wingspan), | 25 pounds |
| Frog | **Goliath** | 1 ft. long, | 10 pounds |

# Animal Words and Phrases in the English Language

Animals have personalities and special traits. People use the animal world to enrich their language. Just the mention of an animal can provide a colorful description of people or events. Here is a partial listing of animal words and phrases along with their meanings.

| | *Meaning* | *Origin* |
|---|---|---|
| **Bee** | A social gathering for work like a sewing bee | Bees are busy animals that work hard together. |

| | Meaning | Origin |
|---|---|---|
| **Black Sheep** | An outcast | The wool of a black sheep has little value because it is difficult to dye. |
| **Clam up** | To be silent | The mouth of the clam is difficult to open. |
| **Crocodile tears** | Fake crying | Legend has it that crocodiles attracted their victims by crying. |
| **Dead as a dodo** | Not alive | Dodo birds are now extinct. |
| **Dog** | To trail persistently | Dogs are used to hunt other animals. |
| **Duck** | To plunge under water, or to dodge | Ducks in water frequently bob their heads beneath the water. |
| **Eager Beaver** | One who is overly enthusiastic | Beavers are known for being extremely hard workers. |
| **Ferret** | To hunt out | Ferrets are animals well-known for hunting rodents. |
| **Fox** | A sly person | Foxes are known for their trickiness. |
| **Get your goat** | To become irritated | Goats were often stabled with thoroughbred racing horses to calm them. Horses who were used to having the goats around would become very upset when the goats were removed. |

| | Meaning | Origin |
|---|---|---|
| **Goose pimples** | Bumps on the skin when one is frightened or cold | The flesh of a goose is pimpled after its feathers have been plucked. |
| **Guinea pig** | Someone who is sacrificed to further a plan | Guinea pigs are commonly used in scientific experiments. |
| **Hightail it** | Make a fast getaway | Rabbits and many other animals raise their tails high when running from danger. |
| **Hold your horses** | Be patient | Horse drivers in American county fair races often started their horses before the race had begun. Spectators would shout "Hold your horses!" |
| **Horsepower** | A unit of power in mechanics | The power a horse uses in pulling. |
| **Pigeonhole** | To file away for future use | Old-fashioned desks had compartments called pigeonholes because they looked like holes in pigeon houses. |
| **Play possum** | To pretend or deceive | Possums (opossums) pretend they are dead when threatened or captured. |
| **Smell a rat** | To suspect something | Cats have the ability to smell rats they cannot see. |
| **Squirrel away** | To save | Squirrels collect food in the summer and fall to eat in the winter. |
| **Weasel words** | A statement that seems to have meaning but does not | Weasels are able to suck out the inside of an egg while leaving the shell whole. |
| **Worm** | A lowly person | Because worms live in the earth and are slow moving crawlers, they are thought to be inferior animals. |

# Animal Sounds

There are virtually silent animals, like the stork, but most make sounds. Some of the names given to the cries animals make are listed below.

| | | | |
|---|---|---|---|
| **Apes** | gibber | **Frogs** | croak |
| **Bears** | growl | **Geese** | cackle |
| **Bees** | buzz | **Grasshoppers** | chirp |
| **Birds** | sing | **Horses** | neigh |
| **Calves** | bleat | **Hyenas** | laugh |
| **Cats** | purr | **Lambs** | bleat |
| **Chickens** | cackle | **Lions** | roar |
| **Cocks** | crow | **Mice** | squeak |
| **Cows** | moo | **Monkeys** | chatter |
| **Dogs** | bark | **Owls** | hoot |
| **Dolphins** | click | **Parrots** | talk |
| **Doves** | coo | **Pigs** | grunt |
| **Ducks** | quack | **Sheep** | baa |
| **Elephants** | trumpet | **Turkeys** | gobble |
| **Fox** | yelp | **Wolves** | howl |

# Animals Who Were First

**AARDVARK**   "Aardy" was the first aardvark born in captivity in America. She was born on September 29, 1967, in the Crandon Park Zoo, Miami, Florida. An aardvark is an African mammal that has ears like a donkey, a tail like a kangaroo, and a long sticky tongue. It feeds on ants and termites.

**CAT**   "Siam" was the first Siamese cat brought into the United States. She was a gift sent to the wife of President Rutherford B. Hayes in November, 1878, by American diplomats in Bangkok, Thailand.

# ANIMALS THE WORLD OVER

**CHIMPANZEE**    **"Washoe"** was the first chimpanzee to learn to communicate in words. She was acquired in 1966 by behavioral psychologists at the University of Nevada in Reno. They taught her the American sign language for the deaf.

**COW**    **"Arlinda Ellen Beecher,"** a Holstein cow raised in Richmond, Indiana, was the first cow to produce over 11,765 gallons of milk in one year (1976).

**DOGS**    **"Buddy,"** a German shepherd, was the first dog to be used as a Seeing Eye dog for the blind. He was trained by his owner, Morris Eustis, in Switzerland in 1920.

**"Rin Tin Tin,"** a German shepherd, was the first dog to earn over a million dollars. He was a movie "character" and his first film was *Where the North Begins,* in 1925.

**"Rover,"** a collie, was the world's first dog movie star. He appeared in a 1902 movie called *Rescue by Rover.*

**GORILLAS**    **"Koko"** was the first gorilla to learn American sign language for the deaf. Born in July, 1971, she was taught by Dr. Franklin Patterson of Stanford University in California.

**"Snowflake"** was the world's first known albino (white) gorilla. She was discovered in Africa in 1966 and sent to the zoo in Barcelona, Spain.

**HORSES**    **"Algonquin"** was the first horse to visit the inside of the White House. He was a pony belonging to President Theodore Roosevelt's son Archie. When Archie came down with the measles, Algonquin was smuggled into the White House to cheer up the bedridden child.

**"Justin Morgan"** was the first horse for whom a new breed was named. He was foaled (born) in 1793 in Massachusetts of unknown lineage. Because of his great intelligence, strength, and speed he was valued as a new breed, the Morgan horse.

**LIGER** *(Half lion, half tiger)*    **"Shasta"** was the first liger born in the United States. She was born on May 6, 1948, at the Hagh Zoo in Salt Lake City, Utah.

**MONKEYS**    **"Able"** and **"Baker"** were the first animals to survive being rocketed into space by the United States government. They were sent aloft in a *Jupiter* rocket on May 28, 1959.

**PANDAS**   "Su-Lin" was the first live Giant Panda to be seen in the United States. She was brought to San Francisco from China in 1936.

"Yvanjing" was the first Giant Panda bred by artificial insemination. She was born in 1978 in the Beijing Zoo in China.

# Migration: Animal Journeys

Migration is a regular, seasonal movement from one part of the world to another by a group of animals. Animals move to find food, a place to breed or a better climate. Mammals migrate in search of food. Fish migrate between fresh and salt water or to different parts of the ocean. Birds usually migrate along regular routes. They are perhaps the most famous migrators. The movement of birds has fascinated scientists, who still don't completely understand how birds find their destinations. Studies have shown that birds use the sun, stars and wind currents to guide them. And yet, birds that have been lost or blown off course are still able to find their homes. Scientists are working to unlock the mysteries of bird and other animal migration. Some of the destinations and distances travelled by animals that are known are listed opposite.

# ANIMAL TRAVELERS:
# WHERE AND HOW FAR THEY GO

## Flyers

| Animal | Distance | Where to and from |
|---|---|---|
| Arctic Tern | 25,000 miles, round trip | North to South Pole |
| Bat | 2,400 miles, round trip | Labrador to Bermuda |
| Golden Plover | 16,000 miles, round trip | Canada to South America |
| Monarch Butterfly | 2,000 miles, round trip | Canada to California |
| Wandering Albatross | 20,000 miles | Circles the whole world west to east |

## Swimmers

| Animal | Distance | Where to and from |
|---|---|---|
| Atlantic Salmon | 6,000 miles in ocean, round trip | St. Lawrence River to Atlantic Ocean |
| Dogfish | 2,500 miles, round trip | Coast of Canada to Mediterranean |
| Emperor Penguin | 1,000–2,000 miles yearly | Antarctica to Weddell Sea |
| Fur Seal | 9,000 miles, round trip | Pribilof Islands to Coast of California (Bering Sea) |
| Green Turtle | 2,800 miles, round trip | South America to Ascension Island (Atlantic Ocean) |
| Humpback Whale | 8,000 miles, round trip | Indian Ocean to Atlantic Ocean |

## Walkers

| Animal | Distance | Where to and from |
|---|---|---|
| Bison | 800 miles | Roam around Northern provinces of Canada |
| Caribou | 800 miles | Northwest Territories to islands in Artic Circle |
| Elk | 200 miles | Roam around Northern provinces of Canada |

# Zoos

## COLLECTIONS OF LIVING ANIMALS

From the earliest times, man has been fascinated by animals and their behavior. Ancient Roman, Egyptian and Chinese emperors all had menageries. These collections of animals were for curiosity or for a show of power. Zoos (zoological gardens) for all people opened in Europe about 200 years ago. Today's zoos are much different from early zoos. They are run for educational, recreational and scientific purposes. They try to provide animals with their natural surroundings. Many hope to preserve rare species by breeding. The following is a list of the oldest and largest zoos in the world and some of the zoos in the United States that are noted for recording firsts in zoo history.

## OLDEST

**EARLIEST KNOWN ZOO**
11th century B.C.—Ling-Yu, "The Garden of Intelligence," was opened in China by the Emperor Wang.

**OLDEST EXISTING ZOO IN THE WORLD**
1752—The Garden at Schönbrunn; Vienna, Austria.

**OLDEST ZOO IN THE UNITED STATES**
1872—The Philadelphia Zoo; Philadelphia, Pennsylvania.

## LARGEST

**LARGEST ZOO IN THE WORLD (MOST ANIMALS)**
The San Diego Wild Animal Park; San Diego, California.

**LARGEST PRIVATE ZOO IN THE UNITED STATES**
The Catskill Game Farm; Catskill, N.Y. (120 miles north of N.Y. City).

**LARGEST URBAN (CITY) ZOO IN THE WORLD**
New York Zoological Gardens; Bronx, N.Y. "The Bronx Zoo" covers 252 acres.

**LARGEST COLLECTION OF AMERICAN RATTLESNAKES**
Staten Island Zoo; Staten Island, N.Y.

**LARGEST COLLECTION OF PARROTS IN THE WORLD**
Busch Gardens; Tampa, Florida.

**LARGEST COLLECTION OF WHALES IN THE UNITED STATES**
Marineland of the Pacific Oceanarium; Palos Verdes, California.

# FIRSTS

**ATLANTA ZOOLOGICAL GARDENS**
**Atlanta, Georgia**
The *first formal zoo school* was established here in 1960.

**CHICAGO ZOOLOGICAL PARK**
**Brookfield, Illinois**
In 1934 this zoo, known as the Brookfield Zoo, introduced the *first free view enclosure.* For the first time in the United States animals were not barred or fenced. Instead, they were separated from visitors by the use of rocks, water, ditches and dry trenches.

**COLUMBUS, OHIO MUNICIPAL ZOO**
**Columbus, Ohio**
The *first gorilla to be born in captivity* was born here. "Colo" was born on December 22, 1956.

**FORT WORTH, TEXAS ZOOLOGICAL PARK**
**Fort Worth, Texas**
This was the *first American zoo to replicate a rain forest.* Its model of a South American rain forest contains native South American animals.

**PHILADELPHIA ZOOLOGICAL GARDENS**
**Philadelphia, Pennsylvania**
In 1938 this zoo opened the *first baby pet zoo* in America. It was a forerunner for today's children's zoos.

**PITTSBURGH'S HIGHLAND PARK ZOOLOGICAL GARDEN**
**Pittsburgh, Pennsylvania**
This was the *first underground zoo* exhibit in America. Animals are shown in their underground burrows. It opened in 1962.

**ST. LOUIS ZOOLOGICAL PARK**
**St. Louis, Missouri**
In 1904 this zoo pioneered the *first open-fronted exhibit of birds.* A huge aviary covered with wire mesh allowed birds to fly freely.

**WASHINGTON, D. C.'S NATIONAL ZOOLOGICAL PARK**
**Washington, District of Columbia**
In 1890 the United States Congress established the *first and only national zoo.*

# Animal Extinction And Endangerment

Since the beginning of life, thousands of animal species have come and gone. Extinction (no longer existing) is a natural process. Dinosaurs no longer exist but man had nothing to do with their disappearance. However, in the last few hundred years, the pace of extinction seems to have speeded up. Man has threatened animal life in three main ways: by hunting certain species too much, by polluting the environment through misapplied technology, and by destroying natural animal living space for man's own use.

The United States government is trying to protect animal life throughout the world. In 1973 it passed a law called the Endangered Species Act. Under the law, animals that are endangered are now protected in order to help them survive.

Saving animals from extinction is important for man. All life forms are interdependent and the loss of one or two of them can greatly hurt man.

Some experts predict animal extinction at the rate of one a minute by 1990. The following is a partial list of the world's extinct and endangered animals.

## EXTINCT AND ENDANGERED ANIMALS

### Amphibians

| *Extinct* | *Endangered* |
| --- | --- |
| Frog, Vegas Valley Leopard | Frog, Pine Barrens |
| | Salamander, Desert Slender |
| | Toad, Houston |

### Birds

| | |
| --- | --- |
| Dodo | Condor, Andean |
| Hen, Heath | Crane, Whooping |
| Parakeet, Carolina | Duck, Labrador |
| Pigeon, Passenger | Eagle, Bald |

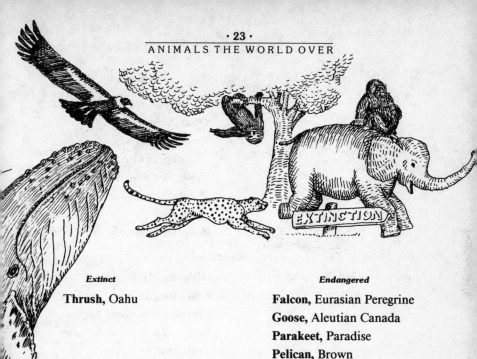

**Extinct**

Thrush, Oahu

**Endangered**

Falcon, Eurasian Peregrine
Goose, Aleutian Canada
Parakeet, Paradise
Pelican, Brown

## Fish

Dare, Grass Valley Speckled
Pupfish, Tecopa
Sucker, Harelip
Topminnow, Whiteline
Troup, Agassiz

Chub, Humpback
Darter, Maryland
Pike, Blue
Pupfish, Warm Springs
Sturgeon, Short Nose
Trout, Gila

## Mammals

Cougar, Wisconsin
Elk, Eastern
Fox, Southern California
Mink, Sea
Sea Cow, Stellars
Whale, Atlantic Great

Bat, Hawaiian
Bear, Brown
Cheetah
Chimpanzee
Deer, Marsh
Elephant, Asian
Gorilla
Jaguar
Kangaroo, Red
Leopard, Snow

*Extinct*                                    *Endangered*

**Monkey,** Black Howler
**Otter,** Southern Sea
**Prairie Dog,** Utah
**Rhinoceros,** Great Indian
**Sloth,** Brazilian Three-toed
**Whale,** Humpback
**Wolf,** Gray
**Zebra,** Mountain

### Reptiles

**Snake,** St. Croix Ground

**Alligator,** American
**Crocodile,** American
**Lizard,** Blunt-nosed Leopard
**Snake,** San Francisco Garter
**Turtle,** Green

# Dinosaurs

Dinosaurs, "terrible lizards," were reptiles who lived on the earth millions of years ago. They were the kings of the earth before any humans existed. Then they disappeared. The reasons for this are still being studied. Scientists have dinosaur bones, footprints, and fossilized eggs to help them unravel the mystery of dinosaurs. Here are some of the most interesting facts known about dinosaurs.

• The **largest** dinosaur was the BRACHIOSAURUS (brack' e' o' sore us), which weighed 100,000 pounds, was 45 feet tall and 80 feet long.
• The **smallest** dinosaur was the COMPSOGNATHUS (Comp-sog-Nay-Thus), which was about 12 inches long and looked like a bird without feathers.
• The **longest** dinosaur was the DIPLODOCUS (dip LOD' o cus) which was almost 90 feet long.
• The **fiercest** dinosaur was the TYRANNOSAURUS REX (tie' ran' o' sore' us) which had sixty long and sharp teeth used to attack and eat other dinosaurs.

- The **largest flying** dinosaur was the PTERANODON (ter' AN' o' don), which had a wingspan of 25 feet (8 meters).
- The **fastest** dinosaur was the HYPSILOPHODON (HIP-si-LOFF-o-donn).
- The **last and largest** meat-eating dinosaur was TYRANNOSAURUS (tie' ran' o' sore' us).

# Animal Pets

If you love animals and would like to have one for a pet, there are many things you should consider. When you take a pet into your home, you are responsible for its well-being for a long time.

The following questions will help you decide if you can be a responsible pet owner. They will also help you decide on the best kind of pet for you.

## A

|  | Yes | No |
|---|---|---|
| 1. Would you love, honor and care for an animal every day for the rest of its life? | ☐ | ☐ |
| 2. Could you pay doctor's bills for sick- and well-animal care? | ☐ | ☐ |
| 3. Would you spay females and neuter males? | ☐ | ☐ |

|  | Yes | No |
|---|---|---|

4. Are you permitted to have animals where you live? ☐ ☐

5. Could you accept an extra three to five dollars tacked onto your grocery bill each week? ☐ ☐

*0–2: Get a pet rock*          *3–4: Think again*          *5: Yes, proceed to Section B*

# B

1. Do you live in a house? ☐ ☐
2. Do you have an unrestricted choice of the type of animal you may have? ☐ ☐
3. Do you have large living quarters? ☐ ☐
4. Will someone be home with the animal most of the time? ☐ ☐
5. Do you have an area where the animal can be safely exercised on a routine basis? ☐ ☐
6. Are you prepared to deal with an animal that may be destructive? ☐ ☐
7. Is your family free of allergy problems? ☐ ☐
8. Do you travel often? ☐ ☐
9. Are you prepared to teach your brothers and sisters how to properly handle an animal? ☐ ☐
10. Do you like to groom animals? ☐ ☐
11. Would you obey leash laws and pooper scooper laws? ☐ ☐
12. Do you establish routines and follow them? ☐ ☐
13. Would you laugh if you found fur in your morning cereal? ☐ ☐
14. Can you live in a house that is less than "hospital clean"? ☐ ☐
15. Do you look forward to getting outside to exercise? ☐ ☐
16. Does another warm body in bed with you at night sound appealing? ☐ ☐
17. Do you want an animal you can pet and handle? ☐ ☐
18. Do you want an animal that will be a companion? ☐ ☐
19. Would you prefer an animal that needs some care daily to one that needs a lot of care twice a week or weekly? ☐ ☐
20. Do you sleep with the windows open? ☐ ☐
21. Are you early to bed, early to rise? ☐ ☐

|  | Yes | No |
|---|---|---|
| 22. Do you prefer a noisy to a quiet living space? | ☐ | ☐ |
| 23. Can you live with stains on your carpet, scratch marks on your chair? | ☐ | ☐ |
| 24. Would you give your pet free access to most areas of the house? | ☐ | ☐ |
| 25. Do you live in a suburban or sparsely populated area? | ☐ | ☐ |

*0–12: Look into caged animals*     *13–20: Cat person!*     *21–25: **Find a breed of dog to match your life-style***

Reprinted with permission of *Animals* Magazine

## A Partial List of Pets

**CAGED ANIMALS: Canaries, gerbils, fish, hamsters, parrots, mice**
These animals are totally dependent on you for food, water and a comfortable environment.

**CAGED ANIMALS THAT ALSO NEED FREEDOM: Guinea pigs, parakeets, rabbits**
These animals depend on you for nourishment and cleaning. When set free, they must be well supervised.

**UNCAGED ANIMALS: Cats and dogs**
They need food and drink but are able to take care of themselves in many ways. They are the most popular pets because they can adapt to the human life-style.

# Books and Magazines for Kids

A treasury of the favorite books of kids, classics for all time, magazines, and little known facts about books can be found here.

> "There are more treasures in books than all the pirates' loot in Treasure Island. . . . and best of all, you can enjoy these riches every day of your life."
>
> —WALT DISNEY

## Book Bits

*In 300 B.C., Ptolemy I of Egypt founded a great library in Alexandria. The library did not contain books as we know them today—instead, it was filled with scrolls of papyrus. The library, which stood for over 400 years, was considered a cultural wonder of its time.

**\*The world's first printed book** was the Diamond Sutra. It was printed with wooden blocks and was published in China in 868 A.D.

**\*The most valuable book in the world** is the Gutenberg Bible which was first printed in 1455, in Mainz, Germany. This bible was the first book ever printed from moveable metal type. It is a huge book with 1,282 sheepskin pages which open to the width of a card table. In 1978 one of the 47 existing copies was sold for $2,400,000. Today, one copy is in the Library of Congress in the U.S., one is in the British Museum in England, and one is in the Biblioteque Nationale in France.

**\*The first children's book printed in English** was a book of rhymes entitled *A Book in Englyssh Metre of the Great Merchant Man Called Dives Pragmaticus.* It was printed by Alexander Lacy of England in 1563.

**\*The world's first children's magazine** was published in 1751 by John Newbery of England. The name of the magazine was *The Lilliputian.*

**\*The first children's library in America** was the Bingham Library for Youth in Salisbury, Connecticut. The library opened in 1803 with 150 books for kids aged 9 to 16 years old.

**\*The World Almanac** was first published in 1868. For a period of 10 years its annual publication was interrupted. In 1886 it was revived by publisher Joseph Pulitzer and has been printed every year thereafter.

**\*The first bookmobile** was a horse-drawn wagon filled with shelves to hold 250 books. These traveling libraries took books to readers in remote rural areas. The bookmobile was the idea and creation of a Maryland librarian in 1905.

**\*The world's largest collection of stored knowledge** is in the Library of Congress, a three-building complex in Washington, D.C. covering 82 acres. There are more than 18 million books, filling 535 miles of shelf space. There are more maps, globes, charts, and atlases there than any other single place on earth. Nearly every phonograph record ever made in the U.S. is kept there. The largest collection of motion pictures in the world is also in this library.

# Children's Choices: The 25 Favorite Books of American Kids

### (SURVEY BY BOOKLIST MAGAZINE, 1982)

| Author | Title |
|---|---|
| Blume, Judy | Superfudge |
| Blume, Judy | Tales of a Fourth Grade Nothing |
| Blume, Judy | Are You There, God? It 's Me, Margaret |
| White, E. B. | Charlotte's Web |
| Blume, Judy | Blubber |
| Silverstein, Shel | Where the Sidewalk Ends |
| Farley, Walter | The Black Stallion |
| Dahl, Roald | Charlie and the Chocolate Factory |
| Rawls, Wilson | Where the Red Fern Grows |
| Blume, Judy | Deenie |
| Tolkien, J. R. R. | The Hobbit |
| Cleary, Beverly | Ramona the Pest |
| Blume, Judy | Forever |
| L'Engle, Madeleine | A Wrinkle in Time |
| Hinton, S. E. | The Outsiders |
| Wilder, Laura Ingalls | Little House on the Prairie |
| Blume, Judy | Tiger Eyes |
| Warner, Gertrude | The Boxcar Children |
| Cleary, Beverly | The Mouse and the Motorcycle |
| Rey, H. A. | Curious George |
| Lewis, C. S. | The Lion, the Witch and the Wardrobe |
| Rockwell, Thomas | How to Eat Fried Worms |
| Dahl, Roald | James and the Giant Peach |
| Silverstein, Shel | A Light in the Attic |
| Cleary, Beverly | Ramon Quimby, Age 8 |

# Fifty Contemporary Classics for Every Child

(COMPILED BY THE AMERICAN LIBRARY ASSOCIATION)

| *Author* | *Title* |
|---|---|
| Alexander, Lloyd | The Book of Three |
| Babbitt, Natalie | Tuck Everlasting |
| Blume, Judy | Are You There, God? It's Me, Margaret |
| Bond, Michael | A Bear Called Paddington |
| Bond, Nancy | A String in the Harp |
| Boston, Lucy M. | The Children of Green Knowe |
| Byars, Betsy C. | The Midnight Fox |
| Cameron, Eleanor | The Court of the Stone Children |
| Cleary, Beverly | Ramona and Her Father |
| Cleaver, Vera and Cleaver, Bill | Where the Lilies Bloom |
| Collier, James L. and Collier, Christopher | My Brother Sam Is Dead |
| Cooper, Susan | The Dark Is Rising |
| Cresswell, Helen | Ordinary Jack: Being the First Part of the Bagthorpe Saga |
| de Jong, Meindert | House of Sixty Fathers |
| Donovan, John | Family |
| Fitgerald, John | The Great Brain |
| Fitzhugh, Louise | Harriet the Spy |
| Fleischman, Sid | Humbug Mountain |
| Fox, Paula | Slave Dancer |
| Greene, Bette | Summer of My German Soldier |
| Greene, Constance C. | Beat the Turtle Drum |
| Hamilton, Virginia | The Planet of Junior Brown |
| Holman, Felice | Slake's Limbo |
| Hunter, Mollie | A Stranger Came Ashore |
| Klein, Norma | Mom, the Wolf Man and Me |
| Konigsburg, E. L. | From the Mixed-Up Files of Mrs. Basil E. Frankweiler |
| Langton, Jane | The Fledgling |

| Author | Title |
|--------|-------|
| Le Guin, Ursula K. | A Wizard of Earthsea |
| L'Engle, Madeleine | A Wrinkle in Time |
| Lewis, C. S. | The Lion, the Witch and the Wardrobe |
| Lively, Penelope | The Ghost of Thomas Kempe |
| Lowry, Louis | Anastasia Krupnik |
| McKinley, Robin | Beauty: A Retelling of the Story of Beauty and the Beast |
| Mathis, Sharon B. | The Hundred Penny Box |
| Merrill, Jean | The Pushcart War |
| Norton, Mary | The Borrowers |
| O'Brien, Robert C. | Mrs. Frisby and the Rats of NIMH |
| O'Dell, Scott | Island of the Blue Dolphins |
| Paterson, Katherine | Bridge to Terabithia |
| Peck, Richard | The Ghost Belonged to Me |
| Pinkwater, Daniel | Lizard Music |
| Rockwell, Thomas | How to Eat Fried Worms |
| Rodgers, Mary | Freaky Friday |
| Selden, George | The Cricket in Times Square |
| Snyder, Zilpha K. | The Egypt Game |
| Speare, Elizabeth G. | The Witch of Blackbird Pond |
| Steig, William | Abel's Island |
| White, E. B. | Charlotte's Web |
| Wiseman, David | Jeremy Visick |
| Yep, Laurence | Dragonwings |

# Magazines for Kids

| Subject | Title | Subscription Address | Features |
|---------|-------|---------------------|----------|
| Art | *Art & Man* (6 issues annually) | 730 Broadway New York, NY 10003 | Full color reproductions of art works; artist of the month; creative art projects. |
| Beauty; fashion | *Seventeen* (monthly) | 850 Third Avenue New York, NY 10022 | Short stories; articles; beauty and fashion tips. |

# BOOKS AND MAGAZINES FOR KIDS

| Subject | Title | Subscription Address | Features |
|---|---|---|---|
| Computers | *Enter* (10 issues a year) | 1 Lincoln Plaza New York, NY 10023 | Only magazine of its kind for teens and pre-teens. Includes hardware and software, reviews, kids' columns and feature stories. |
| Consumer information | *Penny Power* (bi-monthly) | Consumers Union of U.S., Inc. P.O. Box 1906 Marion, OH 43302 | How to be a wise consumer; how to manage your money. |
| Education/ entertainment | *Sesame Street* (10 issues a year) | Box 2896 Boulder, CO 80322 | Sesame Street TV show characters; basic skills for pre-schoolers; "parents page." |
| Fashion | *Young Miss* (10 issues a year) | New Bridge Road Bergenfield, NJ 07621 | Clothing and beauty tips; stories about friendship and romance. |
| Health | *Children's Digest* (9 issues a year) | 1100 Waterway Blvd. P.O. Box 567 Indianapolis, IN 46206 | Articles, puzzles and activities. |
| History | *Cobblestone* (monthly) | P.O. Box 959 Farmingdale, NY 11737 | American history comes alive in themes which are related to historical dates of the month. |
| General interest | *Cricket* (monthly) | P.O. Box 2670 Boulder, CO 80322 | A variety of stories from folk tales to science fiction. |
| General interest | *Lifeprints* (5 issues a year) | Blindskills Inc. P.O. Box 5181 Salem, OR 97304 | This is a unique magazine for teens with limited eyesight or no sight at all. The magazine comes with large print, in braille, and in recorded casettes. |
| General interest | *Ebony Jr.* (monthly) | 820 South Michigan Avenue Chicago, IL 60650 | Stresses accomplishments of young blacks throughout the world. |
| General interest | *Highlights for Children* (11 issues a year) | P.O. Box 269 2300 West 5th Avenue Columbus, OH 43216 | A broad range of topics from science and nature to space and math. |

| Subject | Title | Subscription Address | Features |
|---------|-------|---------------------|----------|
| General interest | *National Geographic World* (monthly) | National Geographic Society 17th and M Streets NW Washington, DC 20036 | Factual stories about animals, sports, hobbies, and kids. |
| Music | *On Key* (6 issues a year) | JDL Publications P.O. Box 1213 Montclair, NJ 07042 | Inspirational articles for young musicians. |
| Reading and writing | *Electric Company* (10 issues a year) | Box 2896 Boulder, CO 80322 | Informative games, interviews and stories. |
| Recreation | *Boys' Life* (12 issues a year) | 1325 Walnut Hill Lane Irving, TX 75062 | Articles on sports, recreation, and scouting. |
| Science | *Odyssey* (monthly) | 625 E. St. Paul Avenue P.O. Box 92788 Milwaukee, WI 53202 | Articles on astronomy and outer space. |
| Science | *Owl* (10 issues a year) | 59 Front Street East Toronto, Ontario Canada M5E1B3 | Science stories from robots to the environment. |
| Science | *3-2-1 Contact* (10 issues a year) | Box 2896 Boulder, CO 80322 | "Factoids" section; coming attractions in science; "Do It" section (puzzles, games); feature articles, including experiments. |
| Nature | *Ranger Rick's Nature Magazine* (monthly) | National Wildlife Foundation 1412 16th Street NW Washington, DC 20036 | Emphasis on wildlife and the environment. |
| Writing | *Stone Soup* (5 issues a year) | Children's Art Fdtn. P.O. Box 83 Santa Cruz, CA 95063 | Stories, book reviews, and artwork—all done by kids. |

# Bridges

The first people to live on earth were nomads who moved from place to place looking for food and shelter. They placed fallen trees across streams in order to pass from one side to the other. These trees were the first bridges. As civilization advanced so did the science of bridge building. New materials and techniques were used to build a variety of longer and stronger bridges. Modern man is able to span great bodies of water with spectacular bridges of steel and concrete.

Bridges inspire authors, poets, playwrights, artists, and photographers who praise them in words and pictures. Bridges are among the most complex, beautiful, and endearing structures built.

# Major Types of Bridges

## FIXED BRIDGES

**BEAM**

This is the simplest type of bridge. It is constructed by laying beams of wood, steel, or concrete across an expanse. A simple example of this type of bridge is a fallen tree lying across a river with both ends resting on the river banks.

**CANTILEVER**

This bridge is made of three beams. Two beams are anchored to the two sides of the river bank. The third is placed between them to close the gap. Each of the anchored beams is called a cantilever.

**SUSPENSION**

A suspension bridge is hung from two or more cables which pass over towers and are then anchored on both sides of the crossing. The first suspension bridges were tightropes strung across rivers.

**ARCH**

An arch bridge curves upward and the ends push outward against a support. It is considered to be an upside-down suspension bridge.

**COVERED**

This is a wooden bridge with a roof built over it to protect it from rot caused by excessive moisture or dryness.

## MOVABLE BRIDGES

**DRAWBRIDGE**
A drawbridge opens upward. The two ends are anchored and the center swings open.

**VERTICAL LIFT**
This bridge moves like an elevator. There is a tower at each end of the span and the span is attached to cables which move the bridge up and down.

**PONTOON BRIDGE**
This is a floating bridge which swings aside to open. It is supported by pontoons (boats) which float on the water.

**SWING SPAN**
A swing bridge opens outward. It is balanced by a pivot pier which is at its center.

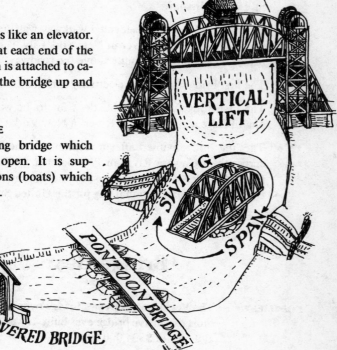

# First in United States Bridges

**1654**   The first toll bridge in the U.S. was built over the Newbury River in Rowley, Massachusetts. The toll was charged for animals to cross. Pedestrians were allowed free passage.

**1785**   The first covered bridge was built over the Connecticut River in Bellows Fall, Vermont.

**1796**   The first suspension bridge was built over Jacob's Creek in Uniontown, Pennsylvania.

**1804** The first pontoon bridge was built over Collins Pond in Lynn, Massachusetts.

**1854** The first bridge to Canada was a suspension bridge built from Niagara Falls, New York.

**1874** The first bridge across the Mississippi River was the Eads Bridge in St. Louis, Missouri.

**1883** The first bridge with an elevated walkway was the Brooklyn Bridge which spans the East River in New York City. Pedestrians cross the bridge on a promenade built above the roadway.

**1883** The first bridge lighted by electricity was the Brooklyn Bridge.

**1909** The first bridge with a double deck for traffic was the Queensborough Bridge across the East River in New York City.

**1976** The first bridge named after a woman was the Betsy Ross Bridge across the Delaware River in Philadelphia, Pennsylvania. (Legend has it that Betsy Ross, a seamstress during the American Revolution, made the first national flag for the United States government.)

# Bridge Bests

**COSTLIEST**      **The Verrazano-Narrows Bridge** over New York Bay is the most expensive bridge ever built. It was completed in 1964 at a cost of $304,000,000.

**MOST FAMOUS**      **Old London Bridge,** which spanned the Thames River in England, is considered the most famous bridge in the English-speaking world.

**HEAVIEST LOAD CARRYING**      **Hell Gate Bridge** over the East River in New York City can withstand the heaviest load of traffic. Built in 1917 for railroad traffic, it can hold up 24,000 pounds per foot, or a 10,000-ton spread.

**HIGHEST**      **The Royal Gorge Bridge** was built 1,053 feet above the Arkansas River in central Colorado. It is the highest bridge above water in the world.

**LONGEST**  **The Lake Ponchartrain No. 2** in New Orleans, Louisiana, is the world's longest bridge. It is 23.87 miles long. Eight miles of the bridge are out of sight of land. The bridge, which spans Lake Ponchartrain, was completed in 1969.

**TALLEST**  **The Golden Gate Bridge** over San Francisco Bay in San Francisco, California, is the tallest bridge in the world. The towers of this suspension bridge extend 745 feet up above the water.

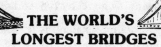

# THE WORLD'S LONGEST BRIDGES

| Type | Name | Location | Length | Date Completed |
|------|------|----------|--------|----------------|
| **Arch** | New River Gorge | U.S.A., Fayetteville, West Virginia | 1,700 ft. | 1977 |
| **Bascule** | Pearl River | U.S.A., Slidell, Louisianna | 482 ft. | 1969 |
| **Beam** | Lake Ponchartrain Number 2 | U.S.A., over Lake Ponchartrain, New Orleans, Louisiana | 23.87 mi. | 1969 |
| **Cantilever** | Quebec Railway Bridge | Canada, over the St. Lawrence River, Quebec City | 1,800 ft. | 1917 |
| **Covered** | Hartland Bridge | Canada, New Brunswick Province | 1,282 ft. | 1899 |
| **Pontoon** | Evergreen Point Bridge | U.S.A., over Lake Washington, Seattle, Washington | 7,518 ft. | 1961 |
| **Suspension** | Humber Bridge | U.K., over the Humbe Estuary in Hull, England | 4,626 ft. | 1977 |
| **Swing Span** | El Ferdan Bridge | Egypt, over the Suez Canal | 552 ft. | 1965 |
| **Vertical Lift** | Arthur Kill Bridge | U.S.A., over the Arthur Channel in Elizabeth, New Jersey | 558 ft. | 1959 |

# Fascinating Facts About Bridges

## FIVE BRIDGES MADE FAMOUS IN LITERATURE

**Boston Bridge** in Boston, Massachusetts, is the subject of "Bridge Over the Charles," a poem by Henry Wadsworth Longfellow.

**Brooklyn Bridge** in New York City is the setting of "A View from The Bridge," a play by Arthur Miller.

**Drina Bridge** in Visegard, Yugoslavia, is the subject of *The Bridge on the Drina,* a Nobel prize-winning novel by Ivo Andue.

**Old London Bridge** in London, England is the subject of "London Bridge Is Falling Down," a nursery rhyme.

**Quebec Bridge** in Quebec, Canada, is the subject of *Alexander's Bridge,* a novel by Willa Cather.

## FIVE BRIDGES MADE FAMOUS IN MOVIES

**The Bridge of San Luis Rey** is a 1945 movie based on a novel of the same name by Thornton Wilder. It is about the collapse of a primitive suspension bridge built by the Inca indians in the Andes mountains of Peru.

**The Bridges at Tokyo-Ri** is a 1954 war movie about the destruction of four North Korean military bridges.

**The Bridge on the River Kwai** is a 1957 movie about a railroad bridge built in Siam (now Thailand), by a British colonel captured by the Japanese in World War II.

**The Bridge** is a 1959 movie about an unnamed bridge defended during World War II by a group of German school boys.

**The Bridge at Remagen** is a 1969 movie about the bridge across the Rhine River that the allied forces crossed into Germany. The crossing became a turning point in World War II.

# FIVE BRIDGES WITH UNUSUAL NAMES

### BRIDGE OF BOILS—LIMA, PERU
An epidemic of bubonic plague broke out among the workmen while they were building this bridge. The disease is characterized by boils (made by the swelling of the lymph nodes). The bridge was named Puente de las Verrugus—the Bridge of Boils.

### BRIDGE OF SIGHS—VENICE, ITALY
This bridge was named for the sighs of unhappy prisoners who used it to cross from their prison to the palace where they were sentenced for their crimes.

### HELL GATE BRIDGE—NEW YORK CITY, U.S.A.
The waters beneath this bridge are so turbulent and treacherous they have been likened to the gates of Hell. Thus, the name Hell Gate Bridge.

### HONEYMOON BRIDGE—NIAGARA FALLS, NEW YORK, U.S.A.
This bridge was located in the one-time "honeymoon capital of America." Because of the number of married couples who honeymooned in Niagara Falls, the bridge was named the Honeymoon Bridge. It was destroyed in 1938 by an ice jam and replaced by the Rainbow Bridge.

### OUTERBRIDGE—STATEN ISLAND, NEW YORK, U.S.A.
It is commonly believed that this bridge was named Outerbridge because of its remoteness from the center of New York City. It was actually named after Eugenius Outerbridge, the first chairman of New York's Port Authority.

# FIVE FAMOUS BRIDGE DISASTERS

**TAY BRIDGE OVER THE FIRTH OF TAY, SCOTLAND**
On December 28, 1979, the bridge collapsed due to a combination of gale winds and faulty construction. A passenger train with 75 people aboard fell into the inlet. There were no survivors.

**QUEBEC BRIDGE OVER THE ST. LAURENCE RIVER, QUEBEC CITY, CANADA**
On August 29, 1907, while the bridge was under construction, part of it collapsed and 82 workers died.

**TACOMA NARROWS BRIDGE OVER PUGET SOUND,
TACOMA, WASHINGTON**
On November 7, 1940, only four months after this bridge was completed, it collapsed from the force of gale winds. There were no lives lost.

**SUNSHINE SKYWAY BRIDGE OVER TAMPA BAY,
ST. PETERSBURG, FLORIDA**
On May 9, 1980, an ocean freighter smashed into an abutment of the bridge. Three cars, one truck and one bus plummetted into the water. Thirty-five people were killed.

**CONNECTICUT TURNPIKE BRIDGE OVER THE MIANUS RIVER,
GREENWICH, CONNECTICUT**
On June 28, 1983, the bridge collapsed due to disrepair, and three motorists were killed. The collapse of this roadway, an important gateway to New England from New York, resulted in major traffic disruption for months.

## FIVE CITIES KNOWN FOR THEIR BRIDGES

| | |
|---|---|
| New York, NY., U.S.A. | 1,420 bridges |
| Sydney, Australia | 1,305 bridges |
| Venice, Italy | 450 bridges |
| Amsterdam, Holland | 300 bridges |
| Osaka, Japan | 250 bridges |

## FIVE STATES IN THE U.S. WITH THE MOST COVERED BRIDGES

| | |
|---|---|
| Pennsylvania | 347 bridges |
| Ohio | 234 bridges |
| Indiana | 152 bridges |
| Vermont | 121 bridges |
| Oregon | 106 bridges |

# FIVE BRIDGES MADE FAMOUS IN PAINTINGS

Pont-Neuf Bridge in Paris, painted by Renoir.
Pont St. Michel Bridge in Paris, painted by Matisse.
A Vermont Covered Bridge, painted by Grandma Moses.
Waterloo Bridge in London, painted by Monet.
Westminster Bridge in London, painted by Whistler.

# FIVE NOTABLE AMERICAN BRIDGE BUILDERS

| Builder | Bridge | Date Completed |
|---|---|---|
| **O. H. Ammann** | Outerbridge, Staten Island, N.Y. | 1928 |
| | Bayonne Bridge, Bayonne, N.J. | 1931 |
| | George Washington Bridge, New York, N.Y. | 1931 |
| | Golden Gate Bridge, San Francisco, Ca. | 1937 |
| | Verrazano-Narrows Bridge, N.Y. | 1969 |
| **James Buchanan Eads** | St. Louis or Eads Bridge, St. Louis, Mo. | 1874 |
| **Roebling John** (Father) and **Washington** (Son) | Allegheny River Bridge, Pittsburgh, Pa. | 1845 |
| | Niagara River Railroad Bridge, Niagara Falls, N.Y. | 1865 |
| | Ohio River Bridge, Cincinnati, Oh. | 1866 |
| | Brooklyn Bridge, N.Y., N.Y. | 1883 |
| **David Steinman** | Florianopolis Bridge, Brazil | 1926 |
| | Carquinez Strait Bridge, Ca. | 1927 |
| | Sydney Harbor Bridge, Australia | 1932 |
| | Triboro Bridge, N.Y., N.Y. | 1936 |
| | Mackinac Straits Bridge, Mi. | 1957 |

# Buildings

Just about anywhere there are people, there are buildings. People live, work, play, and pray in buildings. There has always been a close connection between the structures people build and the way they live. The first buildings of primitive people were simple. Through the ages, however, more elaborate and complicated buildings were made. Simple huts, splendid palaces, and towering skyscrapers are all human expressions of beauty, function, and sometimes folly.

# Buildings Bests

## THE TALLEST STRUCTURES IN THE WORLD

| Type of Structure | Name | Location | Height |
|---|---|---|---|
| Apartment Building | Lake Point Towers | Chicago, Ill., U.S.A. | 645 ft. |
| Cathedral | Ulm | Ulm, West Germany | 528 ft. |
| Factory Chimney | International Nickel Company | Sudbury, Ontario, Canada | 1,250 ft. |
| Hotel | Peachtree Center Plaza | Atlanta, Ga. U.S.A. | 723 ft. |
| Monument | Eiffel Tower | Paris, France | 1,052 ft. |
| Plant Cooling Tower | *(None)* | Uentrop, West Germany | 590 ft. |
| Radio Mast | Warszawa Radio Mast | Plock, Poland | 2,121 ft. |
| Television Tower | KTHI | Fargo, N. D., U.S.A. | 2,063 ft. |
| University Building | M. V. Lomonosov State University | Moscow, U.S.S.R. | 787 ft. |

## TALLEST SKYSCRAPERS AROUND THE WORLD

| Building | Location | Height | Stories |
|---|---|---|---|
| First Canadian Place | Toronto, Canada | 952 ft. | 72 |
| M. V. Lomonosov State University | Moscow, U.S.S.R. | 787 ft. | 32 |
| Mutual Life Citizens | Sydney, Australia | 787 ft. | 70 |
| Palace of Science and Culture | Warsaw, Poland | 758 ft. | 42 |
| Maine Montparnesse | Paris, France | 751 ft. | 64 |
| Ikebokoru | Tokyo, Japan | 741 ft. | 60 |
| Carlton Centre | Johannesburg, South Africa | 722 ft. | 50 |
| Overseas Chinese Banking Corporation | Singapore, Republic of Singapore | 660 ft. | 52 |
| Parque Central Torre | Caracas, Venezuela | 656 ft. | 56 |

## THE FIVE TALLEST SKYSCRAPERS IN THE U.S.

| Building | Location | Height | Stories |
|---|---|---|---|
| Sears Tower | Chicago, Ill. | 1,454 ft. | 110 |
| World Trade Center | New York, N. Y. | 1,350 ft. | 110 |
| Empire State Building | New York, N. Y. | 1,250 ft. | 102 |
| Standard Oil Building | Chicago, Ill. | 1,136 ft. | 80 |
| John Hancock Center | Chicago, Ill. | 1,127 ft. | 100 |

## TALLEST SKYSCRAPERS IN U.S. CITIES

| Building | Location | Height | Stories |
|---|---|---|---|
| Texas Commerce Tower | Houston, Tx. | 997 ft. | 75 |
| First Interstate Bank | Los Angeles, Ca. | 858 ft. | 62 |
| Transamerica Pyramid | San Francisco, Ca. | 853 ft. | 48 |
| U.S. Steel Headquarters | Pittsburgh, Penn. | 841 ft. | 64 |
| John Hancock Tower | Boston, Mass. | 790 ft. | 60 |
| IDS Tower | Minneapolis, Minn. | 775 ft. | 57 |

| Building | Location | Height | Stories |
|---|---|---|---|
| Peachtree Center Plaza Hotel | Atlanta, Ga. | 723 ft. | 71 |
| First International Bldg. | Dallas, Tx. | 710 ft. | 56 |
| Terminal Tower | Cleveland, Oh. | 708 ft. | 52 |

# LARGEST BUILDINGS IN THE WORLD

| Type of Building | Name | Location | Total Floor Space |
|---|---|---|---|
| Arena | Louisiana Superdome | New Orleans, La., U.S.A. | 52 acres |
| Castle (inhabited) | Windsor Castle | England | 51 acres |
| Church | St. Peter's Basilica | Rome, Italy | 162,000 sq. ft. |
| Department Store | Macy's | New York, N.Y., U.S.A. | 50 acres |
| Hotel | Waldorf Astoria | New York, N.Y., U.S.A. | 1,900 rooms |
| Housing Complex | Co-op City | Bronx, N.Y., U.S.A. | 15,000 apartments (1,350 acres) |
| Industrial Plant | Nizhnigtagil Railroad Car & Tank Plant | U.S.S.R. | 204.3 acres |
| Office Building | The Pentagon | Washington, D.C., U.S.A. | 6,500,000 sq. ft. |
| Opera House | Metropolitan Opera House | New York, N.Y. | 3,800 sq. ft. |
| Private House | The Biltmore House | Asherville, N.C., U.S.A. | 250 rooms |
| Museum | Museum of Natural History | New York, N.Y., U.S.A. | 23 acres |
| Synagogue | Temple Emanu-el | New York, N.Y. | 24,000 sq. ft. |
| Theatre | National People's | Peking, China | 12.9 acres |
| Toy Store | Hamleys | London, England | 45,000 sq. ft. |

# Seven Wonders of the Ancient World

| Name | Type of Structure | Location | Remains |
|---|---|---|---|
| **The Pyramids** | Tombs | El Giza, Egypt | Still standing. |
| **Hanging Gardens of Babylon** | Monument | Babylon, Iraq | No ruins remain. |
| **Statue of Zeus** | Statue | Olympia, Greece | All traces of it are lost, except for reproductions on coins. |
| **Temple of Diana at Ephesus** | Temple | Ephesus, Greece (Modern Turkey) | Destroyed by the Goths in A.D. 262. |
| **Mausoleum at Halicarnassus** | Tomb | Bodrum, Turkey | Destroyed by an earthquake in the Middle Ages. |
| **Colossus of Rhodes** | Statue | Rhodes, Greece | Destroyed by an earthquake in 1375 A.D. |
| **Lighthouse at Pharos** | Monument | Alexandria, Egypt | Destroyed by an earthquake in the 13th century. |

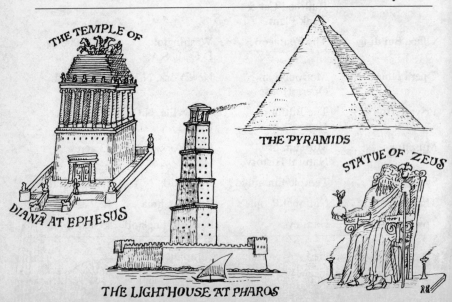

THE TEMPLE OF DIANA AT EPHESUS

THE PYRAMIDS

THE LIGHTHOUSE AT PHAROS

STATUE OF ZEUS

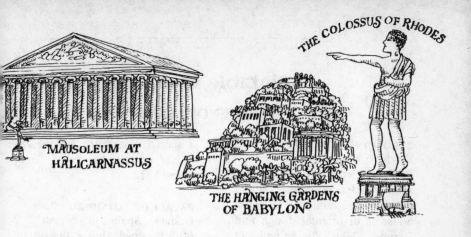

MAUSOLEUM AT HALICARNASSUS

THE COLOSSUS OF RHODES

THE HANGING GARDENS OF BABYLON

# Seven Other Wonders of the World

### COLOSSEUM
**Rome, Italy**
A giant-sized open theatre with a network of arches, vaulted tunnels and stairways with seating for thousands of spectators. Completed in 80 A.D.

### GREAT WALL OF CHINA
**China**
A 3,900-mile wall built of stone, brick, and earth to safeguard the country. The colossal effort it took to build the wall is equal to the labor of a million people working 25 years.

### LEANING TOWER OF PISA
**Pisa, Italy**
An eight-story bell tower with a winding staircase and picturesque marble inlays. The entire building tilts as a result of repeated earth tremors.

### PARTHENON
**Athens, Greece**
A temple constructed of marble and gold which was built 200 feet above the streets of Athens. It featured statues of Greek gods, and carved stone columns. Completed in 432 B.C.

### SANTA SOPHIA
**Istanbul, Turkey**
A Byzantine church noted for its great gold dome and lavish interior. Completed in 537 A.D.

### STONEHENGE
**Salisbury Plain, England**
A group of massive stones standing upright in an open field. How the stones were transported to this location is still a mystery. Built around 2400 B.C.

### TAJ MAHAL
**Agra, India**
An exquisite tomb built in memory of a queen. The building is made of pure white marble. The doors and windows are covered with jewels. Completed in 1654.

# Notable Homes

## TEN SPLENDID HOMES

**BRIGHTON PAVILLION**
**Brighton, England**
Built by George IV, Prince Regent. A "seashore cottage" built at a cost of $15 million. The entire house is of oriental design and features a lavish dining hall and kitchen. Completed 1815.

**CHATEAU OF CHAMBORD**
**Loire Valley, France**
Built by King Francois I. A vacation home consisting of 440 rooms, 350 chimneys, and 75 staircases, built on 14,000 acres of gardens surrounded by a 20-mile wall. Completed 1534.

**HADRIAN'S VILLA**
**Tivoli, Italy**
Built by Emperor Hadrian. This villa included 7 square miles of buildings and gardens enclosed by a wall. A house, theatre, library, and baths were among the buildings set in lovely gardens of trees and flowers. Completed 124 A.D.

**MONTICELLO**
**Charlottesville, Virginia, U.S.A.**
Built by Thomas Jefferson. Thomas Jefferson designed this house which rests on a little mountain (*monticello* in Italian) situated on 5,000 acres of land. The house features a dumbwaiter for bringing wines up from the cellar, and a special passageway for the removal of chamber pots. Completed 1772.

**PALACE OF ALHAMBRA**
**Granada, Spain**
Built by Ibnal Ahmar, the sultan of Granada. The floor space of this unique palace encompasses 9 acres. The sounds of running water can be heard in every palace room. The house was designed to funnel a natural stream through fountains, and reflecting pools were built into all of the rooms. Completed 1358.

**SAN SIMEON CASTLE**
**San Simeon, California, U.S.A.**
Built by William Randolph Hearst. It cost $50 million to build this estate overlooking the Pacific Ocean. It is located on 240,000 acres of land and boasts a house with elevators, pools, movie rooms, and dining halls. Completd 1925.

**SAN SOUCI**
**Cap Haitien, Haiti**
Built by King Henry Christopher. This huge house was built over a mountain stream so that the lower floors would be cooled by running water. The rooms are decorated with lavish paintings and furniture imported from Eu-

rope. The floors are made of marble and mahogany. Completed 1813.

## THE BREAKERS
**Newport, Rhode Island, U.S.A.**
Built by Cornelius Vanderbilt II. This is a 70-room fireproof "summer cottage" built at a cost of $10 million. The elaborate interior includes carved pillars and gold trimmed walls. Sixty overnight guests could be accommodated at one time. It is now a museum. Completed 1895.

## VERSAILLES CHATEAU
**Versailles, France**
Built by King Louis XIV. It took 36,000 men to build this 325 million-dollar house. The Chateau has splendid suites of rooms, private salons, banquet halls, and ballrooms. The Hall of Mirrors, and lavish gardens are among its outstanding features. Completed 1705.

## XANADU
**Orlando, Florida, U.S.A.**
Built by Roy E. Mason. This house was built to be "The Home of the Future." It is constructed of multiple domes made of plastic foam. It provides all the comforts of modern technology, including video monitoring and a computerized kitchen. Completed 1983.

# NINE UNUSUAL HOMES

## ELEPHANT HOUSE
**Margate, New Jersey**
Built by James Lafferty. This is an 8-room house built of wood and coated with tin. This 90-ton house is shaped like an elephant. Completed 1881.

## GHOST-PROOF MANSION
**San Jose, California**
Built by Sarah Winchester. This is a 750-room house designed to fool ghosts. Rooms were built, then torn down over a 38-year period. Fake chimneys, doors, and

staircases which lead to blank walls are among its curiosities. Completed 1922.

## GLASS HOUSE
### New Canaan, Connecticut
Built by Philip Johnson. This is an all-glass rectangular-shaped house. Thin columns of steel support the roof. There are no rooms inside but cabinets are lined up to divide living areas. Completed 1949.

## HOUSE ON THE ROCK
### Spring Green, Wisconsin
Built by Alex Jordan. This house sits on a sixty-foot-high rock overlooking a valley four hundred and fifty feet below. Five hundred tons of mortar and five thousand tons of stone were used in the house; some transported to the top of the rock by electric hoists, some carried up by Alex Jordan. Completed 1960.

## PAPER HOUSE
### Pigeon Cove, Massachusetts
Built by Elis F. Stenman. Approximately 100,000 newspapers were used to construct this house and the furniture within it. The walls were made of layers of pasted and folded newspapers. Papers rolled into different sizes make up the furniture which includes tables, chairs, lamps, and a grandfather clock. Completed 1942.

## HOUSE OF BOTTLES
### British Columbia, Canada
Built by George Plumb. The entire house is constructed of 18,000 liquor, soda, medicine, and beer bottles. Completed 1978.

## PRAIRIE CHICKEN
### Norman, Oklahoma
Built by Herbert Green. This house, built in the shape of a chicken, is made of wooden planks and corrugated metal. Completed 1962.

## REVOLVING HOUSE
### Wilton, Connecticut
Built by Richard Foster. This is a circular-shaped house with rooms shaped like slices of a pie. The house rests on a 3-ton ball bearing and revolves by the power of a 1½ h.p. motor. Completed 1968.

## UNDERGROUND HOUSE
### Fresno, California
Built by Forestiere Baldasera. This 90-room house was dug under the earth by the owner. It took 44 years to complete but cost only $300. Completed 1946.

# Official Homes for Heads of Government

| Country | Name of Home | Head of Government | Location |
|---|---|---|---|
| Australia | The Lodge | Prime Minister | Canberra, Australia |
| Belgium | Chateau de Lachen | King | Brussels, Belgium |
| France | L'Elysee Palace | President | Paris, France |
| Italy | Quiranale | President | Rome, Italy |
| Mexico | Los Pinos | President | Mexico City, Mexico |
| Portugal | Palacio de Belem | President | Lisbon, Portugal |
| Spain | Palacio de la Moncloe | Premier | Madrid, Spain |
| West Germany | Federal Chancellor's Office | Chancellor | Bonn, West Germany |
| United Kingdom | #10 Downing Street | Prime Minister | London, England |
| United States | The White House | President | Washington, D.C., USA |

# A Calendar for Kids

## 365 DAYS OF WORLDWIDE EVENTS, HOLIDAYS, AND BIRTHDAYS

In many countries of the world almanacs were the first books published. These almanacs always included a calendar—a guide to the passing of time.

Although calendars seem very simple, it took many centuries for calendars to evolve as we know them today. This calendar lists a year of worldwide events, holidays, and birthdays. You'll find a reason to celebrate every day of the year, even it it is the one day to do nothing . . . January 16th—National Nothing Day.

**Key to Symbols**

★ **Holidays**

♦ **Events**

⚜ **Birthdays**

## January

**FLOWER: CARNATION**
**BIRTHSTONE: GARNET**

**1**

★ New Year's Day.
★ Haiti, Independence Day, when Haitians honor Jean Jacques Dessalines, the founder of Haiti.
★ Sudan, National Holiday.
♦ The first U.S. Tournament of Roses Parade took place in Pasadena, California in 1886.

**2**

★ Good Luck Day.

◆ Georgia became the 4th U.S. state in 1788.
✿ Betsy Ross, who, legend has it, designed the first American flag, born 1752.
✿ Lucretia Mott, American abolitionist, feminist, born 1793.

**3**

◆ Alaska became the 49th U.S. State in 1959.
✿ J. R. R. Tolkien, English author (*The Hobbit, The Lord of the Rings*), born 1892.

**4**

★ Burma, National Holiday.
◆ Utah became the 45th U.S. state in 1896.
✿ Sir Isaac Newton, English scientist and mathematician, born 1643.
✿ Jacob Grimm, German author of *Grimm's Fairy Tales* (with his brother, Wilhelm), born 1785.
✿ Louis Braille, French inventor of a reading system for the blind, born 1809.

**5**

★ Bird Day, U.S. (for the protection of bird life).
★ George Washington Carver Day, U.S.

**6**

★ Feast of the Epiphany/Twelfth Day (1986).
◆ New Mexico became 47th U.S. state in 1912.
◆ The first around-the-world

commercial airline flight by Pan American Airlines, 1942.

**7**

★ Panama Canal Day in U.S. and Central America.
✿ Millard Fillmore, 13th U.S. president, born 1800.

**8**

★ U.N. World Literary Day.
✿ Elvis Presley, American singer, born 1935.

**9**

◆ Connecticut became the 5th U.S. state in 1788.
✿ Richard Milhous Nixon, 37th U.S. president, born 1913.

**10**

◆ League of Nations founded 1920.

**11**

★ Banana Split Day, U.S.
✿ Alexander Hamilton, first U.S. Secretary of the Treasury, born 1755.

**12**

✿ John Hancock, American patriot, famous for his signature on the Declaration of Independence, born 1737.

**13**

★ Stephen Foster Memorial Day, U.S. Foster was the composer of 175 songs, among them, "Oh! Susanna" and "My Old Kentucky Home."

## 14

✤ Albert Schweitzer, Alsatian (French) missionary, born 1875. Dr. Schweitzer cared for native patients at his hospital in French Equatorial Africa. He was awarded the Nobel Peace Prize in 1956.

## 15

✤ Martin Luther King, American civil rights leader, born 1929.

## 16

★ National Nothing Day, U.S.

## 17

◆ U.S. launched first atomic-powered submarine, the U.S.S. *Nautilus,* in 1954.
✤ Benjamin Franklin, American inventor and statesman, born 1706.

## 18

✤ Daniel Webster, American statesman, born 1782.
✤ A. A. Milne, author of *Winnie-the-Pooh,* born 1882.
✤ Muhammad Ali (Cassius Clay), American heavyweight boxing champion, born 1942.

## 19

✤ Robert E. Lee, American Civil War general, born 1807.
✤ Edgar Allen Poe, American poet ("The Raven," "Annabel Lee") and short story writer ("The Fall of the House of Usher," "The Murders in the Rue Morgue"), born 1809.

## 20

♒ The zodiac sign of Aquarius, The Water Bearer, begins. Those born under the sign are said to be inventive, friendly, and humanitarian.
★ Martin Luther King Day, U.S.
★ Presidential Inauguration Day, U.S. (every 4 years).
◆ First basketball game played in U.S.—Springfield, Mass., 1892.

## 21

✤ Ethan Allen, American patriot and leader of the Green Mountain Boys during the American Revolution, born 1738.

## 22

✤ George Gordon, Lord Byron, English romantic poet ("Childe Harold"), born 1788.
✤ August Strindberg, Swedish playwright ("Miss Julie," "The Dream Play"), born 1849.

## 23

✤ Edward Manet, French artist, born 1832.

## 24

◆ Gold was discovered in Sutter's Mill, California in 1848. The discovery of gold brought 40,000 prospectors to California. Although few of them struck it rich, their presence helped to stimulate economic growth and promote the mining industry in California.
◆ Boy Scouts founded by Robert S. S. Baden-Powell in England, 1908.

## 25

✿ Robert Burns, Scottish poet ("Auld Lang Syne," "Comin' Thro' the Rye"), born 1759.

## 26

★ Australia Day, National Holiday.
♦ Michigan became the 26th U.S. state in 1837.
✿ Douglas MacArthur, American WW II general, born 1880.

## 27

♦ The Vietnam War officially ended, 1973.
✿ Wolfgang Amadeus Mozart, Austrian composer of symphonies, chamber music, and operas, born 1756.

## 28

♦ U.S. Coast Guard established, 1915.

## 29

♦ Kansas became the 34th U.S. state in 1861.
✿ Tom Paine, American political philosopher and writer, born 1737. Paine's pamphlet, Common Sense, 1776, urged American Independence from England.
✿ William McKinley, 25th U.S. president, born 1843.

## 30

✿ Franklin D. Roosevelt, 32nd U.S. president, born 1882.

## 31

✿ Franz Schubert, Austrian composer of symphonies, songs, and piano music, born 1797.
✿ Baseball great, Jackie Robinson, born 1919. Robinson, a member of the Baseball Hall of Fame, was the first black to enter the major leagues.

*Chinese New Year*

# February

**FLOWER: VIOLET**
**BIRTHSTONE: AMETHYST**

## 1

★ National Freedom Day, U.S.
★ Robinson Crusoe Day, U.S.
✿ Langston Hughes, American poet, born 1902.

## 2

★ Groundhog Day, U.S.
✿ James Joyce, Irish short story writer (*Dubliners, Ulysses*), born 1882.

## 3

★ New Zealand Day.
✤ Felix Mendelssohn, German composer of *Songs Without Words,* born 1809.
✤ Elizabeth Blackwell, first American woman doctor, born 1821.

## 4

★ Sri Lanka, National Holiday.
✤ Tadeusz Kosciuszko, Polish war hero of American Revolution, born 1746.
✤ Charles Lindbergh, American aviator, who made the first solo non-stop flight across the Atlantic Ocean, born 1902.

## 5

✤ Adlai Stevenson, U.S. statesman, born 1900.
✤ Hank Aaron, baseball's "Home Run King," born 1934.

## 6

◆ Massachusetts became the 6th U.S. state in 1788.
✤ Babe Ruth (George Herman Ruth), baseball great, born 1895. Ruth, a member of the Baseball Hall of Fame, held over 50 baseball records at the time of his retirement.
✤ Ronald Reagan, 40th U.S. president, born 1911.

## 7

✤ Charles Dickens, English novelist, (*Oliver Twist, Great Expectations*), born 1812.

✤ Frederick Douglass, American abolitionist, born 1817.
✤ Sinclair Lewis, American novelist (*Babbitt, Main Street*), born 1885.

## 8

◆ Boy Scouts of America established in U.S., 1910.
✤ William T. Sherman, American Civil War general, born 1820.
✤ Jules Verne, French novelist (*Around the World in Eighty Days, 20,000 Leagues Under the Sea*), born 1828.

## 9

★ Chinese New Year—Year of the Tiger (1986).
◆ U.S. established National Weather Service, 1870.
✤ William H. Harrison, 9th U.S. president, born 1773.

## 10

✤ Boris Pasternak, Russian poet and novelist (*Doctor Zhivago*), born 1890.

## 11

★ Mardi Gras/Shrove Tuesday, U.S. (1986).
★ National Inventors Day, U.S.
✤ Thomas Alva Edison, American inventor, born 1847.

## 12

★ Lincoln's Birthday, U.S.
★ Ash Wednesday (1986).
✤ Abraham Lincoln, 16th U.S. president, born 1809.

◆ NAACP (National Organization for the Advancement of Colored People), established 1909.
✿ Charles Darwin, English naturalist, born 1809.

## 13

◆ First public school in U.S., the Boston Latin School, opened in 1635.
◆ First magazine in U.S., *The American Magazine,* published in 1741.

## 14

★ St. Valentine's Day, U.S.
◆ Oregon became the 33rd U.S. state in 1859.
◆ Arizona became the 48th U.S. state in 1912.

## 15

✿ Galileo Galilei, Italian astronomer and physicist, born 1564.
✿ Susan B. Anthony, American abolitionist, born 1820.

## 16

★ Lithuania, National Holiday.
◆ First daily television news in U.S. broadcast on NBC, 1948.

## 17

★ Washington's Birthday observed, U.S.
◆ National Congress of Parents and Teachers Association established in U.S. in 1897.
✿ Marian Anderson, American opera singer, born 1902.

## 18

★ Gambia, National Holiday.
◆ Astronomer Clyde Tombaugh confirmed the existence of the planet, Pluto, at Lowell Observatory in Flagstaff, Arizona, 1930.

## 19

♒ The zodiac sign of Pisces, The Fish, begins. Those born under the sign of Pisces are said to be creative, sensitive, and kind.
◆ American Thomas Edison was issued a patent for his invention, the phonograph, 1877.

## 20

◆ John Glenn became the first U.S. astronaut to orbit Earth, 1962.

## 21

◆ First U.S. telephone book was issued to residents of New Haven, Connecticut in 1878.
✿ W. H. Auden, English-American poet, born 1907.

## 22

★ Dominican Republic, National Holiday.
✿ George Washington, first U.S. president, born 1732.
✿ Edna St. Vincent Millay, American poet, born 1892.

## 23

★ Guyana, National Holiday.
✿ Samuel Pepys, English diarist of London's Great Fire, born 1633.

✤ George Frederick Handel, German-English composer of operas, oratorios, and orchestral music, born 1685.

## 24

★ Estonia, National Holiday.
✤ Winslow Homer, American artist, born 1836.

## 25

★ Kuwait, National Holiday.
✤ Enrico Caruso, Italian opera singer, born 1873.
✤ John Foster Dulles, American diplomat, born 1888.

## 26

◆ Grand Canyon National Park established in U.S., 1919.
✤ Buffalo Bill (William F. Cody),

American army scout and Wild West showman, born 1846.

## 27

✤ Sveinn Bjornsson, first president of Iceland, born 1881.
✤ Henry Wadsworth Longfellow, American poet ("The Song of Hiawatha," "The Village Blacksmith"), born 1807.
✤ Ralph Nader, American consumer advocate, born 1934.

## 28

✤ Michael de Montaigne, French writer, first to use the term *essay*, born 1533.

## 29

★ Leap year every four years.
★ Bachelor's Day.

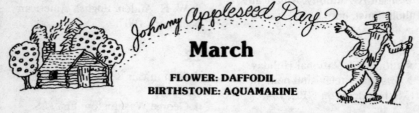

*Johnny Appleseed Day*

# March

**FLOWER: DAFFODIL**
**BIRTHSTONE: AQUAMARINE**

## 1

◆ Ohio became the 17th U.S. state in 1803.
◆ Nebraska became the 37th U.S. state in 1867.
◆ Yellowstone National Park was established as the first U.S. National Park, 1872.

✤ Frederic Chopin, Polish pianist and composer, born 1810.

## 2

✤ Samuel Houston, American frontier hero and statesman after whom Houston, Texas was named, born 1793.

✿ Dr. Seuss (Theodore Geisel), American author (*The Cat in the Hat, The Grinch Who Stole Christmas*), born 1904.

## 3

★ Morocco, National Holiday.
★ Dolls Festival, Japan.
◆ The first laws to protect child workers were passed in U.S., 1842.
◆ Florida became the 27th U.S. state in 1845.
✿ Alexander Graham Bell, Scottish-American inventor of the telephone, born 1847.

## 4

◆ The U.S. Constitution went into effect in 1789.
◆ Vermont became the 14th U.S. state in 1791.
✿ Knute Rockne, famed American football coach, born 1888.

## 5

◆ The Boston Massacre, an attack on American colonists by British troops, 1770.

## 6

★ Ghana, National Holiday.
◆ Mexican siege of the Alamo—Texas annexed. Texas became independent of Mexico in 1836.
✿ Michelangelo Buonarroti, Italian sculptor, painter, and architect, born 1475.

## 7

✿ Luther Burbank, American horticulturist who developed new varieties of potatoes, plums, berries, and flowers, born 1849.

## 8

★ International Women's Day.
✿ Oliver Wendell Holmes, Jr., American jurist, born 1841.
✿ Joseph Lee, American developer of childrens' playgrounds, born 1862.

## 9

◆ Laika, the first dog to travel into space, was launched by the U.S.S.R., 1957.
✿ Amerigo Vespucci, Italian navigator and explorer, for whom the Americas were named, born 1454.

## 10

◆ The Salvation Army was organized in the U.S., 1880.

## 11

★ Johnny Appleseed Day, U.S.

## 12

★ Girl Scout Day, U.S.

## 13

★ Grenada, National Holiday.
◆ The planet Uranus discovered by German-English astronomer, Sir William Herschel, 1781.

## 14

◆ American Eli Whitney was granted a patent for the cotton gin in 1794.

✿ Casey Jones, American railroad engineer, born 1864.
✿ Albert Einstein, German-Swiss-American physicist, who developed theories of relativity, born 1879.

## 15

★ Buzzard Day, the annual return of buzzards to Hinckley, Ohio, U.S.
★ Ides of March (commemorates the assassination of Roman emperor, Julius Caesar, 44 B.C.).
◆ Maine became the 23rd U.S. state in 1820.
✿ Andrew Jackson, 7th U.S. president, born 1767.

## 16

◆ The first docking of one spaceship with another accomplished by the U.S., 1966.
✿ James Madison, 4th U.S. president, born 1751.

## 17

★ St. Patrick's Day.
★ Ireland, National Holiday.

## 18

◆ The first person to walk in space was Soviet cosmonaut Alexei Leonov, 1965.
✿ Grover Cleveland, 22nd and 24th U.S. president, born 1837.

## 19

★ Swallow's Day (the yearly return of the swallows to Capistrano, California).
✿ William Jennings Bryan, American lawyer and political leader, born 1860.
✿ William Bradford, American Pilgrim Father, born 1590.

## 20

🐏 The zodiac sign of Aries, The Ram, begins. Those born under the sign of Aries are said to be adventurous, outgoing, and aggressive.
★ Spring officially begins in Northern Hemisphere; fall begins in Southern Hemisphere, 5:03 P.M. EST (1986).
★ National Teenagers Day, U.S.

## 21

◆ Arthur L. Schalow and Charles H. Townes granted patent for laser, 1958.

## 22

✿ Marcel Marceau, French mime, born 1923.

## 23

★ Palm Sunday.
★ Pakistan, National Holiday.
◆ World Meteorological Organization founded WMO, 1950.
✿ Fannie Farmer, American cooking expert, born 1857.

## 24

★ Agriculture Day, U.S.

## 25

✿ Arturo Toscanini, Italian symphony conductor, born 1867.

**26**

★ Bangladesh, National Holiday.
★ Regatta Day in Hawaii.
✿ Robert Frost, American poet
("Birches"), born 1874.

**27**

◆ Major earthquake, Alaska, 1963.

**28**

★ Good Friday (1986).
◆ Nuclear power accident at Three
Mile Island, Pennsylvania in 1979.

**29**

★ Vietnam Veterans Day, U.S.
✿ John Tyler, 10th U.S. president,
born 1790.

**30**

★ Easter Sunday.
◆ U.S. purchased Alaska from
Russia, 1867.
✿ Vincent Van Gogh, Dutch artist,
born 1853.

**31**

★ Malta, National Holiday.
✿ Rene Descartes, French
philosopher, born 1596.
✿ Franz Joseph Haydn, Austrian
composer of symphonies, chamber
music, songs and oratorios, born
1732.
✿ Robert Ross McBurney,
American YMCA (Young Men's
Christian Association) leader, born
1837.

# April — Pony Express

**FLOWER: SWEETPEA**
**BIRTHSTONE: DIAMOND**

**1**

★ April Fools' Day.

**2**

★ International Children's Book
Day.
✿ Charlemagne, French Ruler,
born 742 A.D.
✿ Hans Christian Anderson,
Danish poet, novelist, and writer of
fairy tales, born 1805.

**3**

◆ The Pony Express began
delivering mail in U.S., 1860.
✿ Washington Irving, American
writer ("The Legend of Sleepy
Hollow," "Rip Van Winkle"), born
1783.

**4**

✿ Dorothea Dix, American social
reformer, born 1802.

★ Senegal, National Holiday.
♦ NATO (North Atlantic Treaty Organization) established in 1949 to settle disputes among member nations through peaceful means.

**5**

❉ Booker T. Washington, American educator and author, born 1856.

**6**

♦ The first modern Olympic games held in Athens, Greece in 1896.
♦ American explorer Robert E. Peary was the first man to reach the North Pole in 1909.
❉ Harry Houdini (Erich Weiss), American magician and escape artist, born 1874.

**7**

★ World Health Day.

**8**

★ Siddhartha Gautama the Buddha, Nepalese philosopher and founder of the religion, Buddhism, born 563 B.C.
♦ Juan Ponce de Leon, Spanish explorer, discovered Florida in 1513.

**9**

★ Czechoslovakia, National Holiday.
♦ The first American public library opened in Peterborough, New Hampshire in 1833.

**10**

♦ ASPCA (The American Society for the Prevention of Cruelty to Animals) established in 1866.

**11**

★ Hungary, National Holiday.
♦ Jackie Robinson became the first black major league baseball player in U.S., 1947.

**12**

♦ American Civil War began with the bombardment of Fort Sumter, Charleston, South Carolina in 1861.
♦ Yuri Gagarin, Soviet cosmonaut, was the first man to travel into space, 1961.

**13**

❉ Thomas Jefferson, 3rd U.S. president, born 1743.

**14**

★ Pan American Day, U.S.
♦ The first edition of Noah Webster's American Dictionary of the English Language published in 1828.

**15**

♦ The British passenger ship, Titanic, sunk after crashing into an iceberg, 1912.
❉ Leonardo da Vinci, Italian artist, scientist, and inventor, born 1452.

**16**

★ Denmark, National Holiday.
❉ Wilbur Wright, American co-

inventor of the ariplane (with his brother, Orville) born 1867.
✤ Charlie Chaplin, British-American silent film star, born 1889.

## 17

★ Syria, National Holiday.
◆ Italian explorer Giovanni da Verrazano, discovered New York Harbor in 1524.
✤ Thornton Wilder, American playwright and novelist, ("Our Town," *The Bridge of San Luis Rey*), born 1897.

## 18

★ Zimbabwe, National Holiday.
★ Israel, National Holiday.
◆ American Paul Revere made his famous midnight ride to warn the colonists of the British march on Concord, Massachusetts, 1775.
◆ San Francisco, California was destroyed by a major earthquake and fire, 1906.

## 19

★ Sierre Leone, National Holiday.
◆ The Battle of Lexington and Concord, an important victory for the colonists in the American Revolutionary War, 1775.

## 20

🐂 The zodiac sign of Taurus, The Bull, begins. Those born under the sign of Taurus are said to be practical, patient, and persistent.
✤ Adolf Hitler, German Nazi dictator, born 1889.

## 21

✤ Charlotte Brontë, English novelist (*Jane Eyre*), born 1816.

## 22

★ Earth Day, U.S.

## 23

✤ William Shakespeare, English playwright and poet ("Hamlet," "Macbeth"), born 1564.
✤ James Buchanan, 15th U.S. president, born 1791.

## 24

★ Passover begins (1986).
★ Secretaries' Day, U.S.
◆ Library of Congress, Washington, D.C. established in 1800.

## 25

✤ Guglielmo Marconi, Italian inventor of the radio, born 1874.

## 26

★ Tanzania, National Holiday.
✤ John James Audubon, American naturalist and painter, born 1785.
✤ Frederick Law Olmstead, American landscape architect, born 1822.

## 27

★ Togo, National Holiday.
★ Afghanistan, National Holiday.
✤ Ulysses S. Grant, 18th U.S. president, born 1822.

## 28

◆ Maryland became the 7th U.S. state in 1788.

✿ James Monroe, 5th U.S. president, born 1758.

### 29

★ Japan, National Holiday.
✿ Hirohito, emperor of Japan, born 1901.

### 30

★ Netherlands, National Holiday.
◆ George Washington was inaugurated as first U.S. president in New York, 1789.
◆ Louisiana became the 18th U.S. state in 1812.

# May

**FLOWER: LILY OF THE VALLEY**
**BIRTHSTONE: EMERALD**

### 1

★ May Day is Labor Day in many parts of Europe.
★ Loyalty Day, U.S.

### 2

✿ Benjamin Spock, American pediatrician, born 1903.

### 3

◆ U.S. airline passenger service began in 1919.
✿ Golda Meir, Israeli leader, born 1898.

### 4

★ Student's Memorial Day, U.S.
✿ Nikolai Lenin, Russian Communist leader, born 1847.

### 5

★ Boy's Day, Japan and Hawaii.
✿ Karl Marx, German philosopher, born 1818.

### 6

◆ Roger Bannister, British doctor and athlete, was the first to run a mile in under 4 minutes, 1954.
✿ Sigmund Freud, Austrian founder of psychoanalysis, born 1856.

### 7

✿ Johannes Brahms, German composer of songs, symphonies, sonatas, and choral music, born 1833.
✿ Peter Ilyich Tchaikovsky, Russian composer, born 1840.

## 8

♦ Spanish explorer, Hernando de Soto, discovered the Mississippi River, 1541.
✤ Harry S. Truman, 33rd U.S. president, born 1884.
✤ Ian Fleming, British creator of Agent 007, born 1908.

## 9

✤ John Brown, American abolitionist, born 1800.
✤ Sir James Barrie, Scottish author of *Peter Pan,* born 1860.

## 10

♦ The first transcontinental railroad in the U.S. completed, 1869.

## 11

★ Mother's Day, international holiday (1986).
♦ Minnesota became the 32nd U.S. state in 1858.
✤ Irving Berlin, American songwriter, born 1888.

## 12

★ National Hospital Day, U.S.
✤ Florence Nightingale, British founder of modern professional nursing, born 1820.

## 13

♦ The first permanent English settlement in America was established, Jamestown, Virginia, 1607.

## 14

★ Paraguay, National Holiday.
♦ American army officers, Capt. Meriwether Lewis and Lt. William Clark began exploration of the Louisiana Territory in 1804.
♦ The first American major league baseball stadium was built in Brooklyn, N.Y. in 1862.
♦ The first U.S. manned space station, *Skylab 2,* was launched, 1973.
✤ Gabriel Fahrenheit, German-Dutch physicist who invented mercury thermometer, born 1686.

## 15

★ Peace Officers Memorial Day, U.S.
✤ Frank Baum, American author of *The Wizard of Oz,* born 1856.

## 16

♦ The first movie "Oscars" were awarded in 1929.

## 17

★ Armed Forces Day, U.S.
★ Norway, National Holiday.
♦ The first Kentucky Derby horse race was held in 1875.
♦ The New York Stock Exchange was founded in 1792.

## 18

♦ Massachusetts became the first state to make school attendance in U.S. mandatory, 1852.
✤ Bertrand Russell, British philosopher, mathematician, and social reformer, born 1872.

## 19

★ Victoria Day, Canada.
✣ Ho Chi Minh, Vietnamese Communist leader, born 1890.

## 20

★ Cameroon, National Holiday.
◆ Henri Rousseau, French artist, born 1844.

## 21

♊ The zodiac sign of Gemini, The Twins, begins. Those born under the sign of Gemini are said to be versatile, witty, and persuasive.
◆ American Red Cross founded by Clara Barton, 1881.
◆ American Charles Lindbergh completed the first solo nonstop transatlantic flight, 1927.

## 22

★ National Maritime Day, U.S. (celebrates first steamboat crossing of the Atlantic Ocean in 1890).
✣ Richard Wagner, German composer of operas, born 1913.
✣ Sir Arthur Conan Doyle, Scottish-English author and creator of Sherlock Holmes, born 1859.

## 23

◆ South Carolina became the 8th U.S. state in 1788.
✣ Carolus Linnaeus, Swedish scientist, known for his system of plant classification, born 1707.

## 24

✣ Queen Victoria, British monarch, born 1819.

◆ The first public telegraph message was sent by Samuel Morse in 1844.

## 25

★ Argentina, National Holiday.
★ Jordan, National Holiday.
✣ Ralph Waldo Emerson, American poet and essayist, born 1803.
✣ Theodore Roethke, American poet, born 1908.

## 26

★ Memorial Day. U.S. honors Americans who died in wars (1986).
✣ Al Jolson, American entertainer, born 1886.

## 27

✣ Amelia Bloomer, American women's rights champion, born 1818.
✣ Julia Ward Howe, American composer of "The Battle Hymn of the Republic," born 1819.
✣ Rachel Carson, American marine biologist and writer, born 1907.

## 28

✣ Jim Thorpe, native American football player and Olympic gold medalist, born 1888.

## 29

◆ Rhode Island became the 13th U.S. state in 1790.
◆ Wisconsin became the 30th U.S. state in 1848.
◆ Sir Edmund Hillary of New

Zealand and Tenzing Norkay of Nepal became the first to reach the summit of Mt. Everest in 1953.
✽ John Fitzgerald Kennedy, 35th U.S. president, born 1917.

**30**

◆ The Hall of Fame of Great

Americans opened at New York University in New York City, 1901.

**31**

★ South Africa, National Holiday.
✽ Walt Whitman, American poet (*Leaves of Grass*), born 1819.

# June

**FLOWER: ROSE**
**BIRTHSTONE: PEARL**

**1**

★ Tunisia, National Holiday.
◆ Kentucky became the 15th U.S. state in 1792.
◆ Tennessee became the 16th U.S. state in 1796.

**2**

★ Italy, National Holiday.
◆ P.T. Barnum's circus began first U.S. tour in 1835.

**3**

✽ Jefferson Davis, President of the Confederate States of America, born 1808.

**4**

★ Tonga, National Holiday.
✽ Robert Merrill, American opera singer, born 1919.

**5**

★ World Environment Day.
★ Seychelles, National Holiday.

**6**

★ Sweden, National Holiday.
◆ D-day, WW II. Allied forces invaded Nazi-held western Europe, 1944.
✽ Nathan Hale, American patriot, born 1755.
◆ World's first drive-in movie theater opened in Camden, N.J. in 1933.

**7**

◆ American frontiersman Daniel Boone began exploring Kentucky in 1769.
✽ Paul Gauguin, French artist, born 1848.

## 8

✿ Frank Lloyd Wright, American architect, born 1869.

## 9

✿ John Howard Payne, American composer of "Home Sweet Home" born 1791.
✿ Cole Porter, American songwriter, born 1893.

## 10

★ Portugal, Camies Memorial Day.
✿ F. Lee Bailey, American trial lawyer, born 1933.

## 11

★ Great Britain, National Holiday.
✿ Ben Jonson, English playwright and poet, born 1572.
✿ King Kamehameha, unifier of Hawaiian islands, born 1758.
✿ Jacques Cousteau, French explorer of the oceans, born 1910.

## 12

★ Philippines, Independence Day.
◆ The Baseball Hall of Fame opened in Cooperstown, New York in 1939.
✿ Anne Frank, German-Dutch author of *The Diary of a Young Girl,* born 1929.

## 13

★ Alexander the Great Memorial Day (honors the ancient Macedonian king).
✿ William Butler Yeats, Irish poet, born 1865.

## 14

★ Flag Day, U.S.
✿ Harriet Beecher Stowe, American author of *Uncle Tom's Cabin,* born 1811.

## 15

★ Father's Day, U.S. (1986).
◆ King John of England signed the Magna Carta, the document on which English law is based, 1215.
◆ Arkansas became the 25th U.S. state in 1836.

## 16

◆ Soviet cosmonaut Valentina Tereshkova became the first woman to travel into space, 1963.

## 17

★ Iceland, National Holiday.
◆ Battle of Bunker Hill, American Revolutionary War, 1775.
◆ Watergate break-in, a U.S. political scandal, 1972.

## 18

◆ Waterloo Day, Great Britain. (remembering the famous Battle of Waterloo, in which the French emperor, Napoleon, was defeated, 1815).

## 19

✿ Lou Gehrig, baseball great, born 1903.

## 20

◆ West Virginia became the 25th U.S. state in 1863.

✣ Lillian Hellman, American writer, born 1905.

## 21

★ Summer officially begins in Northern Hemisphere; winter begins in Southern Hemisphere, 11:30 A.M. EST (1986).
◆ New Hampshire became the 9th U.S. state in 1788.
✣ Jean-Paul Sartre, French philosopher, playwright, and novelist, born 1905.

## 22

 The zodiac sign of Cancer, The Crab, begins. Those born under the sign of Cancer are said to be imaginative, gentle, and emotional.
◆ The voting age in U.S. changed from 21 to 18 in 1970.

## 23

★ Midsummer's Eve, a celebration of summer in Europe.
★ Luxembourg, National Holiday.
◆ English explorer, John Sebastian Cabot, discovered Labrador in 1498.

## 25

◆ Virginia became the 10th U.S. state in 1788.

✣ George Orwell, British novelist (*Nineteen Eighty-Four*), born 1903.

## 26

★ Malagasy Republic and Somalia, Independence Day.
✣ Pearl Buck, American author of *The Good Earth,* born 1892.

## 27

◆ First Newbery medals awarded for excellence in children's literature, 1922.
✣ Helen Keller, American author, born 1880.

## 28

◆ World War I ended with Treaty of Versailles, 1919.
✣ Peter Paul Rubens, Flemish-German artist, born 1577.

## 29

✣ William Mayo, American surgeon, co-founder with his brother, Charles, of the Mayo Clinic, born 1861.

## 30

★ Independence Day, Zaire.

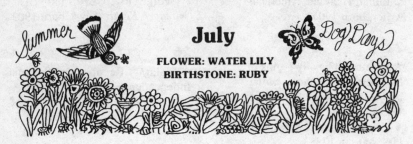

# July

**FLOWER: WATER LILY**
**BIRTHSTONE: RUBY**

## 1

★ Dominion Day, Canada.
★ Half-Year Day, Hong Kong.
◆ The first U.S. postage stamps were issued, 1847.

## 2

✤ Thurgood Marshall, first black U.S. Supreme Court justice, born 1908.

## 3

★ Dog days of Summer (the start of the six hottest weeks of summer in the Northern Hemisphere).
◆ Idaho became the 43rd U.S. state in 1890.
✤ Franz Kafka, Czech-German novelist and short-story writer, born 1883.

## 4

★ Declaration of Independence Day, U.S.
★ Garibaldi Day, Italy.
✤ Calvin Coolidge, 30th U.S. president, born 1872.
✤ Nathaniel Hawthorne, American novelist and short-story writer (*Twice-Told Tales, The Scarlet Letter*), born 1804.

## 5

★ Venezuela, National Holiday.
✤ Daniel Farragut, first admiral of U.S. Navy, born 1801.
✤ P.T. Barnum, American circus showman, born 1810.
✤ Cecil Rhodes, British statesman, businessman, and founder of Rhodes scholarship, born 1853.

## 6

★ Malawi, Republic Day.
✤ John Paul Jones, naval hero of the American Revolution, born 1747.

## 7

★ Solomon Islands, National Holiday.
✤ Marc Chagall, Russian-French artist, born 1887.

## 8

◆ Anniversary of the first passport, issued in U.S., 1796.
✤ John D. Rockefeller, American industrialist and philanthropist, born 1839.

## 9

★ Argentina, Independence Day.

✤ Elias Howe, American inventor of the sewing machine, born 1819.

## 10

★ Bahamas, National Holiday.
◆ Wyoming became the 44th U.S. state in 1890.

## 11

✤ John Quincy Adams, 6th U.S. president, born 1767.

## 12

✤ Henry David Thoreau, American author (*Walden*) and naturalist, born 1817.
✤ George Eastman, American inventor of the camera, born 1854.
✤ Buckminster Fuller, American engineer and architect who designed the geodesic dome, born 1895.

## 13

★ Night Watch Day, the eve of Bastille Day, in France.

## 14

★ Bastille Day. National holiday in France.
✤ Gerald R. Ford, 38th U.S. president, born 1913.

## 15

✤ Rembrandt van Rijn, Dutch artist, born 1606.
✤ Mother Cabrini (Marie Francesca Cabrini), first U.S. citizen named a saint, born 1850.

## 16

◆ The District of Columbia was established as the permanent U.S. capital, 1790.
◆ First parking meter installed in Oklahoma City, Okla. in 1935.
✤ Mary Baker Eddy, American founder of Christian Science movement, born 1821.

## 17

✤ John Jacob Astor, German-American businessman and fur trader, born 1763.
★ Constitution Day, South Korea.

## 18

✤ William Makepeace Thackeray, English novelist (*Vanity Fair*), born 1811.

## 19

◆ The first U.S. Women's Rights Convention held in Seneca Falls, New York, 1920.
✤ Charles Mayo, American surgeon and co-founder with his brother, William, of the Mayo Clinic, born 1865.

## 20

★ Columbia, National Holiday.
◆ The first men to land on the moon were American astronauts Neil Armstrong and Edwin "Buzz" Aldrin, Jr., in 1969.
✤ Francesco Petrarch, Italian poet, born 1304.

## 21

★ Belgium, National Holiday.

♦ A legendary train robbery in U.S. history was masterminded by Jesse James in 1873.

�֎ Ernest Hemingway, American novelist (*For Whom The Bells Tolls, The Sun Also Rises*), born 1899.

## 22

★ Poland, National Holiday.

✤ Emma Lazarus, American poet who wrote the poem engraved on the Statue of Liberty, born 1849.

✤ Stephen Vincent Benet, American poet, born 1898.

✤ Alexander Calder, American sculptor, born 1898.

## 23

❦ The zodiac sign Leo, The Lion, begins. Those born under the sign of Leo are said to be dynamic, generous, and proud.

★ Egypt, National Holiday.

♦ The ice cream cone was invented by Italo Marchioni at the World's Fair in St. Louis, Missouri, 1903.

## 24

✤ Simon Bolivar "The Liberator," South American revolutionary and statesman, born 1783. Bolivar Day, Ecuador and Venezuela.

✤ American aviator, Amelia Earhart, the first woman to fly solo across the Atlantic Ocean, born 1897.

## 25

✤ Louise Brown of Oldham, England, first "test-tube baby," born 1978.

## 26

★ Liberia and Maldive Islands, Independence Day.

♦ New York became the 11th U.S. state in 1788.

✤ George Bernard Shaw, Irish-English playwright ("St. Joan"), born 1856.

## 27

♦ The Korean War ended with the signing of an armistice, 1953.

## 28

★ Peru, Independence Day.

## 29

✤ Booth Tarkington, American novelist (*Penrod, Seventeen*), born 1869.

✤ Benito Mussolini, Italian fascist leader, born 1883.

## 30

★ Marseillaise Day, France.

✤ Emily Brontë, English novelist (*Wuthering Heights*), born 1818.

✤ Henry Ford, American auto manufacturer, born 1863.

## 31

♦ The first U.S. patent ever issued was granted to Samuel Hopkins for processing potash, a substance used in the manufacture of soap and glass, 1790.

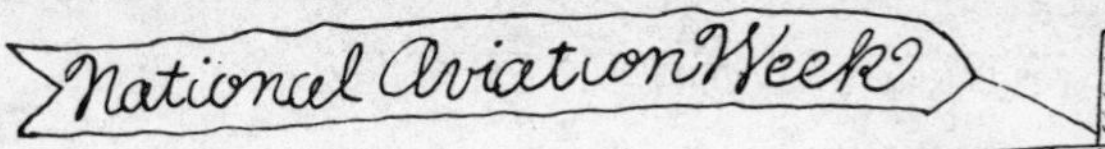


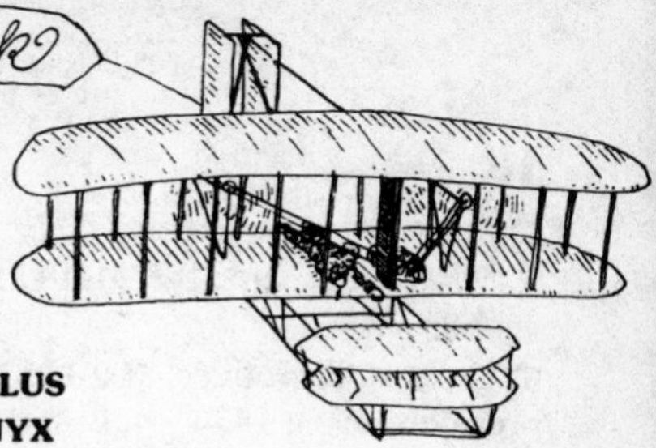

# August

**FLOWER: GLADIOLUS**
**BIRTHSTONE: ONYX**

## 1

★ Jamaica, National Holiday.
★ Switzerland, National Holiday.
♦ Colorado became the 38th U.S. state in 1876.
⚜ William Clark, American explorer and leader of the Lewis and Clark expedition, born 1770.
⚜ Francis Scott Key, American author of the National Anthem, born 1779.
⚜ Maria Mitchell, American astronomer, born 1818.
⚜ Herman Melville, American author of *Moby Dick,* born 1819.

## 2

⚜ Pierre Charles L'Enfant, French designer of the city of Washington, D.C., born 1754.

## 3

♦ Italian explorer Christopher Columbus set sail from Spain on his first voyage and found the Americas, 1492.
♦ The U.S. submarine, *Nautilus,* was the first ship to reach and pass under the North Pole, 1958.

## 4

♦ U.S. purchased Virgin Islands from Denmark, 1917.

## 5

⚜ Guy de Maupassant, French novelist and short story writer, born 1850.
⚜ Conrad Aiken, American writer and critic, born 1889.

## 6

★ Bolivia, National Holiday.
♦ The first atomic bomb dropped by U.S. on Hiroshima, Japan, 1945.
⚜ Alfred Lord Tennyson, English poet, born 1809.

## 7

♦ The first pictures of Earth were sent via U.S. satellite, the *Explorer VI,* 1959.
⚜ Ralph Bunche, American statesman and U.N. official, born 1904.

## 8

★ International Character Day (emphasizes good character).
⚜ Charles Bullfinch, American architect, born 1763.

## 9

★ Singapore, National Day.
♦ Richard M. Nixon, first U.S. president to resign from office, 1974.

## 10

★ Ecuador, Independence Day.
◆ Missouri became the 24th U.S. state in 1821.
✿ Herbert C. Hoover, 31st U.S. president, born 1874.

## 11

★ Chad, Independence Day.
★ Coronation Day, Jordan.

## 12

◆ Airmail service began in U.S. in 1918.
✿ Robert Mills, American architect and designer of the Washington Monument, born 1781.
✿ Katherine Lee Bates, American author of "America the Beautiful," born 1859.
✿ Cecil B. de Mille, film producer and director, born 1881.

## 13

✿ Annie Oakley, American markswoman, born 1860.
✿ Alfred Hitchcock, English-American director of suspense thriller films, born 1899.

## 14

◆ Victory Day (celebrating the ending of World War II with surrender of the Japanese to the Allies, 1945).

## 15

★ Independence Day, India.
◆ The Panama Canal opened in 1914.

◆ The Woodstock Festival, one of the largest rock concerts in history, took place on a farm in Bethel, N.Y. This three-day concert attracted 500,000 fans.
✿ Napoleon Bonaparte, French emperor, born 1769.
✿ Sir Walter Scott, Scottish author of *Ivanhoe*, born 1771.

## 16

★ Korea, National Holiday.
◆ Gold discovered in Klondike region of Alaska, 1896.

## 17

★ Indonesia, Independence Day.
◆ The first to cross the Atlantic Ocean in a balloon were Americans Max Anderson, Ben Abruzzo, and Larry Newman, 1978.
✿ Davy Crockett, American frontiersman and soldier, born 1786.
✿ Samuel Goldwyn, American film producer, born 1882.

## 18

✿ Virginia Dare, first child of English parents born in America, 1587.
✿ Meriwether Lewis, American explorer (Lewis and Clark Expeditions), born 1774.

## 19

★ National Aviation Day, U.S.
✿ Orville Wright, American co-inventor of the airplane with his brother, Wilbur, born 1871.
✿ Ogden Nash, American poet, born 1902.

## 20

★ Constitution Day, Hungary.
✤ Benjamin Harrison, 23rd U.S. president, born 1833.

## 21

◆ Hawaii became the 50th U.S. state in 1959.

## 22

◆ The Lincoln-Douglas debates (between presidential candidates, Stephen Douglas and Abraham Lincoln), a major U.S. political event, took place in 1858.

## 23

✤ The zodiac sign Virgo, The Virgin, begins. Those born under the sign of Virgo are said to be clever, analytical, and perceptive.
★ Rumania, National Holiday.
✤ Edgar Lee Masters, American poet, born 1869.

## 24

◆ Mount Vesuvius erupted in southern Italy, 79 A.D.

## 25

★ Uruguay, National Holiday.
✤ Leonard Bernstein, American composer and conductor, born 1918.

## 26

★ Susan B. Anthony Day.

## 27

✤ Confucius, Chinese philosopher, born c. 551 B.C.
✤ Lyndon Baines Johnson, 36th U.S. president, born 1908.
✤ Theodore Dreiser, American novelist (*An American Tragedy*), born 1871.

## 28

✤ Johann Wolfgang von Goethe, German writer, dramatist, and scientist, born 1749.
✤ Elizabeth Seton, first American-born saint, born 1774.

## 29

◆ South Carolina Senator Strom Thurmond delivered the longest filibuster speech in U.S. Senate history (24 hours, 18 minutes), 1957.

## 30

✤ Roy Wilkins, American civil rights leader, born 1901.

## 31

★ Malaysia Day.
★ Trindad and Tobago, Independence Day.
✤ Maria Montessori, Italian educator, born 1870.
✤ William Saroyan, American author of "The Human Comedy" and "The Time of Your Life," born 1908.

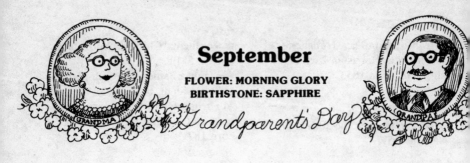

# September

**FLOWER: MORNING GLORY**
**BIRTHSTONE: SAPPHIRE**

*Grandparent's Day*

**1**

★ Labor Day, U.S. (1986).
★ Libya, National Holiday.
◆ World War II began when German leader, Adolf Hitler, invaded Poland in 1939.

**2**

◆ The U.S. Treasury Department was established by Congress in 1789.

**3**

◆ The American Revolutionary War ended with the Treaty of Paris, 1783.

**4**

◆ Barney Flaherty was hired as the first newsboy in the U.S., 1833.

**5**

★ Be Late for Something Day, U.S. (designated by the Procrastinators Club of America).
✾ Louis XIV, King of France, born 1638.

**6**

✾ Jane Addams, American social worker, born 1860.

**7**

★ Brazil, National Holiday.
✾ Grandma Moses (Anna Mary Moses), American artist, born 1860.

**8**

★ International Literary Day.
★ National Pardon Day.
◆ U.S. President Gerald Ford pardoned former U.S. President Richard Nixon for any crimes during his presidency, 1974.

**9**

★ Bulgaria, National Holiday.
◆ California became the 31st U.S. state in 1850.
✾ Leo Tolstoy, Russian author of *War and Peace,* born 1828.

**10**

★ Discovery Day in Hawaii (honors Pacific and Polynesian explorers).
★ Swap Ideas Day—a day for trading ideas with a friend.

**11**

★ Grandparents Day, U.S. (1986).
◆ Henry Hudson, Dutch explorer,

discovered Manhattan Island, New York, 1609.
✤ O. Henry (William S. Porter), American short-story writer, born 1862.

## 12

★ Ethiopia, National Holiday.
★ Respect for the Aged Day, Japan.
✤ Jesse Owens, American athlete, born 1913.

## 13

✤ Walter Reed, American army physician and surgeon, born 1851. (Reed was the first to prove that the disease, Yellow Fever, is transmitted by mosquitoes.)
✤ John J. Pershing, American WWI general, born 1860.

## 14

★ National Anthem Day, U.S.
✤ Alexander von Humboldt, German naturalist and explorer who first suggested building the Panama Canal, born 1767.

## 15

★ Costa Rica, El Salvador, Guatamala, Honduras, Nicaragua, National Holidays.
✤ James Fenimore Cooper, American novelist (*The Last of the Mohicans*), born 1789.
✤ William Howard Taft, 27th U.S. president, born 1857.

## 16

★ Mexico, National Holiday.
★ Cherokee Strip Day in U.S.

(commemorates the Oklahoma land rush in 1893).
◆ The Pilgrims set sail from Plymouth, England, 1620.

## 17

★ Citizenship Day, U.S. (honors new Americans).
✤ Friedrich von Stueben, Prussian officer in the American Revolutionary War, born 1730.

## 18

★ Chile, Independence Day.
◆ George Washington laid the cornerstone of the U.S. Capitol in Washington, D.C. in 1793.

## 19

◆ U.S. President Abraham Lincoln delivered his famous Civil War "Gettysburg Address," 1863.
◆ Mickey Mouse, cartoon character, appeared in his first movie *Steamboat Willie,* 1928.

## 20

★ Harvest Moon Day.
◆ Portuguese explorer, Ferdinand Magellan, sailing under Spanish flags, began the first voyage around the world, 1519.

## 21

★ Belize, National Holiday.
◆ The U.S. Post Office was established in 1789.
◆ President Abraham Lincoln issued the Emancipation Proclamation, freeing all U.S. slaves as of January 1, 1863.

## 22

★ Pen Pal Day all over the world.
❁ Michael Faraday, English scientist and pioneer in the development of electricity, born 1791.

## 23

Autumn officially begins in Northern Hemisphere; spring begins in Southern Hemisphere, 2:59 A.M., EST. (1986).
♈ The zodiac sign of Libra, The Balance, begins. Those born under the sign of Libra are said to be idealistic, artistic, and fair-minded.
★ Native American Day, U.S.
❁ Euripedes, Greek playwright, born c. 480 B.C.

## 24

★ Saudi Arabia, National Holiday.
❁ John Marshall, American lawyer and jurist, born 1755.
❁ F. Scott Fitzgerald, American author of *The Great Gatsby,* born 1896.

## 25

◆ Vasco de Balboa, Spanish explorer discovered and named the Pacific Ocean, 1513.
❁ William Faulkner, American author of *The Sound and the Fury,* born 1897.

## 26

★ Yemen, National Holiday.
◆ U.S. lost "Americas Cup" sailing race to Australia (first loss in 123 years), 1983.

❁ Johnny Appleseed (John Chapman), American apple tree planter, born 1774.
❁ George Gershwin, American composer, born 1898.
★ National Good Neighbor Day, U.S.

## 27

★ Ancestor Appreciation Day, U.S.—a day for reflecting on one's personal ancestry.
❁ Thomas Nast, German-American political cartoonist who created the Democratic Party donkey and the Republican Party elephant, born 1840.
❁ Samuel Adams, American patriot and a signer of the Declaration of Independence, born 1722.

## 28

★ Good Neighbor Day.
◆ Juan Rodriguez Cabrillo, Portuguese explorer, discovered California in 1542.

## 29

◆ Enrico Fermi, Italian physicist who pioneered work on atomic bomb projects, born 1901.

## 30

★ Botswana, National Holiday.
◆ Babe Ruth, American baseball player for the New York Yankees hit his sixtieth home run of the 1927 season.

# October

**FLOWER: CALENDULA**
**BIRTHSTONE: OPAL**

## 1

★ Cyprus, People's Republic of China, and Nigeria, National Holiday.
✻ James Earl Carter, 39th U.S. president, born 1924.

## 2

★ World Vegetarian Day.
★ Guinea, National Holiday.
✻ Mohandas Gandhi, known as the "Father of India," born 1869.

## 3

★ Child Health Day.

## 4

★ Rosh Hashanah, Jewish New Year (1986).
◆ The first manmade satellite, *Sputnik,* was launched by the U.S.S.R., 1957.
✻ Rutherford B. Hayes, 19th U.S. president, born 1822.

## 5

◆ The World Series of baseball was broadcast for the first time on radio, 1921. The New York Giants beat the New York Yankees, five games to three.

✻ Chester A. Arthur, 21st U.S. president, born 1830.

## 6

★ Universal Children's Day.
✻ George Westinghouse, American inventor and manufacturer, born 1846.

## 7

★ German Democratic Republic, National Holiday.

## 8

◆ The great Chicago fire disaster, 1871.
◆ The most disastrous forest fire in recorded history, Peshtigo, Wisconsin, 1871.
✻ Reverend Jesse Jackson, American political and religious leader, born 1941.

## 9

★ Uganda, National Holiday.
★ Fire Prevention Day.
◆ Leif Ericson, Norse explorer, landed in North America in 1000 A.D.
✻ John Lennon, English singer-songwriter and member of rock group, the Beatles, born 1940.

## 10

★ Double Tenth Day, a public holiday in Taiwan (Republic of China).
★ Fiji, National Holiday.
✿ Giuseppe Verdi, Italian composer of operas, born 1813.

## 11

★ Pulaski Memorial Day in U.S. (honors Polish-American Revolutionary War hero).
✿ Eleanor Roosevelt, American first lady and humanitarian, born 1884.

## 12

★ Columbus Day, Spain, Central America, South America.
★ Equatorial Guinea, National Holiday.

## 13

★ Columbus Day, U.S. (observed).
★ Yom Kippur, Jewish Day of Atonement. (1986).
★ Thanksgiving Day, Canada.
◆ U.S. Navy established, 1775.
✿ Molly Pitcher, American Revolutionary War heroine, born 1744.
✿ Margaret Thatcher, British prime minister, born 1925.

## 14

★ National Friendship Day.
✿ William Penn, founder of Pennsylvania, born 1644.
✿ Dwight David Eisenhower, 34th U.S. president, born 1890.

## 15

★ World Poetry Day.
✿ Virgil, Roman poet, born 70 B.C.

## 16

✿ Noah Webster, American creator of a dictionary, born 1758.
✿ David Ben-Gurion, Israel's first prime minister, born 1886.
✿ Eugene O'Neill, American playwright ("Ah! Wilderness"), born 1888.

## 17

★ Black Poetry Day, U.S.

## 18

★ Sweetest Day (a special day for spreading cheer to underprivileged and shut-ins).
✿ Pierre Trudeau, Canadian prime minister, born 1919.

## 19

★ Yorktown Day, U.S. (anniversary of last American Revolutionary War battle).

## 20

✿ Sir Christopher Wren, English architect who designed many new buildings after the Great Fire of London, born 1632.
✿ John Dewey, American educator and philosopher, born 1859.

## 21

★ Somalia, National Holiday.
◆ American, Thomas Edison,

invented the incandescent lamp in 1879.

✣ Samuel Taylor Coleridge, English poet, born 1772.

## 22

★ Austria, National Holiday.
✣ Franz von Liszt, Hungarian composer and pianist, born 1811.

## 23

★ Swallows Day (when the swallows leave Capistrano Mission in California for the winter).
✣ Pele (Edson Arantes do Nascimento), Brazilian soccer great, born 1940.

## 24

🦂 The zodiac sign of Scorpio, The Scorpian, begins. Those born under the sign of Scorpio are said to be intense, mysterious, and individualistic.
★ Zambia, Independence Day.
♦ "Black Thursday," New York Stock Exchange crashed in 1929.
✣ Anton van Leeuwenhoek, Dutch naturalist and "Father of the Microscope," born 1632.

## 25

✣ Pablo Picasso, Spanish artist, born 1881.
✣ Richard B. Byrd, American polar explorer, born 1888.

## 26

★ International Red Cross Day.

## 27

★ St. Vincent and Grenadines, National Holiday.
✣ Niccola Paganini, Italian violin virtuoso, born 1782.
✣ Theodore Roosevelt, 26th U.S. president, born 1858.

## 28

♦ The Statue of Liberty was given to the U.S. by France in 1886.
✣ Jonas Salk, U.S. physician and microbiologist who developed polio vaccine, born 1914.

## 29

★ Turkey, National Holiday.
♦ NOW (National Organization for Women) was organized in 1966.

## 30

✣ John Adams, 2nd U.S. president, born 1735.
✣ Ezra Pound, American poet, born 1885.

## 31

★ Halloween.
★ UNICEF Day (United Nations International Children's Emergency Fund).
♦ Nevada became the 36th U.S. state in 1864.
✣ Juliet Gordon Low, American founder of the Girl Scouts, born 1860.

# November

**FLOWER: CHRYSANTHEMUM**
**BIRTHSTONE: TOPAZ**

Robert Fulton's Steamboat

## 1

★ All Saints Day.
★ Algeria, National Holiday.
★ Antigua and Barbados, National Holiday.
✤ Stephen Crane, American author of *The Red Badge of Courage,* born 1871.

## 2

♦ North Dakota became the 39th U.S. state in 1889.
♦ South Dakota became the 40th U.S. state in 1889.
✤ Daniel Boone, American pioneer and explorer, born 1734.
✤ James Knox Polk, 11th U.S. president, born 1795.
✤ Warren G. Harding, 29th U.S. president, born 1865.

## 3

★ Dominica, National Holiday.
★ Panama, National Holiday.
✤ John Montague, Earl of Sandwich, supposed creator of the sandwich, born 1718.
✤ Stephen Austin, "The Father of Texas," born 1793.
✤ William Cullen Bryant, American poet, born 1794.

## 4

★ Election Day, U.S. (1986).
✤ Will Rogers, American humorist and author, born 1879.

## 5

★ Guy Fawkes Day, Canada and Great Britain.

## 6

✤ James Naismith, Canadian-American inventor of basketball, born 1861.

## 7

★ U.S.S.R., National Holiday.
✤ Marie Curie, Polish-English chemist and physicist, co-discoverer with her husband, Pierre, of radium, born 1867.

## 8

★ U.S.S.R., National Holiday.
♦ Montana became the 41st U.S. state in 1889.
✤ Edmund Halley, English astronomer, first to predict appearance of a comet, born 1656.
✤ Margaret Mitchell, American author of *Gone With the Wind,* born 1900.

## 9

◆ The largest power blackout in history darkened northeast U.S. and Ontario, 1965.
❊ Benjamin Banneker, American astronomer, born 1731.

## 10

★ Hero and Youth Day, Indonesia.
◆ U.S. Marine Corps founded 1798.
❊ Martin Luther, German religious reformer, born 1483.

## 11

★ Veterans Day.
★ Armistice Day, U.S.
◆ Washington became the 42nd U.S. state in 1889.
◆ The Unknown Soldier of WWI entombed at Arlington, Virginia, 1921.

## 12

❊ Elizabeth Cady Stanton, American reformer and leader of the women's suffrage movement, born 1815.
❊ Sun Yat-sen, leader of the Chinese Nationalist Party, born 1866.

## 13

❊ Robert Louis Stevenson, Scottish poet and novelist (*A Child's Garden of Verses, Treasure Island*), born 1850.

## 14

❊ Robert Fulton, American inventor of the steamboat, born 1765.

❊ Claude Monet, French artist, born 1840.
❊ Jawaharlal Nehru, first prime minister of India, born 1889.

## 15

❊ Georgia O'Keeffe, American artist, born 1887.
❊ Marianne Moore, American poet, born 1887.

## 16

◆ Oklahoma became the 46th U.S. state in 1907.
❊ W. C. Handy, American composer, "Father of the Blues," born 1873.

## 17

◆ The Suez Canal in Egypt opened in 1869.
★ Homemade Bread Day, U.S.

## 18

★ Latvia, National Holiday.
◆ U.S. Sea captain, Nathaniel Palmer, discovered Antarctica, 1820.
❊ George Gallup, famous U.S. public opinion pollster, born 1901.

## 19

★ Equal Opportunity Day.
◆ Puerto Rico was discovered by Christopher Columbus in 1493.
❊ James Abram Garfield, 20th U.S. president, born 1831.

## 20

◆ Peregrine White, the first child born in the New England colonies of English parents, 1620.

## 21

★ World Hello Day (learn to say "hello" in 5 different languages).
♦ North Carolina became the 12th U.S. state in 1789.

## 22

♐ The zodiac sign of Sagittarius, The Archer, begins. Those born under the sign of Sagittarius are said to be optimistic, enthusiastic, and outspoken.
★ Lebanon, National Holiday.
♦ U.S. president John F. Kennedy assassinated, Dallas, Texas, 1963.
✣ George Eliot (Mary Ann Evans), English novelist (*Silas Marner, The Mill on the Floss*), born 1819.
✣ Charles de Gaulle, French president, born 1890.

## 23

✣ Franklin Pierce, 14th U.S. president, born 1804.
✣ Boris Karloff, horror movie actor (*Frankenstein, The Mummy*), born 1887.

## 24

★ Zaire, National Holiday.
✣ Zachary Taylor, 12th U.S. president, born 1784.

## 25

★ Suriname, National Holiday.

✣ Andrew Carnegie, American industrialist and philanthropist, born 1835.

## 26

★ Sojourner Truth Memorial Day, U.S. (in honor of American black abolitionists).

## 27

★ Thanksgiving Day, U.S. (1986).
✣ Henry Bacon, American architect of Lincoln Memorial in Washington, D.C., born 1866.

## 28

★ Barbados, National Holiday.
✣ William Blake, English poet ("The Tyger"), born 1757.

## 29

★ Yugoslavia, National Holiday.
♦ The first U.S. Army–Navy football game played in 1890.
✣ Louisa May Alcott, American novelist, born 1832.

## 30

★ St. Andrews Day, Scotland.
✣ Mark Twain (Samuel Clemens), American author (*Tom Sawyer, Huckleberry Finn*), born 1835.
✣ Winston Churchill, British prime minister, born 1874.

# December

**FLOWER: POINSETTIA**
**BIRTHSTONE: TURQUOISE**

## 1

★ Central Africa Republic, National Holiday.
♦ American Rosa Parks began U.S. civil rights movement by refusing to give up her bus seat, Montgomery, Alabama, 1955.

## 2

★ United Arab Emirates, National Holiday.
★ Pan American Health Day.

## 3

♦ Illinois became the 21st U.S. state in 1818.
♦ First human heart transplant performed by Dr. Christiaan Barnard in Cape Town, South Africa, 1967.
❊ Gilbert Stuart, American presidential portrait painter, born 1755.

## 4

♦ The National Grange of Husbandry, U.S. organization of farmers, founded in 1867.

## 5

★ Thailand, National Holiday.

❊ Martin Van Buren, 8th U.S. president, born 1782.
❊ Walt Disney, American film producer and pioneer in animated cartoons, born 1901.

## 6

★ Finland, Independence Day.
★ Feast of St. Nicholas Day, U.S.S.R. and Europe.
❊ Joyce Kilmer, American poet ("Trees"), born 1886.

## 7

★ Ivory Coast, National Holiday.
♦ Delaware became the 1st U.S. state in 1787.
♦ Japanese attacked U.S. fleet at Pearl Harbor, Hawaii, 1941; U.S. entered WWII.
❊ Willa Cather, American author of *One of Ours,* born 1876.

## 8

❊ Eli Whitney, American inventor of the cotton gin, born 1765.

## 9

❊ John Milton, English poet, born 1608.
★ Independence Day, Tanzania.

## 10

★ United Nations Human Rights Day.
◆ Mississippi became the 20th U.S. state in 1817.
◆ First Nobel Peace Prizes awarded in 1901.
✶ Thomas Gallaudet, American pioneer teacher of the deaf, born 1787.
✶ Emily Dickinson, American poet, born 1830.

## 11

★ Upper Volta, Republic Day.
◆ Indiana became the 19th U.S. state in 1816.
◆ UNICEF (United Nations International Children's Emergency Fund) established, 1946.

## 12

★ Kenya, National Holiday.
★ Fiesta of Our Lady of Guadalupe, Mexico.
◆ Pennsylvania became the 2nd U.S. state in 1787.
◆ First transatlantic radio signal sent by Italian, Guglielmo Marconi, 1901.
✶ John Jay, first American Supreme Court justice, born 1745.

## 13

★ Lucia Day in Sweden.
◆ New Zealand discovered by Dutch explorer, Abel Tasmand, 1642.

## 14

◆ Alabama became the 22nd U.S. state in 1819.

## 15

★ Bill of Rights Day in U.S.
✶ Nero, Roman emperor, born 37 A.D.

## 16

★ Boston Tea Party Day in U.S. (American colonists demonstrated against the British in 1773.)
✶ Ludwig von Beethoven, German composer of symphonies, concertos, and sonatas, born 1775.
✶ Jane Austen, English novelist (*Pride and Prejudice*), born 1775.
✶ Margaret Mead, American anthropologist, born 1901.

## 17

◆ Americans Orville and Wilbur Wright made the first successful airplane flight in 1903.
✶ John Greenleaf Whittier, American poet ("Barbara Frietchie"), born 1807.

## 18

◆ New Jersey became the 3rd U.S. state in 1787.
◆ First U.S. commercial nuclear power plant began operating, Shippingport, Pa., 1957.

## 19

◆ Ben Franklin's *Poor Richard's Almanack* first published, 1732.
✶ Leonid Brezhnev, Soviet leader, born 1906.

## 20

◆ U.S. purchased Louisiana Territory from France in 1803.

**21**

★ Forefathers Day (in honor of Pilgrims landing at Plymouth, Mass., 1620).
♦ Winter officially begins in Northern Hemisphere; summer begins in Southern Hemisphere, 11:02 P.M. (1986).
✤ Joseph Stalin, Soviet leader, born 1879.

**22**

The zodiac sign of Capricorn, The Goat, begins. Those born under the sign of Capricorn are said to be hardworking, ambitious, and diplomatic.
★ International Arbor Day.
✤ Giacomo Puccini, Italian composer of operas, born 1858.

**23**

♦ First transistor invented by Americans, J. Bardeen, W. Brattain, and W. Shockley in 1947.
✤ Joseph Smith, American founder of Mormon church, born 1805.

**24**

★ Christmas Eve.

**25**

★ Christmas Day.

**26**

★ Boxing Day in Great Britain.
♦ Radium, co-discovered by Pierre and Marie Curie, 1898.
✤ Mao Tse-tung, Chinese leader, born 1893.

**27**

★ Hanukkah, Jewish Festival of Lights (1986).
✤ Louis Pasteur, French chemist, born 1822.

**28**

★ Nepal, National Holiday.
♦ Iowa became the 29th U.S. state in 1846.
♦ Chewing gum patented by American William Semple, 1869.
✤ Woodrow Wilson, 28th U.S. president, born 1856.

**29**

♦ Texas became the 28th U.S. state in 1845.
✤ Andrew Johnson, 17th U.S. president, born 1808.

**30**

♦ Gadsden Purchase (in which U.S. bought Arizona and New Mexico Territory from Mexico in 1853).

**31**

★ New Year's Eve.
♦ Ellis Island in New York Harbor opened to receive all immigrants to the U.S., 1890.
♦ U.S. President Harry S. Truman officially announced the end of World War II, 1946.

# Communications

This is a handy guide to some of the many ways in which people communicate with each other. Hobo signs, branding symbols, the meanings of colors; all these and more can be found on the following pages.

# Important Events in Communication

**B.C.**

*Before*
**3000**   The Egyptians developed a picture language called hieroglyphics.

*Before*
**1600**   The Phoenicians invented an alphabet.

**300**   Numerals were invented in India.

**A.D.**

**1755**   Samuel Johnson published a dictionary of the English language, the first English dictionary.

**1828**   Noah Webster published the first American dictionary.

**1844**   Samuel Morse sent the first telegraph message.

**1876**   The telephone was invented by American, Alexander Graham Bell.

**1895**   In Italy, Guglielmo Marconi invented the wireless telegraph.

**1927**   Movies with sound first appeared in American theatres.

**1941**   Commercial television began in the United States.

**1957**   The first artificial earth satellite sent back information from space.

**1962**   Television programs were relayed between the U.S. and Europe via the satellite, *Telstar I*.

**1965**   The U.S. launched *Early Bird*, the first commercial communications satellite.

# Signs, Symbols, Language

## BASIC SYMBOLS

| | | | | | |
|---|---|---|---|---|---|
| 1. And | **&** | 8. Equals | = | 16. Multiplied by | ✕ |
| 2. Asterisk | * | 9. Feet | ′ | 17. Number | # |
| 3. At, each | @ | 10. Female | ♀ | 18. Paragraph | ¶ |
| 4. Cents | ¢ | 11. In care of | **c/o** | 19. Parallel | ‖ |
| 5. Degree | ° | 12. Inches | ″ | 20. Prescription | ℞ |
| 6. Divide | ÷ | 13. Is greater than | > | 21. Plus/Positive | + |
| 7. Dollar | **$** | 14. Is less than | < | 22. Ratio of | : |
| | | 15. Male | ♂ | | |

# BASIC SIGNS

1. Animal
   Crossing

2. Barbershop

3. Information

4. Bike Trail

5. No smoking

6. Restaurant

7. Campfire
   allowed

8. Elevator

9. Handicap
   access

10. Hospital:
    First Aid

11. Law

12. Lost and
    Found

13. Mail

14. Medicine

15. No Entry

16. Peace

17. Pedestrian
    Crossing

18. Playground

19. Poison

20. Railroad
    Crossing

# SIGNS

## Braille

### Alphabet of the Blind
People who are blind have a special system for reading. A series of raised dots on paper symbolize letters. They are combined to form words. Fingertips are used to feel this language.

A B C D E F G

H I J K L M N

O P Q R S T U

V W X Y Z

## Sign Language

### Manual Alphabet of the Deaf
In this language, the fingers of the hand are moved to positions which represent the letters of the alphabet. Whole words and ideas are also expressed in sign language.

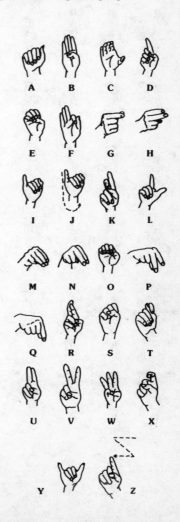

## Morse Code

### Alphabet of Telecommunication
Using this code of dots and dashes, messages are telegraphed over long distances. Each dot is a short sound; each dash is a long sound. Combinations of dots and dashes form the letters of the alphabet.

| | | |
|---|---|---|
| A ·– | J ·––– | R ·–· |
| B –··· | K –·– | S ··· |
| C –·–· | L ·–·· | T – |
| D –·· | M –– | U ··– |
| E · | N –· | V ···– |
| F ··–· | O ––– | W ·–– |
| G ––· | P ·––· | X –··– |
| H ···· | Q ––·– | Y –·–– |
| I ·· | | Z ––·· |

## Semaphore

### Alphabet of Hand Flags

Flags are used to send messages to people who are within seeing range but not within hearing range. This form of communication is commonly used by sailors, lifeguards, and boy scouts.

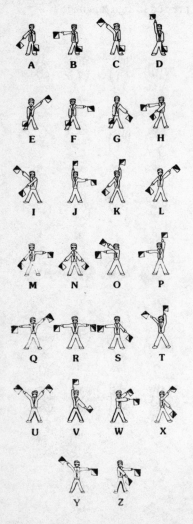

## Hobo Picture Language

Hobos invented their own secret language to communicate with each other. Hobos are homeless people who travel around without money or means, looking for shelter and food as they go.

1. Good road to follow

2. Dangerous neighborhood

3. Nothing good here

4. Good place for a handout

5. Food here, if you work

## Branding Signs

Ranch owners mark their herds with symbols to show ownership. They created a special language of symbols to identify their ranches. Here are some examples.

An upside down brand means "crazy" as in Crazy Heart.

Wings on a brand means "flying" as in Flying V.

A curved line under a brand means "rocking" as in Rocking R.

A curved line over a brand means "swinging" as in Swinging Star.

## Hex Signs

These signs of witchcraft have been used for centuries to ward off trouble or to attract good luck. In the 17th century, the Amish people brought these symbols from Germany to the Pennsylvania farm land where they settled. Today, these symbols are used as decorations rather than for protection.

| | |
|---|---|
| Fertility | Sunshine |
| Rain | Justice |
| Good Luck | Wisdom |
| Against Demons | Against Lightning |

## Roman Numerals

The ancient Romans used a system of letters for counting. Their numbering system is commonly used today on the faces of clocks and to mark chapters in books. The basic Roman numerals and their number values are listed below.

| | | |
|---|---|---|
| I—1 | VI—6 | X—10 |
| II—2 | VII—7 | L—50 |
| III—3 | VIII—8 | C—100 |
| IV—4 | IX—9 | D—500 |
| V—5 | | M—1,000 |

## Symbols of Religion

The major religions of the world have symbols to identify them. Here are seven religions and their most common symbols.

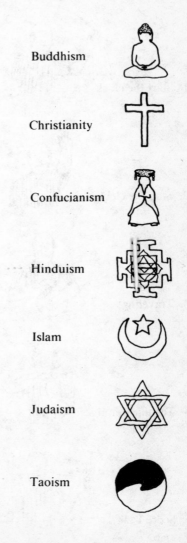

Buddhism

Christianity

Confucianism

Hinduism

Islam

Judaism

Taoism

## Sports Signals

The officials of sports use body language to communicate information about the game to both the players and fans. This list shows five basic signals used in basketball and five used in football.

**BASKETBALL**

1. Start the clock
2. Stop the clock
3. Traveling
4. Technical foul
5. Score/basket

**FOOTBALL**

1. Holding
2. Interference
3. Time-out
4. Safety
5. Touchdown and field goal

# Color Symbols

Colors communicate meaning. For example, a red traffic light means STOP. Colors also express feelings and are often associated with special events.

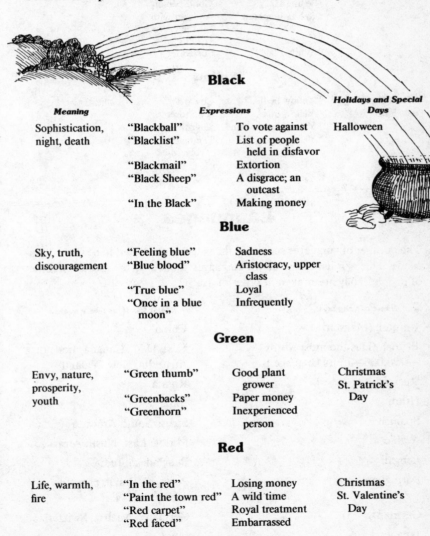

## Black

| Meaning | Expressions | | Holidays and Special Days |
|---|---|---|---|
| Sophistication, night, death | "Blackball" | To vote against | Halloween |
| | "Blacklist" | List of people held in disfavor | |
| | "Blackmail" | Extortion | |
| | "Black Sheep" | A disgrace; an outcast | |
| | "In the Black" | Making money | |

## Blue

| | | | |
|---|---|---|---|
| Sky, truth, discouragement | "Feeling blue" | Sadness | |
| | "Blue blood" | Aristocracy, upper class | |
| | "True blue" | Loyal | |
| | "Once in a blue moon" | Infrequently | |

## Green

| | | | |
|---|---|---|---|
| Envy, nature, prosperity, youth | "Green thumb" | Good plant grower | Christmas St. Patrick's Day |
| | "Greenbacks" | Paper money | |
| | "Greenhorn" | Inexperienced person | |

## Red

| | | | |
|---|---|---|---|
| Life, warmth, fire | "In the red" | Losing money | Christmas St. Valentine's Day |
| | "Paint the town red" | A wild time | |
| | "Red carpet" | Royal treatment | |
| | "Red faced" | Embarrassed | |

## White

| Meaning | Expressions | | Holidays and Special Days |
|---|---|---|---|
| Purity, peace | "White collar" | Office work | Weddings |
| | "White Hat" | Good person | |
| | "White Elephant" | An item with little or no value | |
| | "White Flag" | Surrender | |

## Yellow

| Meaning | Expressions | | Holidays and Special Days |
|---|---|---|---|
| Cowardice, wisdom | "Yellow bellied" | Cowardly | Easter |
| | "Yellow dog" | Scoundrel | |
| | "Yellow journalism" | Sensationalism | |
| | "Yellow streak" | Tendency toward cowardice | |

# Languages

The number of languages spoken in the world is estimated to be in the thousands. This is a list of the major languages spoken by the greatest number of people. They are ranked in order of usage.

| Name of Language | Major locations where spoken |
|---|---|
| Chinese (Mandarin) | China |
| English (Has the most words —790,000—in its language.) | U.S., U.K., Canada, Ireland, Australia, New Zealand |
| Russian | Russia |
| Hindi | India |
| Spanish | Spain, South America |
| Arabic | Middle East, North Africa |
| Bengali | Bengladesh, India |
| Portuguese | Portugal, Brazil, parts of Africa and Asia |
| German | Germany, Austria, Switzerland |
| Japanese | Japan |
| French | France, Belgium, Switzerland, Canada |

# HOW TO SAY HELLO, GOODBYE, AND THANK YOU IN 20 LANGUAGES

| Language | Hello | Goodbye | Thank You |
|---|---|---|---|
| Chinese | Nihow | Tzay-jiann | Shieh-shieh |
| Czech | Dobry den | Sbohem | Dekuji |
| Dutch | Goed dag | Dag | Dank |
| Esperanto (world language) | Saluton | Adiau | Dunkon |
| French | Bon jour | Au revoir | Merci |
| German | Guten Tag | Auf Wiedersehen | Danke |
| Greek | Yaisou | Andio | Bfeharisto |
| Hebrew | Shalom | Shalom | Todah |
| Italian | Bon giorno | Addio | Grazie |
| Japanese | Ohio | Sayonara | Kansha suru |
| Norwegian | God Morgen | Farvel | Takk |
| Polish | Dubry den | Do widzenia | Dziekuje |
| Portuguese | Bom dia | Adeus | Obrigado |
| Rumanian | Buna | Adio | Multumiri |
| Russian | Zdrastvoukee | Do zuidaniya | Spasibo |
| Spanish | Buenos dias | Adios | Gracias |
| Swahili | Jambo | Kwaheri | Asante |
| Swedish | God dag | Adjo | Tack |
| Turkish | Alo | Allah ismarladik | Tchawk |
| Yiddish | Sholem-alé ykhem | Seid ge zund | Dank |

# TEEN TALK

## Thirty Ways to Say "It's Great"

| | | | | |
|---|---|---|---|---|
| ace | cool | groovy | neat | super |
| awesome | decent | hip | nifty | swell |
| all right | dynamite | hot dog! | out of sight | totally |
| "bad" | excellent | keen | outrageous | to the max |
| boss | "fab" | massive | peachy keen | wicked |
| "cat" | far-out | mega | sharp | "word" |

## Fifteen Ways to Say "It's Awful"

| | | |
|---|---|---|
| cruddy | grotty | not so hot |
| crummy | grungy | the pits |
| dinky | mouldy | scuzzy |
| disgusting | nasty | revolting |
| foul | no great shakes | the worst |

# FUN WITH WORDS

## Acronyms

Acronyms are words formed by the first letters of a series of words. Some commonly-used acronyms are:

**AWOL** —Absent Without Leave

**CORE** —Congress of Racial Equality

**ERA** —Equal Rights Amendment

**MOMA**—Museum of Modern Art

**NOW** —National Organization of Women

**OPEC** —Organization of Petroleum Exporting Countries

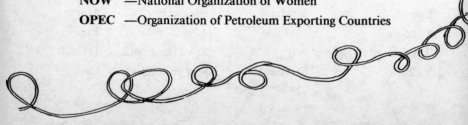

## Palindromes

Palindromes are words or groups of words which can be spelled the same backwards and forwards. The following is an example of a palindrome.

"Able was I ere I saw Elba."
*Attributed to Napoleon.*

## Anagrams

Anagrams are words or phrases that are scrambled to make other words or phrases. Some examples are:

| | | |
|---|---|---|
| **U.S. States anagrams:** | Ha! I do! (Idaho) | End, Ava! (Nevada) |
| | A mine (Maine) | worn key (New York) |
| **Animal anagrams:** | low (owl) | acts (cats) |
| | bare (bear) | sales (seals) |
| | preload (leopard) | |

## Semordnilaps

Semordnilaps are the author Lewis Carroll's version of palindromes. These are words that spell other words when reversed.

| | |
|---|---|
| evil—live | deliver—reviled |
| pin—nip | not—ton |
| repaid—diaper | top—pot |

# Computers, Robots, and Videos

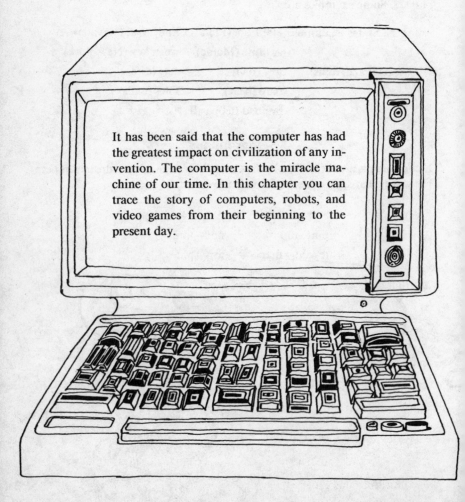

It has been said that the computer has had the greatest impact on civilization of any invention. The computer is the miracle machine of our time. In this chapter you can trace the story of computers, robots, and video games from their beginning to the present day.

# Computers

## COMPUTERS AND PEOPLE

Computers must be told what to do. They cannot think independently of their programming.
People can think, thus making the computer's programming work.

Computers can "see," "hear," and "feel" by the use of electromagnets, photoelectric cells, crystals, and copper wire brushes.
People use eyes, ears, and fingers to see, hear, and feel.

Computers use electricity as their source of energy.
People have brains that use blood glucose for energy.

Computers never forget unless programmed to do so.
People forget without meaning to.

Computers are sensitive machines. They must be protected from extreme temperatures, moisture, dirt, and dust.
People have bodies that adjust to temperature, humidity, dirt, and dust.

Computers have no intelligence of their own.
People have an average intelligence of 100 on the I.Q. scale.

Computers have a memory that can work faster than a person's.
People have a memory that can hold more than a computer's.

## A BASIC GLOSSARY OF COMPUTER WORDS

**Add Time**—The amount of time it takes a computer to do a single addition operation.

**Binary Numbers**—The numbers 0 and 1 are the two (binary) numbers used by a computer. Letters and numbers are combinations of these binary numbers. For example:

|         |         |
|---------|---------|
| A—1000001 | 0—0000 |
| B—1000010 | 1—0001 |
| C—1000011 | 2—0010 |
| D—1000100 | 3—0011 |

**Bit**—Short for binary digit.

**Bug**— A mistake in a computer program. It got it's name when a real bug— a moth— got stuck in a Harvard University computer and the computer stopped working.

**Byte**—A group of eight binary digits used to represent one unit of data in the computer memory. The size of the computer is measured in bytes.

**Chip**—A tiny piece of silicon (sand) which is covered with thousands of passageways (some as long as 24 miles) through which electronic messages travel.

**Computer**—A machine that obeys a list of commands stored in its memory.

**CPU (Central Processing Unit)**—The control center of the computer which organizes all the other parts inside the computer.

**Data**—The information the computer needs to do its work.

**Disk Drive**—This works much like a record turntable. If the program is on a disk, a disk drive is needed to run it.

**Flowchart**—A chart which shows the steps needed in the program.

**Hardware**—All the computer equipment including the computer itself, input and output equipment, disc and tape equipment.

**Input**—The information that goes into the computer. Also, the process of putting information into the computer.

**K**—This is an abbreviation for 1,000. A 10K computer stores 10,000 bytes of computer memory.

**Keyboard**—A row of buttons used to put information into the computer.

**Memory**—The chips in the computer where information and instructions are in binary code.

**Modem**—A device which allows computers to "talk" to one another over the telephone. It turns computer signals into phone vibrations.

**Microprocessor**—A small silicon chip which does the same job as the CPU and main memory of a computer.

**Output**—The information the computer puts out after processing it.

**Program**—A list of orders fed into or stored within the computer.

**RAM (Random Access Memory)**—The part of a computer's memory where information is temporarily stored.

**ROM (Read Only Memory)**—The part of a computer's memory which holds a permanent store of instructions which cannot be erased by the user.

**Software**—Computer programs.

**VDU (Visual Display Unit)**—A screen similar to a TV screen which is used to display computer information.

# A GUIDE TO COMPUTER LANGUAGES

Special languages are used to program computers. There are over 1,000 languages in use today. Ten of the most common ones are listed here.

**ALGOL** is short for Algorithmic Language and is used for scientific purposes.

**BASIC** stands for Beginners All Purpose Symbolic Instruction Code. It is a general purpose language used by students and nonspecialists.

**COBOL** means Common Business Oriented Language. It is the most commonly used language of professionals.

**FORTRAN** stands for Formula Translator and is used for scientific and business purposes.

**JOVIAL** is an acronym for Jules Own Version of the International Algebraic Language. It was invented by Jules Schwartz and is used by the military.

**LISP** stands for List Processor. It was the first language developed for working with artificial intelligence.

**LOGO** is a Greek word which literally means "word." It is used primarily by young children.

**PASCAL** is named after the mathematician Blaise Pascal. It is used for systems development.

**PILOT** stands for Programming Inquiry Learning or Teaching. It uses short, simple commands; a good language for beginners.

**SMALL TALK** is used for communicating with personal computers in a visual way.

# COMPUTER FIRSTS

**1852** The world's first programmer was Lady Augusta Ada Lovelace of England. She worked with Charles Babbage who invented the analytical machine, a forerunner of modern computers. She is credited with telling a machine what to do by using punch cards to program algebraic patterns. The U.S. Department of Defense uses a programming language named ADA in her honor.

**1946** The first electronic computer was made at the University of Pennsylvania. The 30-ton machine stood two stories high and was named ENIAC (Electronic Numerical Integrator and Calculator).

**1951** The first computer animated movies were made at the Massachusetts Institute of Technology.

**1968** The first computer to star in a movie was H.A.L. who was featured in the movie *2001: A Space Odyssey.*

**1970** The first all-computer art exhibit took place at the Jewish Museum in New York City. The show featured computer software.

**1976** The first broadway show to use computers was "A Chorus Line." The computers were used for lighting.

**1977** The first computer camp opened near Simsbury, Connecticut. Sutdents spent the mornings doing nature and sports activities. In the afternoons they were taught computer languages and skills.

**1981** George Guillamo of Valenciennes, France, was the first restaurant owner to use computers to take orders from his customers. Each dining table was equipped with a computer. The menu of the day appeared on the screen and customers typed in their selection.

**1983** Clarkson College in Potsdam, New York, became the first college to require incoming freshmen to purchase a personal computer.

Both superbowl teams, the Washington Redskins and the Miami Dolphins, used computers to call plays.

**1984** The first commercial record made entirely by computer was called "Classical Mosquito." It was conceived and directed by Robb Murray, a composer from Chicago, Illinois.

The first televised computer course was called "Bits and Bytes" and was aired on PBS stations in Canada and the U.S.

# Videos

## A LOOK AT VIDEO GAMES

### ADVENTURE GAMES
The player travels through an adventure world of pictures and words, learning how to survive. The skills needed for this type of game are strategy and puzzle solving. The first adventure game was invented by Crowther and Woods in the 1970s. It was called "Adventure—The Colossal Cave™."

### MAZE GAMES
Players must find their way safely through a maze. The object is to accumulate points as they go. The skills needed for this type of game are good eye-hand coordination and a sense of tactics. "Pac Man™." and "Donkey Kong™." are some of the better known maze games.

### SPORTS GAMES
Many popular sports are available in video games. In some versions the computer is your opponent, in others you play against a friend.

### SPACE GAMES
These are futuristic games in which the action takes place in outer space. They feature high-speed chases and "shoot 'em up" adventure. Timing and scoring points are important in these games. The most famous space game is "Space Invaders™."

### ROLE-PLAYING GAMES
The player in these games must develop a character with special abilities to meet the challenge of the computer's world of adventure. Good reflexes are not important, but strategy and logic are needed to succeed at these games. An example of a role-playing game is "Wizardry™."

### BOARD GAMES
Backgammon, checkers, and chess are among the newly-created computerized board games. In these games a player tries to beat his opponent—the computer.

### DISCOVERY GAMES
These are educational games that teach arithmetic and other thinking skills. One discovery game is LOGO, a computer language developed especially for kids.

# FIRSTS IN VIDEO GAMES

**1962** The first video game was developed when students at the Massachusetts Institute of Technology created "Space War."

**1972** The first arcade game, "Pong™," was made by the Atari Company.

**1973** "Gotcha™," the first video maze game, was developed by Atari.

**1977** The first handheld computer game was "Autorace™," developed by Mattel.

**1982** Pac Man™ became the first video game to inspire a TV show.

**1983** Video games first became available to airline passengers. "Airplay™" was the name of the first video game played in the air.

The first breakfast cereal inspired by a video game was Pac Man™ cereal which was brought out by General Mills.

The Special Olympics for handicapped children added video games to their summer competition.

The Video Game Hall of Fame was established in Ottumwa, Iowa. It honors high-scoring players of arcade coin-operated games.

The first dentist to use video games to distract his patients was Dr. Arthur Zuckerman of New York City. He installed video games on the ceiling of his office so that his patients could play them while he worked on their teeth.

# MOVIES THAT BECAME VIDEO GAMES

Beauty and the Beast        Superman
Conan the Barbarian         The China Syndrome
Jaws                        The Empire Strikes Back
Raiders of the Lost Ark     TRON

# CHARTER MEMBERS OF THE VIDEO HALL OF FAME*

Pong™                       Pac Man™
Space Invaders™             Quest of the Rings™
Asteroids™                  Major League Baseball™

*Sponsored by Electronic Games Magazine. The winners are selected by votes of the readers.

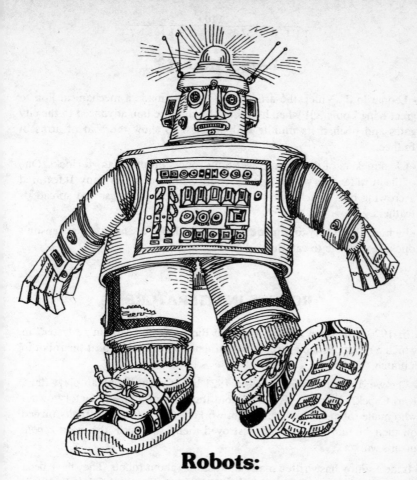

# Robots:

## MACHINES THAT LOOK AND PERFORM LIKE LIVING CREATURES

### ROBOTS IN MYTH AND LEGEND

• King Minos of ancient Crete used a brass robot named Talos to patrol and protect his island. Talos met his fate when an enemy of Minos drained Talos' power by pulling a plug from his foot.

• Daedalus, according to the Greek myths, built strange statues that moved by themselves. The Greek philosopher Plato described Daedalus' figures as so lifelike that they had to be restrained to prevent them from running away.

• In Homer's "Iliad," two robots of pure gold were messengers for Hephaestus, the God of fire.

# EARLY ROBOTS

• Leonardo da Vinci, the artist and inventor, made a mechanical lion to greet King Louis XII when he visited Milan. The lion advanced to the city gates and opened its middle with its claw to show the coat of arms of France.

• Clockmakers of the middle ages built robots into their town clocks. One of the most famous was in the Strasbourg Cathedral in Germany. It featured a crowing bird which opened its beak, flapped its wings, and spread its feathers.

• Eighteenth-century toys made in France included the famous Vaucanson's duck. It was able to eat, drink, "quack," and walk.

# ROBOTS IN LITERATURE

• In 1920, American author Ambrose Bierce wrote "Movon's Master" in which a robot chess player kills his human opponent who beat the robot in a match.

• The word *robot* was first used in 1921 by a Czechoslovakian playwright, Karl Capek. His play, "R.U.R.", told the story of a greedy factory owner who made robots to replace human workers. The robots eventually turned on their human masters and destroyed them. In Czech, the word *robota* means worker.

• Isaac Asimov has written many short stories about robots. They have been collected into two volumes: *I Robot* (1950), and *The Best of Robots* (1964). These stories describe the importance of robots in industry.

# ROBOTS IN FILMS

**The Golem,** 1920. This was the first film to feature a robot.

**Metropolis,** 1926. A female robot was first featured in this film.

**The Day the Earth Stood Still,** 1952. This film shows a spaceship which lands in Washington, D.C., with a robot carrying a vital message for humankind.

**Forbidden Planet,** 1956. A science fiction film classic introducing Robbie the Robot.

**Star Wars,** 1977. This science fiction film introduced R2D2 and C-3PO.

**The Empire Strikes Back,** a 1980 sequel to the successful *Star Wars.*

## FAMOUS WORLD'S FAIR ROBOTS

• The Chicago World's Fair in 1934 featured a robot built by Roland Scaffer. Among other things, his robot could walk, hammer nails, saw tree trunks, and clean windows.

• The largest robot shown at a world's fair was built for Expo '70 in Osaka, Japan. It was twenty-four feet tall.

## TYPES OF ROBOTS

**Automaton**—Any machine that works on its own. For example, a cuckoo clock.

**Android**—A machine built to look or act like a human. For example, Sim One, an artificial hospital patient.

**Cyborg**—Part human, part robot. For example, Steve Austin in the TV show, "The Six Million Dollar Man."

**Droid**—Robots completely devoted to their human masters. For example, R2D2 and C-3PO from *Star Wars.*

**Probots**—Personal robots for home use. For example, Robbie the Robot in the movie, *Forbidden Planet.*

**Robotrix**—A female robot, such as The False Maria in the Fritz Lang movie, *Metropolis.*

## ISAAC ASIMOV'S RULES FOR ROBOTS

1. A robot may not injure a human being.

2. A robot must obey human commands except when the orders conflict with rule #1.

3. A robot must protect itself unless such protection conflicts with rule #1 and rule #2.

# Contests for Kids

Can you catch a greasy pig? How many hot dogs can you eat in one sitting? Can you spell *aardvark?* If the answer to any of these questions is yes, there is a contest for you.

## "THE APPLE SEED POPPING CONTEST"

Contestants are given fresh apples to squeeze in their fists. The one who pops the apple seeds the farthest wins. There is also an Apple Core Throwing Contest in which contestants line up and attempt to throw the apple core the farthest.

PRIZE: Trophies
AGE: 16 and under
LOCATION: Lincoln, Nebraska
DATE: First weekend in October, annually

## "SEVENTEEN MAGAZINE'S ANNUAL ART CONTEST"

Entrants submit one or two samples of artwork by mail. The samples may be no larger than 20 by 26 inches. Each sample must have the entrant's name, address, telephone number, and birth date (month and year) written on the back. A panel of judges selects the winners on the basis of skill, originality, and suitability for publication in the magazine.

PRIZES: Cash to top three winners
AGE: 13 to 20 years old
DATE: Annually
CONTACT:
Art Contest
*Seventeen Magazine*
850 Third Avenue
New York, New York 10022

## "THE BANANA EATING CONTEST"

The contestant who can consume the most bananas in an allotted time, wins the contest.

PRIZES: Ribbons and bananas
LOCATION: Fulton, Kentucky
DATE: August, annually
CONTACT:
International Banana Festival
P.O. 428
Fulton, Kentucky 42041

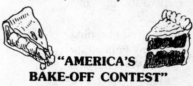

## "AMERICA'S BAKE-OFF CONTEST"

Contestants must submit, in writing, an original recipe using specified Pillsbury products. One hundred and ten finalists are chosen to attend (expenses paid). Each finalist prepares his or her own recipe. The winning recipes are selected for their taste and appearance.

PRIZES: Cash (up to $40,000 for the Grand Prize winner)
AGE: 10 years and over
LOCATION: A major U.S. city is selected for each contest.
DATES: About every two years
CONTACT:
Pillsbury Company
Consumer Affairs
Box 550
Minneapolis, Minnesota 55440

## "THE BUBBLE GUM BLOWING CONTEST"

Each contestant is provided with one stick of bubble gum to be used in the 3 events of this contest: First to Blow a Bubble, Biggest Bubble Blown, Longest Lasting Bubble.

PRIZES: Gum and paperback books
AGE: 5 to 12 years
LOCATION: Main Library, Albany, Oregon
DATE: July, annually
CONTACT:
Children's Librarian
Albany Public Library
1390 Waverly Drive, S.E.
Albany, Oregon 97312

## "CHICKEN FLYING MEET"

The contestants enter their own chicken in one of four weight classes. Each chicken is placed on a roost or launching pad and must take flight within 30 seconds of the starting signal. Chickens may be gently nudged to fly. The flight of the chicken is measured from the base of the roost to the point where the chicken first touches down. The winning chickens fly the longest distance within the flight area.

PRIZES: Cash to the top three contestants in each weight class
AGE: No age limit for chickens or owners
LOCATION: Bob Evans Farm, Rio Grande, Ohio

DATE: Third Saturday in May, annually
CONTACT:
International Chicken Flying Meet Secretary
3776 South High Street
Columbus, Ohio 43207

## "THE CONCH SHELL BLOWING CONTEST"

Contestants bring their own conch shell to compete in this event. There are five age divisions and the winner in each division is selected by a panel of judges for the tone and quality of their blowing. Each contestant performs on stage before an audience.

PRIZES: Trophies
AGE: 4 divisions within the 3 to 17 year old range, and 18 years and over
LOCATION: Key West, Florida
DATE: Last two weeks of March, annually
CONTACT:
"Old Island Days"
Key West, Florida 33040

## "WORLD CHAMPIONSHIP CRAB RACES"

Contestants may bring their own crab or rent one at the contest site. The crabs, prodded by whistlers, blowing or screams, race down a 5-foot track. Contestants are not allowed to touch the crabs during the race. The first crabs to cross the finish line are the winners.

PRIZES: Trophies and cash
AGE: Juniors—under 12 years
   Adults—over 12 years
LOCATION: Crescent City,
   California
DATE: Sunday of Washington's
   Birthday weekend, annually

## "THE ADVANCED DUNGEONS AND DRAGONS FANTASY AND ROLE-PLAYING GAME"

Contestants compete for the title of champion "Dungeon Master." They must create an original pencil and paper design of a dungeon filled with monsters, treasures, tricks, and traps. Each contestant plays a game of the imagination with the judges. The game is played inside the dungeon designed by the contestant. The judges select the winner on the basis of dungeon design and role-playing.

PRIZES: Trophies
AGE: No Limit
DATE: Annually
CONTACT:
   T.S.R. Hobbies, Inc.
   P.O. Box 726
   Lake Geneva, Wisconsin
   53147

## "JUNIOR WORLD DUCK-CALLING CONTEST"

Contestants attempt to reproduce vocally four kinds of duck calls: comeback call, feed call, hail call, and mating call. The winners are selected by a panel of judges.

PRIZES: Cash
AGE: 14 and under
LOCATION: Stuttgart, Arkansas
DATE: November 25, annually
ENTRY FEE: $12.00

## "THE WHITE HOUSE EASTER EGG ROLL"

Thousands of contestants wait in line to participate in this event. Eight kids compete at one time, each using a spoon to push a colored egg down an 8-foot lane. One in every 8 is a winner and all entrants receive prizes.

PRIZES: Each contestant is given
   a remembrance for
   participating.
AGE: 8 years old and under,
   accompanied by an adult
LOCATION: South lawn of White
   House, Washington, D.C.
DATE: Monday after Easter
   Sunday, annually

## "FENCE PAINTING, NATIONAL TOM SAWYER DAY"

Contestants for the event are selected by local contests held in their home states. Judges for the national championship score each contestant in three categories: costume (authentic Tom Sawyer garb), speed (how fast contestant whitewashes a 4' x 5' fence and runs to finish line), and painting quality (uniformity and coverage of whitewash).

PRIZES: Cash and traveling Trophy displayed in the state capitol building of winner
AGE: 10 through 13
LOCATION: Hannibal, Missouri
DATE: Fourth of July, annually
CONTACT:
Hannibal Jaycees
P.O. Box 484
Hannibal, Missouri 63401

## "INTERNATIONAL FROG RACING & JUMPING CONTEST"

Contestants may enter their own frog or rent a frog at the contest site. The frogs allowed in the competition are bullfrogs, toadfrogs and springfrogs, measuring 4 inches from nose to tail. The first to cross the finish line in the frog race, wins. The frogs may be coaxed with dull-edged instruments. In the Jumping Contest the frog that jumps the furthest distance in 3 jumps, wins.

PRIZES: Trophies
AGE: No limit
LOCATION: Payne, Louisiana
DATE: Saturday of third weekend in September, annually

## "THE GREASY PIG SCRAMBLE"

Each contestant tries to catch a pig greased with peanut oil, hold on to it, and drag it across the finish line. The first one to succeed wins the contest.

PRIZE: The pig
AGE: 14 and under
LOCATION: Dothan, Alabama
DATE: Mid-October
CONTACT:
Peanut Festival
Dothan, Alabama 36302

## "THE HOT DOG EATING CONTEST"

Contestants are provided with hot dogs and the winner is the one who can eat the most hot dogs within a certain time limit.

PRIZE: Ribbons
AGE: No age limit
LOCATION:
Nathan's at Coney Island
1310 Surf Avenue
Brooklyn, New York 11224
DATE: Fourth of July, annually

## "INTERNATIONAL JUGGLER ASSOCIATION'S JUNIOR CHAMPIONSHIP"

The juggling contest is a staged event held in a theatre. An audience and a panel of 7 judges watch a 3-minute free style performance by each contestant. The winner is selected for juggling ability, stage presentation, and costume.

PRIZE: Trophy
AGE: 16 and under
LOCATION: Annual I.J.A. convention site
DATE: Third week of July, annually
CONTACT:
I.J.A.
P.O. Box 383
New York, New York 10040

## "THE WORLD CHAMPIONSHIP LOG ROLLING CONTEST"

Contestants in this event compete two at a time, in a series of eliminations. The contestants try to maintain their balance on a floating log. The winners are the ones who stay on the log after their opponents topple into the water. The contestant who "out-rolls" all the competitors is the champion.

PRIZES: Trophies
AGE:
Juniors: 9 and under
Intermediates: 10–13
Seniors: 14–18

LOCATION: Hayward, Wisconsin
DATE: Last weekend in July, annually
CONTACT:
Telemark Lodge
Hayward, Wisconsin 54843

## "THE NATIONAL MARBLES TOURNAMENT"

Boys and girls compete separately in this tournament. Each contestant must qualify for the competition by first winning local tournaments. "Ringers" is the contest game. The champion in each division must win a series of round robin play.

PRIZES: Trophies
AGE: 14 and under
LOCATION: Wildwood, New Jersey
DATE: Last week of June, annually
CONTACT:
Chamber of Commerce
Wildwood, New Jersey 08260

## "NOW YOU'RE COOKING CONTEST"

Contestants submit a planned menu, using specific food products. There are four categories of competition: Dinner for Two, Family Dinner, American Regional, and Party for Friends. Contestants mail their menus (each entrant must have a school sponsor whose signature accompanies the entry). Six finalists are chosen in each category. They travel, expenses paid, to the "cook-off," which is held at the Culinary Institute of America. The winners are selected for the taste, appearance, originality, nutrition, and creativity of their menus.

PRIZES: Cash and school tuition
AGE: 13 through 19
LOCATION: Hyde Park, New York
DATE: Fall, annually
CONTACT:
Seventeen Magazine
Education Division
850 Third Avenue
New York, New York 10022

## "THE MILK DRINKING CONTEST"

The contestant who can drink a container of milk in the quickest time wins the contest. The entrants compete within specified age divisions.

PRIZES: Ribbons
AGE: 3 to 18 (3 divisions)
LOCATION: Los Angeles County Fair
Los Angeles, California
DATE: End of September, annually
CONTACT:
Milk Drinking Contest
(L.A. Fair)
P.O. Box 388
Industry City, California 91747

## "THE PEANUT RECIPE CONTEST"

Contestants submit an original recipe using peanuts. Fifteen finalists are selected to bring in their prepared recipe. A panel of judges selects a winner on the basis of taste and appearance.

PRIZES: Cash
AGE: 16 and under
LOCATION: Dothan, Alabama
DATE: Mid-October
CONTACT:
National Peanut Festival Association
Dothan, Alabama 36302

## "THE PET ROCK RACE AND COSTUME CONTEST"

Contestants race their own rocks down a 16-foot incline. The owner of the rock that rolls the furthest, without rolling off course, wins the race. In the Best-Dressed Rock Contest, a panel of judges selects the rock with the most creative garb.

PRIZES: Cash, trophies, ribbons
AGE: 3 divisions: under 10, 10–13, 14–18
LOCATION:
Logan County Fair
Logan, Colorado
DATE: Beginning of August, annually

## "THE NATIONAL ROTTEN SNEAKER CHAMPIONSHIP"

Contestants wear their naturally-worn sneakers and parade in front of a panel of judges. Ten finalists are selected. They must jump up and down in front of judges to prove wearability of sneakers. The judges select the most rotten, yet wearable, pair of sneakers.

PRIZES: New sneakers and foot powder
AGE: Under 18
LOCATION: Montpelier, Vermont
DATE: First day of Spring
CONTACT:
Recreation Department
Montpelier, Vermont 05602

## "THE SUN HERALD SAND SCULPTURE CONTEST FOR SCOUTS"

Teams of Boy Scouts and Girl Scouts participate in this event. The sculptures must relate to the theme of that year's contest. Contestants are provided with a limited area of space and are given five hours to create their sculptures. A panel of judges determines winners based on creativity and execution.

PRIZES: Trophies and cash to winning troop
AGE: Cub Scouts, Brownies, Boy Scouts, Girl Scouts
LOCATION: Biloxi, Mississippi
DATE: Third week in September, annually
CONTACT:
Gulf Publishing, Inc.
Director of Marketing
Biloxi, Mississippi 39530

## "THE NATIONAL SEWING MONTH CONTEST"

Entrants compete in one of two contest categories: apparel and crafts. A 5″ x 7″ photo of the entry must be mailed with an entry form (available at sewing stores throughout the country) to the contest site. Twenty-five finalists are chosen in each category and in each age division. Their finished products are mailed to the contest site where a panel of judges selects winners for creativity and sewing ability.

PRIZES: Cash
AGE: 14 and under, 15 to 21, and 3 older divisions
DATE: September through November, annually
CONTACT:
American Home Sewing Association
Suite 1007
1270 Broadway
New York, New York 10001

## "THE WORLD CHAMPIONSHIP SNOW SHOVEL RIDING CONTEST"

Each contestant must ride a coal shovel down a 153-foot snow-covered hill. The one with the fastest time wins. Boys and girls compete separately.

PRIZES: Trophies
AGE: 13 and under
LOCATION: Ambridge, Pennsylvania
DATE: Third week in January
CONTACT:
Beaver County Tourist Prom. Agency
14th and Church Street
Ambridge, Pennsylvania 15003

## "ALL AMERICAN SOAP BOX DERBY"

Contestants race their homemade soap box derby cars down a 953-foot course. The wooden or fiberglass cars must be built to specifications listed in the official rule book. All contestants must first win local races in order to compete.

PRIZES: Scholarships, trophies, jackets, helmets and T-shirts; a week at Derby Downs Camp
AGE: 2 divisions, Junior 10–12, Senior 12–15
LOCATION: Derby Downs, Akron, Ohio
DATE: Second Saturday of August, annually
CONTACT:
All American Soap Box Derby
789 Derby Downs Drive
Akron, Ohio 44309

## "THE NATIONAL SPELLING BEE"

Contestants are asked to spell, out loud, a series of words. The entrant who "out-spells" the others wins. Every contestant is sponsored by a daily or weekly newspaper and he or she must win local and regional spelling bees to compete in the national contest.

PRIZES: Trophies
AGE: Under 16
LOCATION: Washington, D.C.
DATE: Late May, early June, annually
CONTACT:
National Spelling Bee
1100 Central Trust Tower
Cincinnati, Ohio 45202

## "SEVENTEEN MAGAZINE'S FICTION CONTEST"

Entrants submit original stories between 1,000 and 3,000 words in length by mail. The stories must be typed (double spaced) with the name and address of the entrant on each page. There is no limit to the number of stories each contestant may submit. The editors of the magazine select the winners on the basis of literary worth, originality, naturalness of dialogue, characterization, and suitability for publication in the magazine.

PRIZES: Cash to the top three
winners; six honorable
mentions
AGE: 13 through 19
DATE: Summer, annually
CONTACT:
Fiction Contest
*Seventeen Magazine*
850 Third Avenue
New York, New York 10022

## "THE UGLY DOG CONTEST"

Contestants bring their ugly dogs to
this event where a panel of judges
select the ugliest dogs in two categories: Mutt and Pedigree. The two
winners may return the following
year to participate in the "Ring of
Champions" where mutt and pedigree dogs compete together for the
title of "The Ugliest Dog."

PRIZES: Trophies
LOCATION: Petaluma, California
DATE: Springtime, annually
CONTACT:
Chamber of Commerce
Petaluma, California 94952

## "ATARI'S VIDEO GAME CONTEST"

Each year a video game by Atari is
selected for tournament competition. Contestants participate in a
series of eliminations. Winners are
determined by the highest scores.
The top six contestants in each category advance to the finals.

PRIZES: Cash
AGE: Juniors: 18 and under
Seniors: 18 and over
DATE: No set date
LOCATION: Major cities
throughout the world are
selected for each year's
tournament
CONTACT:
Atari Inc.
1265 Borregas Avenue
P.O. Box 427
Sunnyvale, California 94086

# Food

The subject here is kids' favorite foods. You can find out about the first ice cream sundae and how the hot dog got its name. Among other fanciful facts about food, you'll find a fast food calorie counter.

# Fanciful Facts About Food

## How Five Foods Were Created

1. The first doughnuts with holes were made by a 15-year-old, Hanson Crockett. He was a baker's apprentice working in Camden, Maine, in 1847. One day he noticed a rawness in the middle of his fried cakes. He cut out the soggy centers and made the first ring doughnuts. They became very popular and were made by hand until the first doughnut cutter was invented in 1872.

2. The ice cream sundae was first made in E. C. Berner's ice cream parlor in Two River, Wisconsin, around 1890. One of Berner's customers suggested that he pour chocolate syrup over a scoop of ice cream in a dish. This ice cream treat was a hit but was originally sold only on Sundays, hence the name.

3. Peanut Butter was the creation of a St. Louis doctor who was trying to improve the diets of his patients. He spread mashed peanuts on bread and suggested that his patients eat this nutritional, high protein, inexpensive food.

4. The popsicle was first called an "epsicle." It was named after its creator, Frank Epperson of San Francisco, California. One cold night in 1905, Epperson accidentally left a mixing stick in a glass of lemonade on his windowsill. The following morning, the lemonade was found frozen into the first known "ice lollipop." The "epsicle" became a "popsicle."

5. The first potato chips were made in a fit of frustration. George Crumb was a chef working at the Moon Lake Lodge in Saratoga Springs, New York. One evening in 1835, a customer kept sending french fries back to the kitchen complaining they were too thick and too soft. Finally, the chef took a potato, sliced it wafer thin, fried it, and personally served the first potato chips to the satisfied customer.

 ## Five Facts About Hamburgers

1. The first "hamburgers" were eaten by the Tartars, a Mongol people in 13 A.D. Their version of the "hamburger" was raw, shredded goat, camel, or horsemeat made into a patty.

2. The first major hamburger chain was White Castle, which was established in 1921. The White Castle hamburger was shaped into a thin 2 ½-inch square and sold for 5 cents.

3. An American-style hamburger sold in countries such as England, France, Italy, and Japan may contain a high proportion of pork and possibly rabbit and horsemeat plus fat and cereal fillers. This is because beef is not as readily available in those countries as it is in the U.S.

4. A degree of "Bachelor of Hamburgerology" is awarded to all graduates of McDonald's Hamburger University in Elk Grove, Illinois. All managers and owners of McDonald's restaurants must earn this degree.

5. Raw chopped meat patties were first seasoned and cooked in Hamburg, Germany. The Germans called them "Deutsche" or beefsteak. When introduced to America, they were first known as Hamburg steaks and later called Hamburgers.

## How Five Foods Got Their Names

1. The cracker was named by Josiah Bent of Milton, Massachusetts. It was in the early 1890s when he baked an extra crispy batch of biscuits. They crackled when eaten so he called them crackers.

2. Crackerjacks are a combination of popcorn and peanuts which are coated with candy. When a salesman of the Bueckheim Brothers' Candy Company first tasted this confection, he exclaimed "crackerjack!" The Bueckheims then decided to call their creation *Crackerjacks.*

3. French fries are not named after the country of France. "Frenched" means to cut into narrow strips, before frying. These long, thin potatoes are named for the cooking term.

4. The hot dog got its name from Chicago newspaper cartoonist Tad Dorgan. One day in 1906, Dorgan was attending a baseball game in New York's Polo Grounds. He drew a sketch of frankfurters making them look like dachshunds on buns. Beneath the cartoon he wrote, "Hot Dogs."

5. Ketchup originated in China. The Chinese made a spicy sauce of fish broth and mushrooms which they called ke-tsiap. Sailors brought the recipe for this sauce to England where tomatoes were added. The name for them became *kechup.*

## How Five Fruits Were Named

1. Bartlett pears were called "bon chretien" in France where they originated. They became known as Bartlett pears in the U.S. when Enoch Bartlett first sold them here.

2. A boysenberry is a cross between a blackberry, a loganberry, and raspberry. It is named after Rudolph Boysen, who first bred this berry in 1920.

3. Elberta peaches are named in honor of the wife of Samuel Rumph, who developed this variety of peach in 1870.

4. Loganberries were created by Judge James Harvey Logan in 1881, when he crossed a raspberry and a blackberry.

5. Newton Pippin is a breed of apple named in 1666 after Issac Newton, the English scientist, who used an apple to demonstrate the law of gravity.

## Five Facts About the Most Famous Meal Served in the U.S.—Thanksgiving

1. The Pilgrims entertained 92 Indian guests at the 1621 event.

2. The first Thanksgiving meal was a breakfast.

3. Boiled eel, lobster, roasted pigeon, and stuffed cod were served at the meal.

4. The Indians brought turkeys, pumpkins, sweet potatoes, and cranberry sauce to the celebration.

5. The Pilgrims had their first taste of popcorn which was prepared for them by the Indian brave Quadequina, son of Massasoit.

## How Five Candies Were Named

1. Baby Ruth candy bars were named for Ruth, the daughter of President Grover Cleveland, who died tragically at the age of 12. The candy company's president, a long time friend of President Cleveland, decided to honor "Baby Ruth" by naming the candy bar after her.

2. The unique shape of lifesavers came about by accident. In 1912 Cleveland candy maker, Clarence Crane, took his new candy recipe to a pill factory to have it pressed into discs. The machine mistakenly pressed out little rings of candy. Crane liked the new shape which reminded him a life preserver. He decided to sell them as they were and call them "lifesavers."

3. M&Ms were named after the last initial of their creators, Forrest Mars and Bruce Murries. In 1940, they created this candy for the U.S. military.

4. Tootsie Rolls were a creation of Leo Hirschfield, a New York candymaker, who named them after his six-year-old daughter, whom he nicknamed "Tootsie."

5. Milky Ways were named after the star galaxy by their creator, Frank C. Mars. He had great success in selling his candy after he gave them the name "Milky Way."

## Five Facts About Soft Drinks

1. Carbonated water, the basis for modern soft drinks, was first made by an Englishman, Joseph Priestley, in 1772. By adding carbonic gas to water, Priestley was able to duplicate nature's bubbling water.

2. The first sweetened carbonated drink was ginger ale. It was created in Ireland by Dr. Cantrall in 1850.

3. Coca cola syrup was first made in 1886 by pharmacist John Pemberton of Atlanta, Georgia. He created the syrup as a cure for headaches and hangovers. His employee, William Venable, who worked at the pharmacy soda fountain, added carbonated water to the syrup and made the first coca cola soft drink. There are fifteen ingredients in Coca Cola. Fourteen of them are well known, but one which is called 7x is still a well-guarded secret.

4. Hires root beer began as an herb tea. It was concocted by Charles Hires, a pharmacist from Philadelphia. In 1876, at the World's Fair, he sold a package of dry herbs, bark, and roots, to be brewed at home. By 1886, Hires root beer was sold in bottles.

5. The first sugar-free soft drink was made by Hyman Kirsch of Brooklyn. New York in 1952. He called his diet soft drink, No-cal Soda.

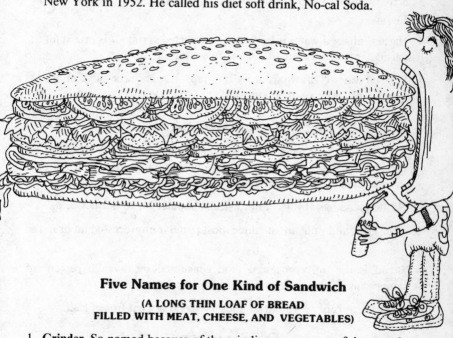

## Five Names for One Kind of Sandwich
### (A LONG THIN LOAF OF BREAD FILLED WITH MEAT, CHEESE, AND VEGETABLES)

1. **Grinder.** So named because of the grinding movement of the mouth required to eat this sandwich.

2. **Hero.** This name refers to the "hero-size" appetite needed to consume this large sandwich.

3. **Hoagie.** Because the workers at *Hog Island* Shipyard in Philadelphia ate these sandwiches for lunch, the sandwiches were nicknamed "hoggies" and later "hoagies."

4. **Poor Boy.** This is a name used by New Orleans nuns who distributed this kind of sandwich to hungry, homeless boys.

5. **Submarine.** The shape of this sandwich is similar to the shape of a submarine.

## Five Kinds of Bottled Water

1. Distilled water is vaporized and condensed to remove all minerals.

2. Soda water, also known as club soda, is tap water which has been charged with carbon dioxide gas.

3. Natural spring water is bottled at a natural spring or other pure water source.

4. Natural mineral water is bottled at a protected spring. It is prized for its particular mineral content and is often naturally bubbly.

5. Purified water is drawn from wells or taps. It is cleansed of all minerals; specific minerals are then replaced.

## Five Facts About Food Consumption

1. The most popular meat in the world is lamb or mutton from sheep. In the United States, however, a relatively small amount of lamb is consumed. Beef is the meat favored by Americans.

2. White bread has always been the most popular bread in the world.

3. Beef, eggs, and milk are the three most popular unprocessed foods in the U.S.

4. Bread is the only processed food consumed by over 90 percent of Americans.

5. Over 95 percent of American households do not eat frozen fruit.

## Five Food Terms

1. **Enriched foods** have nutrients restored which have been lost in processing.

2. **Fortified foods** have vitamins and minerals added to them to make them more nutritious.

3. **Junk foods** are foods which have sugar or fat as the main ingredient. For example, candy is mainly sugar, and potato chips are mostly fat.

4. **Kosher foods** are certain foods which are prepared under the supervision of a rabbi, according to Jewish dietary laws.

5. **Natural foods** are unprocessed foods which have no preservatives, or artificial colors or flavors.

## Five U.S. Names for a Carbonated Drink

1. **Soft drink**—in the South
2. **Pop**—in the Midwest and West
3. **Soda**—in the Northeast
4. **Tonic**—Boston
5. **Seltzer**—New York City

## Five Myths About Foods

1. Eating beets will make one's blood redder.
2. Bread and potatoes are fattening foods.
3. Brown eggs are more nutritious than white eggs.
4. Honey is less fattening than sugar.
5. Sweets cause adolescent acne.

## Five Names for Pancakes

1. Hoe cakes
2. Flapjacks
3. Griddle cakes
4. Hot cakes
5. Silver dollars

## Five Foods Columbus Brought Back from the New World

1. Corn
2. Peppers
3. Pineapples
4. Pumpkins
5. Sweet Potatoes

## Five American Regional Dishes

1. New England Clam Chowder
2. Texas Beef Enchiladas
3. Florida's Key Lime Pie
4. California Burger
5. Maryland Crab Cakes

## Five Facts About Chocolate

1. The first people to drink chocolate were the Mayans and Aztecs, natives of Central America.
2. Chocolate, in the form of cacao beans, was once used as money in South America.
3. It is said that Montezuma, the Aztec king, drank 50 cups of chocolate a day.
4. Hernando Cortez, the Spanish explorer, first brought chocolate from Mexico to Europe in the early 1500s.
5. Casanova, the famous 18th-century Italian lover, drank chocolate as a love potion.

# Meats

Meat is often the main course at a major meal. How the meat is prepared and how it tastes, varies according to the part of the animal used. The following lists are of the major animals used for food and the variety of meats people consume.

## VEAL

This meat comes from a calf (a baby cow).

| Cow Part | Meat Cut |
|---|---|
| Shoulder | Roast |
| Ribs | Chops, cutlets |
| Loin | Chops, cutlets |
| Leg | Roast, scallopine |
| Breast | Roast |
| Shank | Stew meat |

## PORK

This meat comes from a pig.

| Pig Part | Meat Cut |
|---|---|
| Shoulder Butt | Shoulder chops, rib chops |
| Fat Back | Lard, salt pork, tenderloin |
| Loin | Chops, roast |
| Ham | Roasts, fresh or smoked |
| Side | Bacon |
| Spareribs | Pork ribs |
| Picnic | Picnic ham |

## LAMB

This meat comes from sheep less than a year old.

| Lamb Part | Meat Cut |
|---|---|
| Shoulder | Roast |
| Back | Rib chops, crown roast |
| Loin | Saddle roast, steak |
| Leg | Roast |
| Breast | Roast |

## MISCELLANEOUS MEAT CUTS

**Brains**—Organ meat of beef, lamb, pork, and veal.

**Heart**—Organ meat of beef, lamb, poultry, and veal.

**Kidney**—Organ meat of beef, lamb, pork, and veal.

**Liver**—Organ meat of beef, lamb, poultry, and veal.

**Sweetbreads**—The thymus glands of young animals, usually calves.

**Tongue**—Muscle meat of beef, lamb, pork, and veal.

**Tripe**—Lining of the inner stomach of a cow.

## BEEF

This meat comes from a male cow known as a steer.

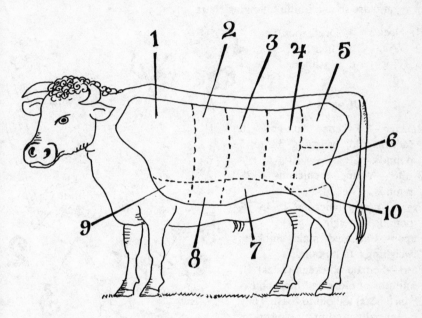

| Cow Part | Meat Cut | Cow Part | Meat Cut |
|---|---|---|---|
| 1. Chuck | Pot roast, ground chuck | 5. Rump | Roast |
| 2. Rib | Prime rib, short rib (for BBQ) | 6. Round | Roast, ground round |
| 3. Short loin | Steaks (porterhouse, T-bone, tenderloin) | 7. Flank | London Broil |
| | | 8. Plate | Braised beef, hamburger |
| 4. Sirloin | Sirloin steak, roast | 9. Brisket | Boiling beef, corned beef |
| | | 10. Shank | Soup and stew meat |

## POULTRY

Domesticated fowl such as chickens, turkeys, ducks, and geese are known as poultry. The cuts of meat from these birds are all labeled in the same way, and are shown in the following chart.

1. Neck
2. Wing
3. Thigh

4. Drumstick/Leg
5. Breast
6. Wishbone

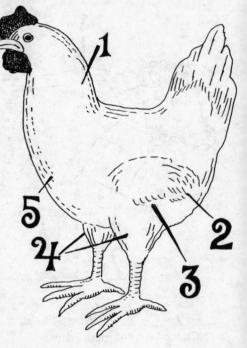

### What Is a . . .

**Roaster**—Chickens under 8 months old, weighing 3½ to 5 pounds.

**Broiler**—Young chickens 2½ pounds in weight.

**Fryer**—Young chickens 2½ to 3½ pounds in weight.

**Capon**—Castrated male chickens weighing 6 to 8 pounds.

**Fowl**—Female chickens (hens) 10 months or older and male chickens (cocks) too old to roast. They are usually used in making soup.

# Bread

Bread is a universal food. It is made in many shapes and prepared in many ways. Below is a sampling of breads from around the world.

| Origin | Bread Name |
|---|---|
| American | Sourdough, white bread |
| Armenian | Filo bread |
| Chinese | Dumpling, steamed buns |
| Danish | Pastries |
| English | Muffin, cottage loaf |
| Finnish | Flat bread |

| Origin | Bread Name |
|--------|-----------|
| French | Croissant, baguette |
| German | Zwieback, Christmas stollen |
| Greek | Easter bread |
| Indian | Paratha, pooris |
| Irish | Soda bread |
| Italian | Twist bread, pizza |
| Japanese | Shina fu |
| Jewish | Bagel, challah |
| Mideastern | Pita bread |
| Mexican | Tortillas |
| Native American | Acorn bread, Navaho fried bread |
| Scottish | Baps, scones |

# Fast Food Calorie Counter

| Food | Calories |
|------|----------|
| **Chicken** | |
| Kentucky Fried Chicken Original Recipe Dinner | 830 |
| Church's Chicken Snack | 316 |
| **Fish Sandwiches** | |
| Burger King Whaler | 486 |
| Gino's fish sandwich | 445 |
| Hardee's fish sandwich | 468 |
| McDonald's Filet-o-Fish | 402 |
| **Hamburgers** | |
| Burger King Whopper | 631 |
| McDonald's Big Mac | 541 |
| Wendy's Old Fashioned Hamburger | 472 |
| Hardee's Cheeseburger | 335 |
| **Hot Dogs** | |
| Dairy Queen Brazier Dog | 273 |
| Friendly Frank | 370 |
| Hardee's hot dog | 346 |
| **Pizza** | |
| Pizza Hut (2 slices, plain) | 340 |

| Food | Calories |
|------|----------|
| **Roast Beef Sandwiches** | |
| Arby's Junior Roast Beef | 220 |
| Hardee's Roast Beef | 390 |
| Jack-in-Box Steak Sandwich | 428 |
| Rustler Steak Sandwich | 369 |
| **French Fries** | |
| Burger King regular | 209 |
| McDonald's small | 211 |
| Wendy's regular | 327 |
| **Beverages** | |
| Burger King's Vanilla Shake | 336 |
| Friendly's Vanilla Shake | 520 |
| McDonald's Chocolate Shake | 364 |
| **Others** | |
| Dairy Queen Onion Rings | 300 |
| McDonald's Apple Pie | 300 |

# Inventions

From tapemeasures to TVs, the many gadgets people use had to be invented by someone. Many fascinating facts can be found among the inventors and inventions.

## Inventions A-Z

| Invention | Inventor | Year Patented |
|---|---|---|
| Airplane with motor ("Flying Machine") | Orville Wright; Wilbur Wright | 1906 |
| Aspirin ("Acetylsalicylic Acid") | Hermann Dresser; Felix Hoffman | 1889 |
| Ball point pen | John J. Loud | 1888 |
| "Cash Register and Indicator" | James Ritty; John Ritty | 1879 |

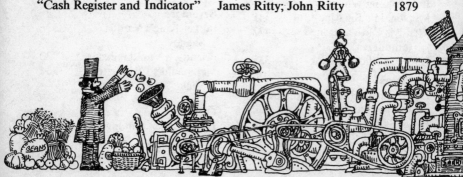

| Invention | Inventor | Year Patented |
|---|---|---|
| Cosmetics (modern) | George Washington Carver | 1925 |
| Cotton gin | Eli Whitney | 1794 |
| Cylinder lock (Door lock) | Linus Yale, Jr. | 1844 |
| Diesel Engine | Rudolf Diesel | 1898 |
| Dresser Trunk | Lillian Russel | 1912 |
| Electric Razor ("Shaving Implement") | Jacob Schick | 1928 |
| Frozen Foods (packaged) | Clarence Birdseye | 1930 |
| Icemaking Machine | John Gorrie | 1851 |
| Ironing Board | Sarah Boone | 1892 |
| Laser | Arthur L. Schawlow Charles H. Townes | 1960 |
| "Life Raft" | Frederick S. Allen | 1881 |
| Mason Jar ("Improvement in Screw Neck Bottles") | John L. Mason | 1858 |
| Matches (friction) | Alonso D. Phillips | 1836 |
| "Microphone" | Emile Berliner | 1880 |
| Motion Picture Projector | Thomas A. Edison | 1892 |
| "Motor Carriage" | Henry Ford | 1901 |

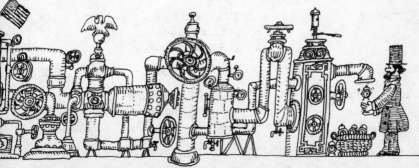

| Invention | Inventor | Year Patented |
|---|---|---|
| Navigable Balloon | J. Etienne; J. Montgolfier | 1783 |
| Nuclear Reactor | Enrico Fermi Leo Szilard | 1955 |
| Nylon | Wallace H. Carothers | 1937 |
| Phonograph | Thomas A. Edison | 1877 |
| Pasteurization | Louis Pasteur | 1873 |
| Refrigeration | Jacob Perkins | 1834 |
| Revolver | Samuel Colt | 1836 |
| Rocket Engine | Robert H. Goddard | 1914 |
| Safety Pin | Walter Hunt | 1849 |
| Sewing Machine | Elias Howe, Jr. | 1846 |
| "Speaking Telegraph" | Thomas A. Edison | 1892 |
| Steamboat | Robert Fulton | 1811 |
| Stethoscope | William Ford | 1882 |
| Suspenders | Samuel Clemens (Mark Twain) | 1871 |
| Tape Measure | Alvin J. Fellows | 1868 |
| Telegraph Signs | Samuel F. B. Morse | 1840 |
| Telephone | Alexander Graham Bell | 1876 |
| Television | Philo T. Farnsworth | 1930 |
| Typewriter | C. Latham Sholes; Carlos Glidden; Samuel W. Soule | 1868 |
| Vacuum Cleaner | Ives W. McGaffey | 1869 |
| Videotape Recorder | Charles P. Ginsburg; Shelby Anderson, Jr.; Ray M. Dolby | 1960 |

| Invention | Inventor | Year Patented |
|---|---|---|
| Vulcanized Rubber | Charles Goodyear | 1844 |
| Washing Machine | Chester Stone | 1827 |
| Wireless Telegraph | Guglielmo Marconi | 1896 |
| Zipper | Whitcomb Judson | 1893 |

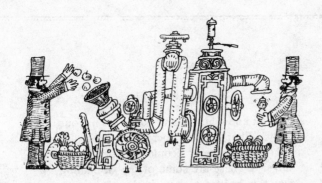

# Medicine

Do you know how many bones are in your body? What kind of doctor is a nephrologist? What ancient people first performed surgery? These are some of the fascinating facts you can learn about in this chapter on Medicine.

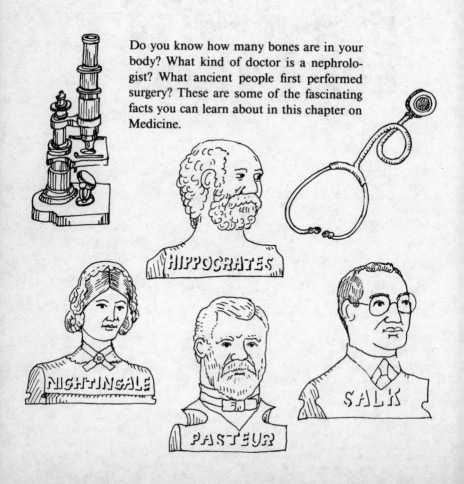

# Medical Milestones

**B.C.**

**2700** The Chinese emperor Shen-Nung is the first to use acupuncture.

**1500** The Egyptians describe diseases and surgery on papyrus scrolls.

**600** The Hebrews are the first to make laws for cleanliness and diet.

**400** Hippocrates, the Greek physician known as the "father of doctors," writes an oath for doctors. By taking this oath, doctors promise to follow certain medical values and ethics.

**A.D.**

**190** Galen of Greece, physician of the Roman Empire, writes about the functions of body organs. His system of medicine is followed for over a thousand years.

**1590** Invention of the microscope by Dutch optician Zacharias Janssen.

**1628** William Harvey of England describes how blood circulates.

**1683** Dutch naturalist Anton van Leeuwenhoek is the first to see and describe bacteria through a microscope.

**1796** Edward Jenner of England develops the first successful vaccination against smallpox.

**1819** French doctor Rene Laennec invents the stethoscope.

**1849** Elizabeth Blackwell becomes the first woman in the U.S. to gain an M.D.

**1854** Florence Nightingale, an English nurse, starts the profession of trained nursing.

**1859** French chemist Louis Pasteur is the first to write about the "germ theory" of disease.

**1864** Louis Pasteur discovers pasteurization, a process which kills harmful bacteria in liquids.

**1865** Joseph Lister of England is the first to perform an antiseptic (germ-free) operation.

**1895** Discovery of X-rays by German physicist, William Roentgen.

**1900** Sigmund Freud, an Austrian doctor, founds modern psychoanalysis.

**1921** First microsurgery (an operation using a microscope and miniature tools) is performed in an operation of the middle ear.

**1928**   Alexander Fleming of Scotland discovers penicillin.

**1953**   Beginning of cryogenics (super cold) in surgery with a successful operation performed by U.S. physician Henry Swan.

**1954**   Dr. Jonas Salk of the U.S. develops the polio vaccine.

**1954**   The first organ (kidney) transplant is performed at Peter Bent Brigham Hospital in Boston.

**1967**   South African doctor Christiaan Barnard performs the first human heart transplant.

**1972**   Beginning of the use of medicine in outer space, testing the effects of space travel on the human body.

**1972**   The CAT scan first shows clean pictures of cross sections of the body. (CAT stands for Computer Assisted Axial Tomography.)

**1978**   The world's first baby conceived in a test tube outside the mother's body is born in Oldham, England. Her name is Louise Joy Brown. Artificial skin is developed by Flow Laboratories, Inc., a biomedical company in Virginia.

**1982**   The first artificial heart is implanted in a human by surgeon, William Devries.

**1983**   More than three million artificial body parts are implanted in humans.

**1984**   The first electronic hearing system is implanted in a deaf person.

**1984**   The first computer system to produce artificial joint design is developed at the Hospital for Special Surgery in New York City.

# Stories Behind Common Health Aids

### ASPIRIN

The most widely-used pain killer in the world is aspirin. It was perfected by German researchers Felix Hoffman and Hermann Dresser in 1899. It was first sold under the trade name Bayer Aspirin in 1905 by prescription only, and in powder form. By 1915, tablets of aspirin were sold over the counter.

### BAND-AIDS

The first adhesive bandages were made by Earl Dickson, an employee of Johnson & Johnson. He designed them for his wife who was prone to cuts and scrapes. The company liked these bandages, named them Band-Aids, and began selling them in 1921.

**EYEGLASSES**
The first people known to wear eyeglasses were the 13th-century Mongols. These eyeglasses were made of convex-shaped quartz with frames of tortoise shells. In the 1700s, Benjamin Franklin came up with the idea of combining farsighted and nearsighted glasses into one pair of bifocal glasses. The first contact lenses were made in the 1880s, even though Leonardo da Vinci had thought of them as early as the 1500s.

**THERMOMETER**
The very first thermometer to measure heat was invented by Galileo. Santorio, a friend of Galileo, was inspired by Galileo's invention and invented the clinical thermometer to record body temperature. Today it is the most widely-used medical tool in the world.

**TOOTH CLEANERS**
The first known instrument to clean teeth was the toothpick. It was used as early as 3000 B.C. by the Sumerians who had toothpicks made of gold. The toothbrush may have been invented by the Chinese in the 15th century. The first toothbrushes used in Europe were said to be made by a London prisoner, William Addis, about 1770.

# A Doctor Directory

**Allergist**—Treats allergies.

**Anesthesiologist**—Puts patients to sleep before surgery.

**Cardiologist**—Treats heart ailments.

**Dermatologist**—Treats the skin and its diseases.

**Endocrinologist**—Treats the glands such as the thyroid and adrenal which secrete body hormones.

**Gastroenterologist**—Specializes in diseases and disorders of the digestive system.

**Gerontologist**—Treats diseases of old age.

**Hematologist**—Treats blood diseases.

**Immunologist**—Specializes in the body's defense system against infection and disease.

**Nephrologist**—Treats kidney disorders.

**Obstetrician**—A doctor who cares for women throughout pregnancy.

**Ophthalmologist**—Treats the eye and its diseases.

**Orthodontist**—A dentist who specializes in straightening teeth.

**Orthopedist**—Treats disorders of bones and muscles.

**Otolaryngologist**—Treats ailments of the nose, throat, and ears.

**Pathologist**—Studies the cause, development, and manifestations of disease.

**Pediatrician**—Specializes in the care and treatment of infants and children.

**Psychiatrist**—Treats illnesses and disorders of the mind.

**Radiologist**—Uses X-rays for medical diagnosis.

**Rheumatologist**—Treats diseases of body joints.

**Urologist**—Treats the urinary tract of the body.

# Body Facts

• There are more than 26 billion cells in a newborn baby.

• More than two-thirds of body weight is made up of fluids.

• There are over 650 muscles in the body, from the tiny ones that move the eyelids to the powerful ones that move the legs.

• The brain is the body's main control center. Messages are sent from the brain to the body at a rate of 240 miles per hour.

• Some body reflexes are:

> Sneezing—which clears dirt from the nose,
> Coughing—which clears mucus from the throat,
> Yawning—which brings more oxygen to the lungs, and
> Shivering—which warms the body.

• The main organ of balance is in the inner ear.

• The skin is one of the body's most important parts. It weighs about 6 pounds, is waterproof, and helps protect the body from dirt and germs.

• It takes 24 hours for food to travel over 30 feet through your body.

• The eyes weigh 1½ ounces each. Both eyes move together. They are always in motion, even during sleep.

• Adults have 32 teeth. There are three kinds of teeth for chewing food: the incisors chop it, the canines tear it, and the molars grind it up.

• There are 206 bones in the body:

     Arm—32
     Leg—31
     Skull—29
     Spine—26
     Chest—25

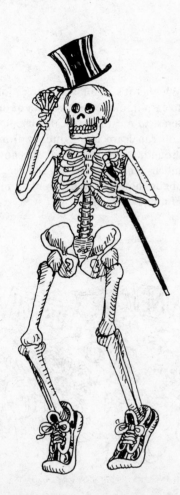

# Money

Whether it's an allowance, or a job to earn it, money is a subject of interest to most kids. In this chapter you can learn about money from around the world, find out how much a half a yard is, and learn about some of the different forms of money.

# Paper Money

• The Chinese were the first to use paper as money. They introduced paper money in the 8th century A.D.

• Plates for the first paper money printed in the U.S. were designed and engraved by Paul Revere in 1775.

• Washington, D.C. is the only place in the United States where paper money is printed.

• U.S. dollar bills are made of linen and cotton woven with red and blue threads.

• The average life span of a $1 bill is 14 months. The average life span of a $5 bill is 2 years. Fiftys and $100 bills usually last 5 years.

• Sixty percent of the paper currency printed in the U.S. is in $1 bills.

• The U.S. Treasury keeps a record of every bill ever printed. They do this by keeping a list of all serial numbers.

• The first female pictured on U.S. paper currency was Martha Washington who appeared on the 1886 one dollar bill.

• Each U.S. bill has a portrait of a president or historical American.

• The back side of each U.S. bill pictures an event in American history or a government building.

• The serial number of each U.S. bill is printed twice.

• The dates of each U.S. bill tell the year the bill was designed.

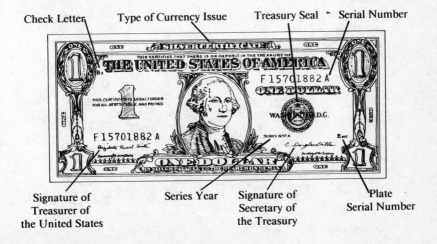

Check Letter  Type of Currency Issue  Treasury Seal  Serial Number

Signature of Treasurer of the United States    Series Year    Signature of Secretary of the Treasury    Plate Serial Number

# Coins

• The ancient Lydians were the first to use coins as money. They began the practice in 1700 B.C. (Lydia was a country in what is Turkey today.)

• The first dollar widely used in colonial Amerca was a Dutch coin bearing the likeness of a lion. It was brought to America by Dutch settlers in 1620.

• The first U.S. mint was established by George Washington. Washington contributed his own household silver candlesticks and dishes to be melted down into coins because of a silver shortage.

• The first American common coin to have a president's portrait was the Lincoln penny. In 1909 it was issued to commemorate the 100th anniversary of President Abraham Lincoln's birth.

• The first nickels were minted in 1866. Prior to that time, 5-cent coins were called half dimes and were made of silver.

• The design of any U.S. coin may not be changed more often than 25 years.

• The largest mint in the world is in Philadelphia, Pennsylvania.

• The largest U.S. coin is the Eisenhower dollar.

• All American coins are marked with "In God We Trust" and "E Pluribus Unum." The motto means "One out of many," thought to be a reference to the unity of the states. They are also marked with the following:

    Date of Issue

    U.S.A.

    Designer's initials

    Mint marking

        D for Denver

        S for San Francisco

        P or no mark for Philadelphia

# Money Around the World

## BASIC UNITS OF MONEY IN 20 COUNTRIES

| Country | Unit | Country | Unit |
|---------|------|---------|------|
| Austria | schilling | Jordan | dinar |
| Brazil | cruzeiro | Laos | kip |
| Canada | dollar | Mexico | peso |
| Denmark | krone | Morocco | dirham |
| France | franc | Netherlands | guilder |
| Great Britain | pound | Portugal | escudo |
| Greece | drachma | Russia | ruble |
| India | rupee | Spain | peseta |
| Italy | lira | West Germany | deutsche mark |
| Japan | yen | Zambia | kwacha |

# Forms of Money

**Bonds** are loans of money to governments or private companies. That money is returned to the bondholder with interest, after a certain amount of time.

**Checks** are like letters to the bank. They tell the bank to give some of your money to someone as payment.

**Credit cards** are used by people who want to pay for something at a later time. The card is an identification card which is shown to the seller. The owner of the card signs a sales slip and usually receives the bill for his or her purchase in the mail.

**Money orders** are issued by the U.S. Post Office. They can be bought for a small fee. They are most often used by people without checking accounts who want to send money safely through the mail. Money orders can be cashed at any U.S. Post Office.

**Stocks** are shares in a large company. When the company makes money the stockholder makes money.

# Money Talk

The following are money terms and what they mean.

**Almighty dollar**—This phrase was first used by writer, Washington Irving, in 1836 when he wrote "the almighty dollar, that great object of universal devotion throughout our land."

**Bearish**—Falling prices, particularly in the stock market. Bears are known to slap their enemies down.

**Bill**—A word for paper money.

**Bullish**—Rising prices, particularly in the stock market. Bulls are known to toss their enemies up.

**Hush money**—Money paid to keep someone quiet.

**Kitty**—A sum of money collected from a group of people to be used for a certain purpose.

**Mad money**—Extra money to be used frivolously.

**Moneybags**—A person with a great deal of money.

**Money talks**—Money influences people.

**Piggybank**—First named after the clay called pygg from which early Americans made coin banks. Later these clay coin banks were made into the shape of pigs.

**Smart money**—Money wisely invested.

**Two bits**—The first American silver dollar was modeled after the Spanish "piece of eight." When used, this silver dollar was often broken off into two bits ($.25) or four bits ($.50).

**Worth his salt**—The Romans once paid their soldiers' salaries in salt. Today this term means a person is worth one's wages.

# Money Slang

|  |  |
|---|---|
| **Money** — | bills, bread, dough, green, lettuce |
| **$1** — | ace, bean, buck, one-spot, single |
| **$5** — | fin, fiver |
| **$10** — | sawbuck, ten-spot |
| **$20** — | double sawbuck |
| **$50** — | half a yard |
| **$100** — | benji, C-note, yard |
| **$500** — | five bills, five Cs, half a G |
| **$1000** — | a grand, a G, a large |

# Money Places to Visit

**CHICAGO MERCANTILE EXCHANGE**
**30 South Wacker Drive**
**Chicago, Illinois 60606**
The visitors gallery is open to the public from 7:15 A.M. to 3:15 P.M. Visitors can see the action on the trading floor where commodities (i.e., grains, metals, and livestock) are bought and sold. Guided tours are available by reservation. The guides explain the workings of the commodities exchange.

**DENVER MINT**
**320 West Colfax**
**Denver, Colorado 80204**
The mint conducts a 20-minute tour Monday through Friday, 8:30 A.M. to 3:00 P.M. There is an exhibit of coins and a balcony from which visitors may look down on money-making operations.

**FORT KNOX**
**Fort Knox, Kentucky 40121**
Visitors are not allowed inside this high security building. They may tour the nearby army base and view the large granite, steel, and concrete building which holds a large amount of the U.S. government's gold. Approximately 150 million ounces of gold are stored in this depository.

**HOMESTAKE MINE**
**Box 875**
**Lead, South Dakota 57754**
This is a privately owned gold mine which conducts a 1¼-hour walking tour for the public. Visitors can view the surface workings of the mine and the final processing of gold.

**NEW YORK STOCK EXCHANGE**
**20 Broad Street**
**New York, New York 10005**
Visitors are allowed in the observation gallery from 10:00 A.M. to 3:00 P.M. Monday through Friday to watch the activities of trading stocks. A guide is available to explain how to read the ticker tape.

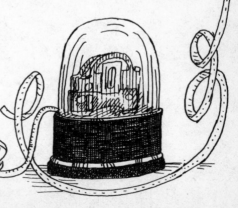

**PHILADELPHIA MINT**
**5th and Arch Streets**
**Philadelphia, Pennsylvania 19106**
Visitors are allowed to take self-guided tours on weekdays from 9:00 A.M. to 4:30 P.M. Coin exhibits are on display and coin production can be viewed.

**SAN FRANCISCO MINT**
**55 Mint Street**
**San Francisco, California 94175**
Visitors may not view coin production at this mint. However, visitors are offered a movie, which tells the story of the San Francisco mint, and a museum, which features a replica of the gold rush days.

**SUTTER'S MILL AND MARSHALL**
**GOLD DISCOVERY STATE**
**HISTORICAL PARK**
**P.O. Box 265**
**Coloma, California 95613**
Visitors may take a self-guided tour through the museum which contains a replica of the original mill where gold was first discovered in the U.S. There are dioramas which show the many uses of gold throughout history.

# Museums

Famous and offbeat collections found in the United States are listed in this chapter. Whether your interest is baseball cards or stuffed animals, there's a museum for you.

# Must-See U.S. Museum Collections

**AIRCRAFT**
**National Air and Space Museum**
**Independence Ave. (4th & 7th St.)**
 **SW**
**Washington, D.C. 20560**
This museum features aircraft ranging from the Wright brothers' original plane and Lindbergh's *Spirit of St. Louis,* to World War II fighter planes and the *Apollo II* spacecraft. People's early interest in flight can be viewed in the collection of Chinese kites and balloons.

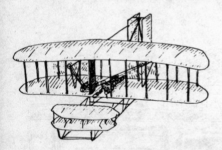

**AUTOMOBILES**
**Henry Ford Museum**
**20900 Oakwood Boulevard**
**Dearborn, Michigan 41821**
This museum is famous for its collection of automobiles. There are more than 200 old cars, including Henry Ford's first car, the 1907

Rolls Royce Silver Ghost, and the 1914 Detroit Electric.

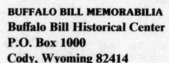

**BASEBALL CARDS**
**Metropolitan Museum of Art**
**5th Ave. and 80th St.**
**New York, New York 10028**
The Print Room of this museum houses the world-famous Burdick collection of baseball and tobacco cards. It is the largest and most extensive collection of baseball cards available for viewing in the U.S.

**BUFFALO BILL MEMORABILIA**
**Buffalo Bill Historical Center**
**P.O. Box 1000**
**Cody, Wyoming 82414**
The personal items of Buffalo Bill Cody including guns, saddles, clothing, and trophies can be found in this museum. In addition, artifacts from his traveling show, among them Annie Oakley's fringed rawhide outfit, are on display here.

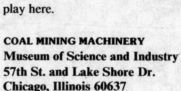

**COAL MINING MACHINERY**
**Museum of Science and Industry**
**57th St. and Lake Shore Dr.**
**Chicago, Illinois 60637**
A full-sized reproduction of a coal mine is on display here. Visitors enter the mine in a real mine hoist. A guided tour explains the machinery and technology used in modern mining methods.

## COMPUTERS
**The Computer Museum**
**300 Congress St.**
**Boston, Massachusetts 01752**
Computers made of tinker toys, huge obsolete computers, and the very latest home computers are all on display at this museum. It is a one-of-a-kind collection that takes both a serious and humorous look at computers.

## CIRCUS WAGONS
**Circus World Museum**
**426 Water St.**
**Baraboo, Wisconsin 53913**
Over 100 circus wagons are on display in this museum. It is the world's largest collection of circus wagons and is situated on land once owned by the Ringling Brothers. Circus parades, aerial arts, and clown shows are also featured at this museum.

## DINOSAURS
**Carnegie Museum of**
  **Natural History**
**Carnegie Institute**
**4400 Forbes Ave.**
**Pittsburgh, Pennsylvania 15213**
The museum's Dinosaur Hall houses one of the world's best exhibits devoted to dinosaurs. Mounted dinosaurs include the finest allosaurus ever found, a protoceratops with its egg, and a Tyrannosaurus rex.

## DOG ARTWORK
**The Dog Museum**
**New York Life Insurance Bldg.**
**51 Madison Ave. (26th & 27th St.)**
**New York, New York 10010**
Dogs have been prominent in artwork for centuries, from early cave paintings to modern works. This exhibit is devoted entirely to dogs and includes bronze sculptures, 18th-century paintings, and photographs.

## DOLLS
**Margaret Woodbury Strong**
  **Museum**
**One Manhattan Square**
**Rochester, New York 14607**
More than 19,000 dolls of every type and fashion from all over the world are on display here. There are also thousands of doll houses, miniature houses, trains and toys to delight kids and grown-ups alike.

## FIRST LADIES' GOWNS
**National Museum of**
**American History**
**Constitution Ave. (12th &**
**14th St.) NW**
**Washington, D.C. 20560**
Every U.S. president's wife is featured in this exhibit. Life-size replicas of the women dressed in their inaugural gowns are displayed in period settings.

## FLAGS
**National Museum of**
**American History**
**Constitution Ave. (12th &**
**14th St.) NW**
**Washington, D.C. 20560**
Among the many flags displayed is the original "Old Glory" which inspired Francis Scott Key to write the words for the U.S. national anthem, "The Star-Spangled Banner."

## KIDS
**Children's Museum**
**P.O. Box 3000**
**Worth Meridian**
**Indianapolis, Indiana 46206**
This is the largest children's museum in the world. There are more than 75,000 objects kids can touch or handle. Visitors can sit at the

wheel of a racing car or ride an 80-year-old merry-go-round.

## MECHANICAL MUSIC
**Musical Museum**
**Main St.**
**Deansboro, New York 13328**
The world's largest collection of mechanical music machines is housed in this 17-room museum. Nickleodeons, organ grinders, and rice organs are displayed, and classical and ragtime are among the musical styles they play.

## OCEANS
**Planet Ocean**
**3975 Richenbachen Causeway**
**Miami, Florida 33149**
At this museum you can see a real iceberg, step into a hurricane, and look through the jaws of a shark. Action exhibits based on the ocean and its animals are displayed here.

## POLICE MEMORABILIA
**New York City Police Academy**
**Museum**
**235 East 20th St.**
**New York, New York 10003**
Exhibits here include police uniforms and equipment, as well as weapons captured by police from famed gangster Al Capone and other criminals.

## SEAGOING VESSELS
**Mystic Seaport Museum**
**Greenmanville Ave.**
**Mystic, Connecticut 06355**
This museum is devoted to Amer-

ican sailors and sailing. On exhibit are whaling ships, carved figureheads, anchors, harpoons, and all types of objects related to the shipping and whaling trade.

## STUFFED ANIMALS
**Foster's Bighorn**
**143 Main Street**
**Rio Vista, California 94571**
Known as the world's largest "inert zoo," this collection of stuffed animals includes examples of rare and

extinct species. This huge collection is worth over 3 million dollars.

## TRAINS
**National Museum of Transport**
**3015 Barrett Station Rd.**
**Saint Louis, Missouri 63122**
Classic steam locomotives, early diesels, Pullman sleeping cars, lavish dining cars, cabooses, and early refrigerated cars are some of the sights for train lovers to see at this museum.

## TROLLEYS
**Seashore Trolley Museum**
**Drawer A**
**Log Cabin Rd.**
**Kennebunkport, Maine 04046**
One of the world's most complete collections of street and railway vehicles can be seen here. Many are on display, but some are in service on the museum's demonstration railway and road.

# Music

Rock, Pop, Reggae, Folk, Country, Jazz, Swing. If you like music, these pages will "sing" with things you'll want to know.

# Music Trivia

1. What is the most popular Christian hymn in the U.S.?
   ANSWER: "Abide With Me."
2. What is the most popular musical instrument in the U.S.?
   ANSWER: More Americans play the piano than any other instrument.
3. What composer has written the most million-selling singles in pop music?
   ANSWER: Paul McCartney.
4. What is the most frequently sung song in the world?
   ANSWER: "Happy Birthday to You" written by the American sisters Patty and Mildred Hill in 1893.
5. Who is the person generally credited with the first solo recital?
   ANSWER: Franz Liszt, a piano virtuoso who lived in Hungary in the 1800s.
6. Who won the most Grammy Awards (given for artistic achievement in the recording field) in one year?
   ANSWER: Michael Jackson, who won 8 for the year 1983.
7. Who was the first recording artist to win a gold record?
   ANSWER: Perry Como in 1958 for his song "Catch A Falling Star."
8. Who is the best-selling classical pianist in recording history?
   ANSWER: Polish-born Arthur Rubinstein, who first played in the U.S. in 1906. He has become one of the most widely-loved U.S. concert pianists selling more than 10 million of his 200 recordings.
9. What is the biggest and most powerful musical instrument?
   ANSWER: The pipe organ. The largest pipe organ on record is the Auditorium Organ in Atlantic City, New Jersey, which has 33,112 pipes and the volume of 25 brass bands.
10. What orchestra has given more concerts than any other in the world?
    ANSWER: The New York Philharmonic began playing in 1842. In 1982 it played its 10,000th concert and has performed over a thousand more since then.
11. Who was the most famous violin maker in history?
    ANSWER: Antonio Stradivarius (1644–1737) of Italy. No one has been able to duplicate the sound of his violins. It is not known whether his formula for varnish, the sap applied to the wood, or the wood itself is the secret to his violins. Today, a Stradivarius violin is worth over $450,000.
12. What was the first opera ever composed?
    ANSWER: *Dafne* by Jacopo Peri of Florence, Italy in 1597.

13. What instrument do most kids in most marching bands want to play?
    ANSWER: The drums.
14. Where is the capital of jazz in the United States?
    ANSWER: New Orleans, Louisiana.
15. What was the first Broadway musical written and produced by blacks?
    ANSWER: *Shuffle Along* by Eubie Blake and Nobel Sissle in 1921.
16. What music is played when the president of the U.S. appears in public?
    ANSWER: "Hail to the Chief."
17. What was the first music video nominated for an Academy Award (given for excellence in motion pictures)?
    ANSWER: *Thriller* by Michael Jackson.
18. Who was the most successful music group ever?
    ANSWER: The Beatles sold over a hundred million singles and a hundred million albums.
19. What was the first television station to feature video music exclusively?
    ANSWER: Music Television (MTV) began in 1981 as a 24-hour, seven-day-a-week rock channel playing video songs only.
20. What was the greatest selling classical record?
    ANSWER: *Switched-on Bach* by Walter Carlos (1968) featuring many of Bach's best known works played on the Moog Synthesizer.
21. Is there such a thing as a one-man orchestra?
    ANSWER: Yes, a "Symphonytron" which is an electronic instrument, allows a player to perform a symphony written for many instruments on a single machine.

# Gold Record Chart

This is a list of the number of records that must be sold to win a gold record in countries around the world.

| Country | Number of Singles | Country | Number of Singles |
|---|---|---|---|
| Australia | 50,000 | Italy | 1,000,000 |
| Austria | 100,000 | The Netherlands | 100,000 |
| Canada | 75,000 | Poland | 250,000 |
| Denmark | 50,000 | Spain | 100,000 |
| Finland | 10,000 | Sweden | 100,000 |
| France | 500,000 | United Kingdom | 500,000 |
| Hungary | 100,000 | U.S.A. | 1,000,000 |
| Ireland | 100,000 | West Germany | 1,000,000 |

# Musical Notes

## Five Musicians Who Influenced Popular Music

Bill Haley and His Comets—Rock
'n' Roll
Woody Guthrie—Folk Music
Ray Charles—Rhythm and Blues
Dave Brubeck—Modern
Progressive Jazz
Bob Marley—Reggae Music

## Five Funny Song Titles

"The Purple People Eater"—1958
"Does Your Chewing Gum Lose
Its Flavor on the Bedpost
Overnight?"—1961
"The Monster Mash"—1962
"Itsy Bitsy Teenie Weenie Yellow
Polka Dot Bikini"—1960
"A Boy Named Sue"—1968

## Five Grammy Award-Winning "Records of the Year"

1980 "Sailing," sung by
Christopher Cross
1981 "Bette Davis Eyes," sung by
Kim Carnes
1982 "Rosanna," sung by Toto
1983 "Beat It," sung by Michael
Jackson
1984 "What's Love Got to Do
with It," sung by Tina Turner

## Top Five Performers with the Most Pop Hits (1953–1983)

Elvis Presley
The Beatles
James Brown
Pat Boone
Fats Domino

## Kids' Five Favorite Broadway Musicals

1. Annie
2. Grease
3. Oklahoma
4. Oliver
5. West Side Story

## Five Musical Groups with Animal Names

The Beatles
The Byrds
The Eagles
The Monkees
The Turtles

## Five Musical Groups with Food Names

The Electric Prunes
Meat Loaf
The Flying Burrito Brothers
The Strawberry Alarm Clock
Vanilla Fudge

## Five Kings of Music

"The King"—Elvis Presley
"King of Swing"—Benny Goodman
"King of Ragtime"—Scott Joplin
"King of Mountain Music"—Roy Acuff
"King of the Twelve-String Guitar"—Leadbelly (Huddie Ledbetter)

## Five Queens of Music

"Queen of Soul"—Aretha Franklin
"Queen of the Blues"—Dinah Washington
"Queen of Country Music"—Mother Maybelle Carter
"Queen of Folk Music"—Joan Baez
"Queen of Rock"—Janis Joplin

## Five Firsts in Rock 'n' Roll

• The first to use the term rock 'n' roll was Alan Freed, a disc jockey from Cleveland. In 1952 he changed the name of his radio show to "Morning Rock 'n' Roll House Party."

• The first national rock 'n' roll hit was "Sh-Boom (Life Would Be A Dream)" by the Chords. It was recorded in 1954.

• The first rock film was *Blackboard Jungle*. This 1955 movie featured the hit song "Rock Around the Clock" by Bill Haley and His Comets.

• The first to win a Gold Record for a rock 'n' roll single was Elvis Presley for his 1958 hit "Hard Headed Woman."

• The first Broadway rock musical was *Hair* which opened in 1968.

## Five Kinds of Songs

**Aria**—A song with an instrumental accompaniment. Arias appear most commonly in operas.
**Ballad**—A folk song that tells a story.
**Carol**—A traditional song heard at Christmastime or on other holidays.
**Round/Canon**—A song in which all parts and voices have the same melody, each starting at a different time (e.g., "Row Row Row Your Boat . . .").
**Shanty**—A song sung by sailors in earlier times to help them keep a rhythm as they worked.

## Five Song Titles That Became Popular Sayings

"The Times They Are A-Changin'," Bob Dylan
"Give Peace A Chance," John Lennon and Paul McCartney
"Say It Loud 'I'm Black and I'm Proud'," James Brown
"You Are The Sunshine of My Life," Stevie Wonder
"I Can't Get No Satisfaction," Mick Jagger and Keith Richards

## Five Kinds of Rock Music

| Music | Examples of Musicians |
|---|---|
| Heavy Metal (Hard Rock) | Van Halen |
| New Wave | The Pretenders |
| Pop Rock | Olivia Newton-John |
| Punk | The Clash |
| Country Rock | The Stray Cats |

## Five Kinds of Jazz Music

| Music | Examples of Musicians |
|---|---|
| Boogie Woogie | Jelly Roll Morton |
| Blues | Bessie Smith |
| Dixieland | The Preservation Hall Band |
| Progressive | Miles Davis |
| Ragtime | Scott Joplin |

## Five Kinds of Country Music

| Music | Examples of Musicians |
|---|---|
| Bluegrass | Bill Monroe |
| Cajun | Doug Kershaw |
| Country and Western | Hank Williams |
| Country Gospel | The Oak Ridge Boys |
| Western Swing | Bob Wills and the Texas Playboys |

# Classical Musical Notes

## Five Music Professions

A **composer** writes music.

A **conductor** directs the performances of a chorus, band or orchestra.

A **performer** either plays an instrument or works as a solo or group artist.

A **teacher** works in a school or gives private lessons.

A **tuner** tunes musical instruments.

## Five Forms of Classical Music

**Ballet**—A story danced to music, usually with scenery and costumes.

**Concerto**—A work for one or more solo instruments and orchestra.

**Opera**—A play or story that is sung and acted. An opera is usually staged with costumes, scenery, a chorus, and an orchestra.

**Oratorio**—A religious story put to music and usually performed by a chorus without scenery and costumes.

**Symphony**—A long musical composition for orchestra.

## Five Great Composers for Young People

**Robert Schumann,** a German who lived in the 1800s, was one of the first to write piano pieces for children. Among his works are "Album for the Young" and "Scenes from Childhood."

**Peter Ilyich Tchaikovsky** was a Russian composer who lived from 1840 to 1893. He composed the music for *The Nutcracker,* a ballet loved by children.

**Johannes Brahms,** 19th-century German composer, wrote a now-famous lullaby, which has been sung by parents to babies for over a hundred years.

**Sergei Prokofiev,** who lived in Russia from 1891–1953, composed *Peter and the Wolf,* a classic favorite of kids.

**Aaron Copeland,** a modern American composer, wrote an opera for children to perform entitled *The Second Hurricane.*

## Five Notable Music Festivals

**The Aspen Festival** takes place in Aspen, Colorado every summer. Concerts, recitals, and chamber music are performed.

**The Bayreuth Festival** is held in Bayreuth, Germany every July and August. The festival is dedicated to the music of Richard Wagner's operas.

**The Berkshire Festival,** also known as Tanglewood, is held near Lenox, Massachusetts every July and August. Operas, chamber music, and concert performances of the Boston Symphony Orchestra are featured.

**The Edinburgh Festival** is known for the variety of its music. It presents operas, ballets, and concerts every year from late August into September.

**The Salzburg Festival** in Salzburg, Austria is dedicated to the music of Mozart although other composers' works are included in the festival. It runs from late July through August every year.

## Five Famous National Anthems

• "God Save the King," the royal anthem of Great Britain, is called the "anthem of anthems." Its melody is one of the most popular tunes in the world. Germany, Denmark, Sweden, Switzerland, and the U.S. all have national songs written to its tune. "My Country Tis of Thee" is the American national song which is sung to this melody.

• The national anthem of Austria is considered to be one of the most beautiful. "Got Erhaltz" (May God Save) was composed by the great Austrian composer, Joseph Haydn.

• "The Marseillaise," is the national anthem of France. Next to "God Save the King," it is the best-known national anthem. It was written by Claude Joesph Rouget de Lisle, a loyal subject of King Louis XVI. However, it was later used against the king as the song of the revolutionaries. In 1795 it became the official anthem of France.

• The words to "The Star-spangled Banner" were written by Francis Scott Key in 1814 when he watched the British bomb Fort McHenry near Baltimore. It was not until 117 years later in 1931 that a law was passed making "The Star-spangled Banner" the National Anthem of the U.S.

• The tiny country of Vatican City has an anthem. It is called the "Marcia Pontificale" and was composed by Charles Gounod for Pope Pius IX in 1846. It became the official papal anthem in 1949.

# The Orchestra

The orchestra is made up of four families of musical instruments. There are usually about 100 instruments in a standard orchestra.

## STRING INSTRUMENTS

About two-thirds of the orchestra is made up of instruments in the string family. The sounds of these instruments are made by drawing a bow across the strings or by plucking them.

### VIOLIN

A four-stringed instrument, it is the smallest instrument in this family. Violins are the largest group of instruments in the orchestra; about thirty-six are in a standard orchestra.

### VIOLA

An instrument like the violin, the viola is only one-seventh larger in size. The tone of the viola is lower than the violin. There are usually eight to ten violas in an orchestra.

### CELLO

Twice the size of the viola, the cello is held between the knees. Its tone is eight notes lower than the viola and there are usually ten to twelve celli in an orchestra.

### DOUBLE BASS

The largest stringed instrument, it stands six feet tall. The player stands or sits on a high stool to play it. There are eight to ten in an orchestra.

### HARP

The oldest instrument in the string section, the harp is also the only stringed instrument not in the violin family. Instead of four strings it has forty-seven, and it has seven pedals. The harp is not always played in an orchestra.

SEATING PLAN OF A

# WOODWIND INSTRUMENTS

These instruments were named because they were originally made of wood and played by blowing wind into them. Today, they are still played in the same manner but many are made of metal rather than of wood. The notes are produced by pressing on the keys of the instrument.

## FLUTE

This instrument is about two feet long and is held horizontally when played. The tones are made by pressing keys with the fingers. There are three in an orchestra.

## PICCOLO

This instrument is a half-size flute that plays notes higher than the flute. There is one in an orchestra.

## OBOE

A two-foot-long instrument, it is held vertically when played. The oboe is a double-reed instrument, meaning it has a mouthpiece made of two pieces of cane wood tied around a small tube. There are three in an orchestra.

## ENGLISH HORN

A kind of oboe, this instrument is five notes lower and is one-and-a-half times the size of an oboe. There is one English horn player in an orchestra.

## CLARINET

This is a single-reed instrument. There are three in an orchestra.

## BASS CLARINET

Twice as large as a clarinet, this instrument plays eight notes lower. It is used occasionally in an orchestra.

## BASSOON

An eight-foot-long instrument, it is doubled over to make it easier to handle. There are two in an orchestra.

## DOUBLE BASSOON/CONTRA BASSOON

This instrument is sixteen feet long but doubled four times to make it shorter. It plays the lowest notes of the woodwind instruments. There is one double bassoon player in an orchestra.

BRASS STRING BASSES INDS VIOLAS TOR CELLOS HARP YPICAL SYMPHONY ORCHESTRA

# BRASS INSTRUMENTS

All of the instruments in this family are made of metal. They are blown to make music.

## TRUMPET

This instrument is played by pressing three valves. The tube of a trumpet is eight feet long but is coiled around so the instrument is shorter and easier to handle. There are four trumpet players in an orchestra.

## FRENCH HORN

There are three valves in a French horn which are pressed to produce different tones. The tube of this instrument is sixteen feet long and coiled around to make it managea-ble. There are three French horn players in an orchestra.

## TROMBONE

This instrument has no valves. The tones are produced by moving the slide back and forth while blowing into the instrument. A standard orchestra has three trombones.

## TUBA

The heaviest and largest of brass instruments, its mouthpiece covers the mouth of most players. If the tube of this instrument were uncoiled it would stretch five feet. The tone, made by pressing valves, is very low. There is one tuba player in an orchestra.

# PERCUSSION INSTRUMENTS

## DRUMS

Snare drums are 16 inches across, the smallest in the drum family. Bass drums are four times larger than the snare. Kettle drums look like enormous kettles. There are three to four in an orchestra, each producing different tones.

## TRIANGLE

The simplest instrument in the orchestra, it is made of steel shaped into a triangle. It tinkles like a bell when struck with a metal rod.

## CYMBALS

Two brass plates which are clapped together to make a crashing sound.

## GONG

A large brass plate four to five feet across, which is hung in place and played with a wooden mallet.

# PEOPLE WHO ARE IMPORTANT TO THE ORCHESTRA

• **The composer** writes the music the orchestra plays. The parts for all the various instruments are written by the composer.

• **The conductor** interprets the music and directs the performance of the orchestra. The conductor must be able to read all the musical parts at once.

• **The concertmaster** is the first violinist and is the lead musician in the orchestra. The concertmaster helps the conductor train and rehearse the musicians in the orchestra.

• **The copyist** makes the music for each member of the orchestra to read.

• **The librarian** is responsible for arranging the chairs, music stands, and music for each member of the orchestra.

• **The manager** makes the arrangements for the performances of the orchestra. A manager schedules performing dates and makes all travel and hotel arrangements for the orchestra when it travels.

# Ten Italian Musical Terms

1. **A capella** (ah cah-pel' lah)—Unaccompanied choral singing.

2. **Adagio** (ah-dah' jo)—Slowly.

3. **Allegro** (ah-lay' groh)—Fast and lively.

4. **Crescendo** (creh-shen' doh)—Growing louder.

5. **Decrescendo** (day-creh-shen' doh)—Growing softer.

6. **Forte** (for' tay)—Loud.

7. **Largo** (lar' goh)—Slow.

8. **Legato** (lay-gah' toh)—Smooth and connected. To be played with no interruptions between notes.

9. **Staccato** (stah-cah' toh)—Sharply detached, one note from another.

10. **Tutti** (toot' ee)—The part of a composition in which all the instruments or voices perform together.

# Milestones in Recording History

**1877** Thomas Alva Edison of Menlo Park, New Jersey, first recorded sound on December 6th. The tune he recorded was "Mary Had a Little Lamb."

**1888** The first popular artist to make a recording was 12-year-old Josef Hoffman, a pianist. He recorded a brief passage at the Edison Laboratories in New Jersey.

**1903** The first "unbreakable" record was made by Nicole Freres. He made it out of cardboard covered with shellac.

**1927** The first record changer was introduced by The Victor Talking Machine Company of New Jersey.

**1936** Billboard published the first pop record sales chart.

**1949** The first 45-rpm record was made by RCA.

**1953** The first rock 'n' roll song made the Billboard charts. The song was "Crazy Man Crazy" sung by Bill Haley and His Comets.

**1954** Les Paul built the first multi-track (8-track) tape recorder. He also discovered the technique of echo or delay which revolutionized the sound of recording.

**1954** Tape cartridges were invented by George Eash, a Los Angeles engineer.

**1958** Stereo LPs were first marketed in the U.S.

**1959** The first album sold without the name of the artist on the front or back of the album cover was For LP Fans Only by Elvis Presley.

# Native Instruments Around the World

| Instrument | Country of origin | Instrument | Country of origin |
|---|---|---|---|
| 1. Alpenhorn | Switzerland | 6. Marimba | Guatemala |
| 2. Bagpipe | Scotland | 7. Sitar | India |
| 3. Balalaika | Russia | 8. Spike Fiddle | Thailand |
| 4. Cimbalon | Hungary | 9. Steel Drums | West Indies |
| 5. Gusla | Yugoslavia | 10. Trompong | Bali |

# People

The people in this chapter are famous; heroes who have overcome handicaps or those who have said unforgettable things. Some are the subjects of legends.

## People Who Conquered Handicaps and Achieved Greatness

### Sequoya

Sequoya was born in a Cherokee village in Tennessee in 1775. At a very early age Sequoya lost the use of one of his legs. His lameness prevented him from running and hunting with the other young braves, so he decided to spend his time drawing and painting. His drawings expressed his ideas. Soon he became interested in the way European settlers expressed their ideas—with written words or "talking leaves." Sequoya decided to dedicate his life to making a written system of communication for his people. After years of difficult and often discouraging work, he invented an alphabet of symbols known as "syllabary." Sequoya was able to teach his entire tribe to use the syllabary. As a result, the Cherokees were the first native Americans to read and write their language.

## Louis Braille

When he was just 15 years old and blind, Louis Braille invented a system of writing which has been used by millions of blind people the world over. Louis was born in France in 1809 with normal eyesight. But when he was 3 years old he accidentally punctured one of his eyes. Infection set in and in a short time he lost the sight in both eyes. At the age of 13 he was attending a special school for the blind when he learned about a system called "night writing." It was meant for the blind but proved to be a cumbersome and difficult system. Louis was fascinated with the idea of inventing a writing system the blind could read. He worked on his idea for two years, after which he had developed the raised dot system called Braille.

## Thomas Edison

Thomas Edison is known to most people as the inventor of the light bulb, phonograph, and the motion picture projector. However, what is not known are the difficult years of his life when he was thought to be learning disabled. Edison was born in Ohio in 1847. Because of sickness and many family moves he did not enter school until he was 8 years old. His teachers were extremely frustrated with Thomas. They told his mother that he was a dreamer and could not learn. Thomas was taken out of school after a very short time and that was the only formal schooling he ever had. School was

a painful experience for Thomas. His parents had faith in him, however, and his mother took up the task of teaching him. He was, as she thought, extremely bright. By the age of 10 he was spending hours in his basement doing scientific experiments. Edison grew up to be called "the genius of his time." His inventions have affected the lives of people all over the world.

## Charles Steinmetz

Born in Germany in 1865, Charles Steinmetz was one of the most brilliant electrical engineers of the past century. At birth, Steinmetz was hunchbacked and dwarfish. His severe handicap did not prevent him from having a happy and productive life. As a young man, he studied mathematics, science, and engineering at a German University where he was an outstanding pupil. Later he moved to the United States where he worked for a major electrical company. His inventions and work with electricity made the growth of modern electrical power possible.

## Helen Keller

Helen Keller was born in Alabama in 1880. When she was a 20-month-old baby, she became very sick with a high fever. The fever lasted a few days; when it passed, Helen was left without her sight or hearing. No doctor was able to reverse the tragic effects of her illness. Helen was to live the rest of her life in a dark and soundless world. Her parents weren't able to communicate with her and she was unable to learn from them, so she became a frightened, troublesome, and unhappy child. When she was 7 years old, her parents hired a woman named Anne Sullivan, a special teacher, to help her. After some time, Anne was able to communicate with Helen by using the sense of touch. Anne spelled out words with her fingers pressed into the palm of Helen's hands. It was a great breakthrough for Helen, and one which totally changed her life.

Helen went on to graduate with honors from college. She then dedicated her life to the needs of handicapped people by becoming their spokesperson and by raising money for schools and research. Helen also wrote several books, including *The Story of My Life* and *Midstream—My Later Life*. These inspiring books tell of the struggles and needs of handicapped people as seen through the life of one, Helen Keller.

## Paul Wittgenstein

Paul Wittgenstein was born in Vienna, Austria to a family of music lovers. He studied piano when he was a youngster and by the time he was 21 he had begun a career as a pianist. Then, World War I broke out and he was enrolled in the army. During the war, Paul was wounded in the right arm. His arm had to be amputated. It seemed as if his career as a pianist was at an end. But Paul knew what he wanted in life and that was to be a concert pianist. After the war he began to practice left-handed piano playing. Eventually he was able to play as well with one hand as he had once played with two and he became a well-loved concert pianist. His playing inspired several great composers of his time to write original left-handed music for him.

## Kate Smith

Kate Smith, who was born in Virginia in 1909, was blessed with a great singing voice and a perfect sense of pitch. As a young child it was her goal in life to become a professional singer. But when Kate was 14 years old she developed a gland disorder which caused her to gain weight. Doctors were unable to help her and, despite her own efforts to control her weight, she became very heavy. Kate became depressed and embarrassed, and she stopped singing. Her parents encouraged her to find another career. They felt that the public would not accept a person of her size as a performer. But Kate's grandmother urged her to forget about being heavy and to work on her voice and her career. Kate then decided to pursue the life of a singer. It was what she most wanted in life and her heaviness would not stand in her way. First, she entered and won amateur singing contests. Then, she moved on to Broadway. Eventually, she became a world-renowned recording and performing artist. Today she is still famous for her singing of "God Bless America." No wonder President Franklin D. Roosevelt once introduced her by saying, "This is Kate Smith. This is America."

## Stevie Wonder

Singer/songwriter Stevie Wonder was born Steveland Judkins Morris in Michigan in 1950. He was blind at birth and his family was poor. However, Stevie never let his blindness stop him from composing and performing music. As a very young boy, he was given a harmonica by his family barber. At the young age of 13 he recorded his first hit song "Fingertips." Today, he is a wealthy and famous performer. Stevie Wonder has proven his theory that a handicap is a handicap only if a person lets it be one.

## Wilma Rudolph

Wilma Rudolph was born in 1940 in Tennessee. When she was four years old she became ill with scarlet fever followed by pneumonia. She was so sick that her parents feared for her life. Fortunately, the doctors were able to save her, but her illness left her without the use of one leg. It was thought that she could never walk again. Wilma's mother was determined to help her overcome her handicap. Years of treatment, braces, special shoes, and sheer determination paid off. Wilma was able to walk again. When she could walk she began to run. Her running took her to the 1960 Olympics where she became the second American woman in history to win three gold medals in a single Olympics.

## Itzhak Perlman

Itzhak Perlman was born in Tel Aviv, Israel in 1945. When he was 4 years old he was infected by polio, a disease which crippled him for life. At an early age Itzhak began to play the violin. He had a great gift for music and refused to let his crippled legs keep him from becoming a performer. At the

age of 10 he gave his first concert. A talent scout from the United States saw him play and convinced him to go to the U.S. where he appeared on television. He was a great success and his career took off. Today Itzhak Perlman is a world-renowned concert violinist. He walks on stage with the aid of crutches and struggles into his chair, but he plays the violin with brilliance and beauty.

# Who Said What
### FAMOUS WORDS OF FAMOUS PEOPLE

AESOP,
*Greek fable writer.*

"Do not count your chickens before they are hatched."

JULIUS CAESAR,
*Roman emperor.*

"The die is cast."

WILLIAM SHAKESPEARE,
*English playwright.*

"Sink or swim."

BENJAMIN FRANKLIN,
*U.S. statesman.*

"A penny saved is a penny earned."
"Nothing is certain but death and taxes."

ALEXANDER POPE,
*English poet.*

"A little learning is a dangerous thing."

JOHN PAUL JONES,
*Scottish naval hero of
the American Revolution.*

"I have not yet begun to fight."

ABRAHAM LINCOLN,
*U.S. president.*

"You can't fool all of the people all the time."

FRANKLIN D. ROOSEVELT,
*U.S. president.*

"The only thing we have to fear is fear itself."

DOUGLAS MACARTHUR,
*U.S. Army general.*

"I shall return."

WILL ROGERS,
*U.S. humorist.*

"I never met one (a man) I didn't like."

HUMPHREY BOGART,
*U.S. movie actor.*

"Tennis anyone?"

ANNE FRANK,
*German Jewish girl;
victim of the Nazis.*

"In spite of everything I still believe that people are really good at heart."

JOHN F. KENNEDY,
*U.S. president.*

"Ask not what your country can do for you; ask what you can do for your country."

YOGI BERRA,
*U.S. baseball player.*

"The game isn't over till it's over."

NEIL A. ARMSTRONG,
*U.S. astronaut.*

"That's one small step for man, one great leap for mankind."

WALTER CRONKITE,
*U.S. newsman.*

"And that's the way it is."

P. T. BARNUM,
*American showman.*

"There's a sucker born every minute."

KNUTE ROCKNE,
*U.S. football coach of
Notre Dame.*

"When the going gets tough the tough get going."

THOMAS PAINE,
*American political
philosopher.*

"These are the times that try men's souls."

# Famous People: Real and Legendary

## REAL PEOPLE

**ANNIE OAKLEY** —A renowned sharpshooter with a rifle and shotgun, she traveled with Buffalo Bill's Wild West Show for 17 years. She was born Phoebe Anne Oakley Mozee in Ohio in 1860 and died in 1926.

**CAPTAIN KIDD** —William Kidd was born in Scotland in 1645. As a seaman he was hired to protect ships from piracy. However, he became a pirate. He was convicted of piracy and hanged in London in 1701.

**CLEOPATRA** —A true Egyptian queen, she was born in 69 B.C. and died in 30 B.C. For 30 years she fought with her brother, Ptolemy, for control of Egypt. Finally she allied herself with Roman emperor, Julius Caesar, who defeated her brother in war. She married Mark Antony, Julius Caesar's successor.

**DAVY CROCKETT** —A great hero of frontier America, Crockett was born in Tennessee in 1786. He fought in Indian wars, served in the U.S. House of Representatives, and died in 1836 defending the Alamo in Texas.

**GERONIMO** —Geronimo was born in Arizona in 1829. He was an Apache chief known for his raids on white settlers. He finally surrendered to U.S. troops in 1886 and thereafter became a prosperous farmer. He died in 1909.

**JESSE JAMES** —This notorious U.S. outlaw was famous for his train and bank robberies. He was born in Missouri in 1847, and was killed by one of his own gang members in 1882.

**POCAHONTAS** —She was born in Virginia in 1595 and died in 1617. Pocahontas saved the life of the English settler, Captain John Smith, and helped to keep relationships friendly between the English settlers of Jamestown, Virginia and the Indians. She married John Rolfe, a Jamestown settler.

**SITTING BULL** —A Sioux Indian from South Dakota, he was a leader in the Indian resistance that led to the famous Battle of Little Bighorn. Also a famous medicine man, he later toured with Buffalo Bill's Wild West Show. He was born in 1831 and died in 1890.

**TOM THUMB** —Charles Sherwood Stratton was an American midget who became known by his circus name, General Tom Thumb. When fully grown, he was 2 feet tall and weighed 70 pounds. He joined P. T. Barnum's traveling show and became a world-famous show business personality. Tom Thumb was born in Connecticut in 1838. He died in 1883 at the age of 45.

## LEGENDARY PEOPLE

**PAUL BUNYAN** —A U.S. folk hero of the 1800s, Paul Bunyan and his Blue Ox, Babe, were created by American lumberjacks. He was said to be able to cut down a mile of trees with one swing of his ax. He was also given credit for creating the Rocky Mountains and the Grand Canyon.

**DRACULA** —The story of Dracula, the Transylvanian count who was a vampire, was written by the British novelist, Bram Stoker (1847–1912).

**FU MANCHU** —The Chinese criminal genius was created by Englishman Sax Rohmer (1883–1959) who wrote 13 books about Fu Manchu.

**ROBIN HOOD** —An English folk hero of the Middle Ages, he was said to live in Sherwood Forest where he robbed from the rich and shared his spoils with the poor. His story has been told in books and movies. Although many have tried, no one has yet been able to prove that he really existed.

**ROBINSON CRUSOE** —He was created by the English novelist Daniel Defoe. The story of Robinson Crusoe was based on the real-life experience of a Scottish sailor named Alexander Selkirk, who lived alone on the island of Juan Fernandez in the Pacific Ocean for four years before he was eventually rescued.

**ROMEO AND JULIET** —These two famous lovers of Verona, Italy married against the wishes of their families. After their deaths, the feuding families made a peace. The characters were created by Matteo Bandello, a 16th-century Italian writer. Their story was made famous by William Shakespeare, who wrote a play about them.

**SHERLOCK HOLMES** —This famous English private detective was a character who first appeared in Arthur Conan Doyle's, *A Study in Scarlet*. In over 50 stories published from 1892–1915, Holmes is portrayed as an exceptional detective who wears a dressing gown, smokes a pipe, and plays a violin.

**TARZAN** —This famous man of the jungle was a creation of Chicagoan Edgar Rice Burroughs. Burroughs was born in 1875 and wrote 23 Tarzan books before his death in 1950.

**THE THREE MUSKETEERS** —These courageous young men of 17th-century France, who worked for King Louis XII, were characters created by French author, Alexander Dumas. Dumas wrote this popular adventure story in 1844.

**UNCLE SAM** —The U.S. government is often symbolized by a tall, white-haired bearded man, known as Uncle Sam. Sam Wilson supplied meat to the U.S. Army in the War of 1812. He stamped the barrels of meat "U.S." and people said it stood for "Uncle Sam." This nickname was an unfriendly term used by people who were against the war. In 1816, the nickname appeared in a book called *The Adventures of Uncle Sam*. The costume of stars and stripes was a creation of an 1830 cartoon.

# Famous Name Changes

## REAL NAMES OF TEN FAMOUS PEOPLE

| | |
|---|---|
| **Billy the Kid** | William H. Bonney (1859–1881), U.S. outlaw. |
| **Bloody Mary** | Mary I (1516–1558), Queen of England. |
| **Buffalo Bill** | Colonel William F. Cody (1846–1917), U.S. buffalo hunter, Indian scout, and showman. |
| **Calamity Jane** | Martha Jane Burke (1852–1903), U.S. frontier woman. |
| **Confucius** | K'ung Fu-tzu (551 B.C.–479 B.C.), Chinese philosopher. |
| **Diamond Jim Brady** | James Buchanan Brady (1856–1917), U.S. financier. |
| **Adolf Hitler** | Adolf Schicklgruber (1889–1917), German dictator. |

| Johnny Appleseed | John Chapman (1774–1845), U.S. apple tree planter. |
| Mark Twain | Samuel Clemens (1835–1910), U.S. writer. |
| Muhammed Ali | Cassius Marcellus Clay (1942– ), U.S. boxer. |
| O. Henry | William Sidney Porter (1862–1910), U.S. short-story writer. |

## REAL NAMES OF TEN POPULAR CELEBRITIES

| Alan Alda | Alphonso D'Abruzzo |
| Woody Allen | Allen Steward Konigsberg |
| Cher | Cherilyn Sarkisian |
| Alice Cooper | Vincent Furnier |
| Howard Cosell | Howard Cohen |
| John Denver | Henry John Deutschendorf, Jr. |
| Redd Foxx | John Sanford |
| Elton John | Reginald Dwight |
| Donna Summers | LaDonna Gaines |
| Stevie Wonder | Steveland Judkins Morris |

# Presidents of the U.S.

There have been forty men who have served as president of the United States. The highlights of their terms of office, their sporting interests, and little known facts about these men are included in this chapter.

# Presidential Achievements

| *Name and Years in Office* | *Highlights of Administration* |
| --- | --- |
| **1. George Washington**<br>1789–1793<br>1793–1797 | Created Department of Foreign Affairs, national bank, patent laws, Post Office, Treasury Post Office and the Treasury; Bank of U.S. Chartered. |
| **2. John Adams**<br>1797–1801 | Established the Library of Congress, Marine Corps, Navy, and public health services. |
| **3. Thomas Jefferson**<br>1801–1805<br>1805–1809 | Purchased Louisiana Territory; authorized the Lewis and Clark expedition; ended African slave import; established Army Corps of Engineers. |
| **4. James Madison**<br>1809–1813<br>1813–1817 | Issued first war bonds; U.S. defeated England in War of 1812. |
| **5. James Monroe**<br>1817–1821<br>1821–1825 | Purchased Florida; issued Monroe Doctrine (a warning to Europe to stop colonizing America); Missouri Compromise (slave state issue). |
| **6. John Quincy Adams**<br>1825–1829 | Opened western America for settlement with the buiding of canals, highways, and railroads. |
| **7. Andrew Jackson**<br>1829–1833<br>1833–1837 | Introduced "spoils system" by which friends were awarded government jobs; reopened U.S. trade with West Indies. |
| **8. Martin van Buren**<br>1837–1841 | Created independent treasury system to deal with economic panic of 1837. |
| **9. William Henry Harrison**<br>1841 | Died a month after taking office. |
| **10. John Tyler**<br>1841–1845 | Annexed Texas; established uniform election day; signed treaty with China. |

| *Name and Years in Office* | *Highlights of Administration* |
|---|---|
| **11. James Knox Polk**<br>1845–1849 | Established the Department of the Interior; purchased California, New Mexico, Arizona, Nevada, Utah, and parts of Colorado; settled Oregon boundary dispute with Great Britain. |
| **12. Zachary Taylor**<br>1849–1850 | Signed a treaty with Hawaiian Islands; Compromise of 1850 (slave state issue); died after 16 months in office. |
| **13. Millard Fillmore**<br>1850–1853 | Sent Commodore Perry to Japan to open trade with U.S.; Fugitive Slave Law enacted (runaway slaves must be returned to owners). |
| **14. Franklin Pierce**<br>1853–1857 | Signed treaty with Japan; Gadsden Purchase of Mexico border land; Kansas Nebraska Act (state choice on slavery issue). |
| **15. James Buchanan**<br>1857–1861 | Dred Scott decision by Supreme Court deprived Congress of the right to end slavery; South Carolina seceded from the U.S. |
| **16. Abraham Lincoln**<br>1861–1865 | Issued Emancipation Proclamation which freed slaves; Civil War fought; established Department of Agriculture; proclaimed Thanksgiving Day as national holiday; assassinated. |
| **17. Andrew Jackson**<br>1865–1869 | Purchased Alaska; 14th Amendment passed to establish the rights of U.S. citizens. |
| **18. Ulysses S. Grant**<br>1869–1873<br>1873–1877 | Created Department of Justice; transcontinental railroad completed; financial panic, political scandals. |
| **19. Rutherford B. Hayes**<br>1877–1881 | Women allowed to practice law before the Supreme Court; the last Federal troops were withdrawn from the South. |
| **20. James A. Garfield**<br>1881 | Established American Red Cross; assassinated after 199 days in office. |
| **21. Chester A. Arthur**<br>1881–1885 | Signed treaty with Korea; civil service reform act passed; standard time adopted. |

| *Name and Years in Office* | *Highlights of Administration* |
|---|---|
| **22. Grover Cleveland** 1885–1889 and **24.** 1893–1897 | Interstate Commerce Commission established; gold standard maintained; western U.S. homesteaded. |
| **23. Benjamin Harrison** 1889–1893 | Sherman Antitrust Act passed, which broke up business monopolies. Six states entered U.S.: Washington, Idaho, Montana, Wyoming, North Dakota and South Dakota. |
| **25. William McKinley** 1897–1901 | Spanish-American War won, whereby U.S. acquired Philippines, Puerto Rico, and Guam from Spain; Hawaii annexed by U.S.; assassinated. |
| **26. Theodore Roosevelt** 1901–1905 1905–1909 | Created Department of Commerce and Labor; Pure Food and Drug Act and Meat Inspection Act passed to protect consumers; Panama Canal Zone leased to U.S. for use of the canal. |
| **27. William Howard Taft** 1909–1913 | Established postal banks and parcel post; Congress given power to tax citizen incomes. |
| **28. Woodrow Wilson** 1913–1917 1917–1921 | Purchased Danish West Indies (now U.S. Virgin Islands); FTC and Federal Reserve System created; 19th Amendment (women's voting rights) passed; World War I began. |
| **29. Warren G. Harding** 1921–1923 | Created Bureau of the Budget; first immigration quota passed; political scandals. |
| **30. Calvin Coolidge** 1923–1925 1925–1929 | Created the Foreign Service and U.S. Radio Commission; U.S. citizenship granted to American Indians. |
| **31. Herbert C. Hoover** 1929–1933 | Created Veterans Administration; adopted "Star-Spangled Banner" as the National Anthem; economic depression. |
| **32. Franklin D. Roosevelt** 1933–1937 1937–1941 1941–1945 | Brought U.S. out of Great Depression; U.S. entered WW II; Government reform and expansion through programs such as the Social Security Act and Minimum Wage Laws. |

| *Name and Years in Office* | *Highlights of Administration* |
| --- | --- |
| **33. Harry S. Truman**<br>1945–1949<br>1949–1953 | U.S. dropped atom bomb on Japan; WW II ended; Korean War began; North Atlantic Treaty Organization (NATO) established; Truman Doctrine (halted Russian expansion into Europe and Asia). |
| **34. Dwight D. Eisenhower**<br>1953–1957<br>1957–1961 | Korean War ended; racial integration of schools enforced; created National Aeronautics and Space Administration (NASA) which launched first U.S. satellites. |
| **35. John F. Kennedy**<br>1961–1963 | Created Peace Corps; established "hotline" (direct telephone line between Soviet and U.S. leaders); forced Russia to remove missiles from Cuba; first man launched into space; assassinated. |
| **36. Lyndon B. Johnson**<br>1963–1965<br>1965–1969 | Escalated U.S. involvement in Viet Nam; passed legislation on civil rights and tax reduction; established anti-poverty and conservation programs. |
| **37. Richard M. Nixon**<br>1969–1972<br>1972–1974 | First man on the moon; established relations with the Peoples Republic of China; ended Viet Nam War; political scandal and resignation from office of president. |
| **38. Gerald R. Ford**<br>1974–1977 | President Nixon pardoned; passed Federal Campaign Reform Act; proposed statehood for Puerto Rico. |
| **39. James E. Carter**<br>1977–1981 | Pardoned Viet Nam draft resisters; led negotiations for peace in the Middle East; signed treaty which gave the Panama Canal back to Panama in the year 2000. |
| **40. Ronald W. Reagan**<br>1981–1984<br>1984– | Lifted controls on oil pricing; instituted a freeze on hiring new government employees; ordered U.S. invasion of Grenada. |

# Singular Facts About U.S. Presidents

**Arrested**    President Ulysses S. Grant was stopped by a policeman while he was driving his carriage through Washington, D.C. He was issued a ticket for speeding. Rather than appear for a court trial, Grant paid a fine of $20.

**Bachelor**    President James Buchanan was the first bachelor elected to the presidency. He never married and was known as the bachelor president. His niece, Jane Lane, served as "first lady" during his administration.

**Gourmet**    President Thomas Jefferson was an excellent cook and food lover. He is credited with introducing ice cream, waffles and spaghetti to America.

**Heaviest**    President William Taft was 6 feet tall and weighed between 300 and 350 pounds.

**Horse at the White House**    President Zachary Taylor, a war hero, brought his favorite horse, "Whitey," with him when he moved into the White House. The horse was allowed to graze and run on the White House lawn.

**Impeached**    President Andrew Johnson was the only president to be impeached. He was later acquitted, by one vote, of the charges of usurping the law, corrupt use of the veto power, interference at elections and misdemeanors. He served out the rest of his term.

**Inaugurated in 2 Cities**    On April 30, 1743, President George Washington was inaugurated in New York City, the nation's first capital. He took his second oath of office in Philadelphia, Pennsylvania, the second U.S. capital city. He was the only president inaugurated in two different cities.

**Inventor**    President Abraham Lincoln was the only U.S. president to patent an invention. He received patent 6469 for a floatable device to allow steamboats to pass over shallow waters. He was awarded the patent in 1849, twelve years before he was elected president.

**Longest Lived**
President John Adams was the president who lived the longest. He died on July 4, 1826 at the age of 90. He became president when he was 61 years old, served for 4 years, and lived for 25 years after his term.

**Longest Term of Office**
President Franklin D. Roosevelt was the only president to be elected 4 times. He served for 12 years and 39 days and died while still in office. In 1951 a law was passed to limit the office of president to two terms.

**Married in the White House**
President Grover Cleveland was the only president to be married in the White House. When elected, he was a bachelor, but on June 2, 1886, he married Frances Folson at a ceremony which took place in the White House.

**Most Children**
President John Tyler had more children than any other U.S. president. His first child, Mary, was born in 1815. His last child, Pearl, was born in 1860. All together Tyler sired fifteen children. His first wife, Letitia Christian, bore eight children. After her death, his second wife, Julia Gardiner, gave birth to seven more children.

**Name on the Moon**
President Richard Nixon is the only president whose name is inscribed on a plaque on the moon. The plaque was left on the moon by the Apollo II astronauts.

**Oldest Inaugurated**
President Ronald Reagan was the oldest person to be elected president. He was 69 years, 349 days old when he took the oath of office. He was reelected at age 74.

**Resigned**
President Richard Nixon was the only president to resign from office. During his second term, he bowed to the pressures of the nation and Congress to resign or face impeachment because of the "Watergate" scandal. His resignation officially took place at noon on August 9, 1974. Vice-President Gerald Ford became the next president.

**Shortest Term of Office**
President William H. Harrison died after serving only 32 days as President. He caught a chill during his inaugural ceremonies and later died of pneumonia.

**Smallest**
President James Madison was the shortest man to serve as President. He was 5 feet, 4 inches tall and weighed about 100 pounds.

**Sworn in
by Father**

The only president to be sworn into office by his father was Calvin Coolidge. Upon the sudden death of President Harding, the then vice-president took the oath of office before his father, John, a notary public. The event took place at their home in Plymouth, Vermont at 2:47 A.M. on August 3, 1923.

**Tallest**

President Abraham Lincoln was a towering 6-foot, 4-inch man. He was the tallest U.S. president.

**Unknown**

The only man to be U.S. president for a day was David Rice Atchison. There was no official president for one day after President Polk's term expired and President Taylor's began. For religious reasons, Taylor would not be sworn in on a Sunday. So, from noon on Sunday, March 4 until noon on Monday, March 5, 1849, Atchison, the president of the Senate, was the head of state.

**Youngest**

President Theodore Roosevelt was the youngest person to serve as president. When President McKinley was assassinated, Vice-President Roosevelt took the oath of office. He was 42 years and 10 months old.

**Youngest
Elected**

The youngest person to be elected to the presidency was John F. Kennedy. He was 43 years and 236 days old when he took the oath of office.

# Favorite Sports of the Presidents

| President | Favorite Sport(s) |
| --- | --- |
| George Washington | Billiards, canoeing, cockfighting, exploring, fishing, horse racing, hunting, riding. |
| John Adams | Horseback riding, hunting, ice skating, swimming, townball (early version of baseball). |
| Thomas Jefferson | Fishing, horse racing, horseback riding, running, swimming, walking. |

| President | Favorite Sport(s) |
|---|---|
| **James Madison** | Walking. |
| **James Monroe** | Fishing, horseback riding, hunting, swimming. |
| **John Quincy Adams** | Billiards, horse racing, horseback riding, swimming, walking. |
| **Andrew Jackson** | Cockfighting, horse racing, horseback riding. (He kept a stable of thoroughbreds on the White House lawn.) |
| **Martin Van Buren** | Horseback riding, walking. |
| **William Henry Harrison** | Horseback riding. |
| **John Tyler** | Horseback riding, marbles. |
| **James Polk** | None, he was sickly. At age 14 he had a serious operation on his stomach. |
| **Zachary Taylor** | Horseback riding, hunting, swimming. |
| **Millard Fillmore** | None, he was forbade participation in sports because he had to work 12 to 15 hours a day as a weaver helping his father. |
| **Franklin Pierce** | Swimming, walking. |
| **James Buchanan** | Hunting, walking. |
| **Abraham Lincoln** | Billiards, cockfighting, marbles, walking, weight lifting, wrestling. |
| **Andrew Johnson** | None. He wasn't particularly interested in sports. |
| **Ulysses S. Grant** | Baseball, diving, horse racing, skating, swimming. |
| **Rutherford Hayes** | Croquet, hunting. |
| **James Garfield** | Billiards, horseback riding, walking. |
| **Chester Arthur** | Canoeing, fishing, hunting, swimming. |
| **Grover Cleveland** | Billiards, fishing, hunting. |
| **Benjamin Harrison** | Hunting, ice skating, fishing, baseball. |

# PRESIDENTS OF THE U.S.

| President | Favorite Sport(s) |
|---|---|
| **William McKinley** | Fishing, golf, horseback riding, ice skating, swimming, walking. |
| **Theodore Roosevelt** | Boxing, exploring, horseback riding, hunting, jujitsu, mountain climbing, polo, rowing, tennis, walking, wrestling. |
| **William Howard Taft** | Baseball (He was the first President to throw out the ball to open a major league baseball season), golf. |
| **Woodrow Wilson** | Baseball, football, golf, walking. |
| **Warren G. Harding** | Golf, table tennis, tennis. |
| **Calvin Coolidge** | Fishing, mechanical horse riding, trap shooting, walking. |
| **Herbert Hoover** | Baseball, fishing, football. |
| **Franklin D. Roosevelt** | Canoeing, fishing, football, golf, horseback riding, rowing, running, sailing, swimming. |
| **Harry Truman** | Fishing, walking. |
| **Dwight D. Eisenhower** | Baseball, boxing, fishing, football, golf, horseback riding, hunting. |
| **John F. Kennedy** | Baseball, fishing, football, golf, sailing, swimming, tennis, touch football. |
| **Lyndon B. Johnson** | Boating, golf, horseback riding, hunting, swimming, walking. |
| **Richard Nixon** | Bowling, golf. |
| **Gerald Ford** | Golf, running, sailing, swimming, skiing. |
| **Jimmy Carter** | Canoeing, fishing, running, softball. |
| **Ronald Reagan** | Horseback riding, swimming. |

# U.S. Presidents Depicted on Money

## COINS

| | | |
|---|---|---|
| 1 cent | Penny | Abraham Lincoln |
| 5 cents | Nickel | Thomas Jefferson |
| 10 cents | Dime | Franklin Delano Roosevelt |
| 25 cents | Quarter | George Washington |
| 50 cents | Half-Dollar | John F. Kennedy |
| $1.00 | Dollar | Dwight D. Eisenhower |

## PAPER CURRENCY

| | |
|---|---|
| $1 | George Washington |
| $2 | Thomas Jefferson |
| $5 | Abraham Lincoln |
| $20 | Andrew Jackson |
| $50 | Ulysses S. Grant |
| $500 | William McKinley |
| $1,000 | Grover Cleveland |
| $5,000 | James Madison |
| $100,000 | Woodrow Wilson |

## U.S. SAVINGS BONDS

| | |
|---|---|
| $25 | George Washington |
| $50 | Franklin Delano Roosevelt |
| $75 | Harry S. Truman |
| $100 | Dwight D. Eisenhower |
| $200 | John F. Kennedy |
| $500 | Woodrow Wilson |
| $1,000 | Theodore Roosevelt |
| $5,000 | William McKinley |
| $10,000 | Grover Cleveland |

# Religions of the World

Buddhism, Christianity, Confucianism, Hinduism, Islam, Judaism and Taoism are seven major world religions to be found in this chapter. You can find out for yourself how they teach men to be good—each one in its own way.

"Every religion is good that teaches man to be good."
— THOMAS PAINE,
*American Statesman*

# Religions of The World

## BUDDHISM

• Founded about 500 B.C. by Prince Siddhartha Gautama (the Buddha) near Benares, India.

• Practiced mainly in Ceylon, Japan, and India.

• The symbol of this religion is an eight-spoked wheel. Each spoke represents a step toward peace of mind and an end to suffering. It is called the "eightfold path."

Step 1—Right knowledge
Step 2—Right intention
Step 3—Right speech
Step 4—Right conduct
Step 5—Right means of livelihood
Step 6—Right effort
Step 7—Right mindfulness
Step 8—Right concentration

• The sacred book is the *Tripitaka,* a collection of Buddha's teachings.

• There are no gods but Buddhists worship images of Buddha.

• Followers practice yoga and meditation.

• Buddhists believe that people are born and reborn over and over again. When they achieve enlightenment they are finally freed from all desire and the cycle of rebirth. They have then reached Nirvana.

## CHRISTIANITY

• Founded by followers of Jesus Christ after 4 A.D.

• The most popular religion in the world. Over one-fifth of world's population follow one of its sects.

• Practiced mainly in Europe, North America, and South America.

• The holy book is the *Bible* which consists of the Old Testament and New Testament (Christ's life and teachings).

• There are hundreds of Christian groups called denominations. Their beliefs and practices vary.

• Christians believe in one God and in Jesus Christ as the son of God. God redeemed the sins of humans when Jesus Christ was crucified and died on the cross. He then ascended to heaven as the son of God.

• In Christian teaching the soul lives after the body dies. The soul goes to heaven to live with God or to hell for eternal damnation.

# CONFUCIANISM

• Founded in China in the 6th century B.C. by Confucius (K'ung Fu-tzu).

• Practiced in China, Japan, and Mongolia.

• Believe in heaven, ancestor worship, and many gods.

• Sacred books, the *Analects* (*Lun Yu*) and the *Wu Ching* (fire classics), ancient Chinese writings.

• Believe in afterlife with ancestors in heaven.

• No clergy.

# HINDUISM

• Began, c. 1500 B.C.; the founder is unknown.

• Practiced mainly in India.

• Hindus are born to their religion. There are no converts.

• The sacred text is the *Veda,* a collection of myths, epic stories, and rituals.

• There are hundreds of gods and goddesses, enough so that each family has a favorite to honor.

• Followers believe in a cycle of birth and rebirth. Each life is determined by past deeds called Karma. (The concept of Karma is also shared by Buddhists.)

# ISLAM

- Founded in 622 A.D. by Mohammed, the Prophet, in Medina, Arabia.

- Followers of Islam are called Moslems.

- Practiced from West Africa to Indonesia.

- The holy book is the *Koran,* which contains the words of God (Allah) as told by Mohammed.

- Islam means submission to Allah. All the earth belongs to Allah which is why Moslems pray on the ground.

- Followers believe their bodies die but their souls live forever in heaven or hell.

- The five pillars of faith of Islam are:

    1. Belief in Allah.

    2. Prayer 5 times a day.

    3. Donating to charity.

    4. Fasting one day during the month of Ramadan.

    5. Making a pilgrimage to Mecca at least once in a lifetime.

# JUDAISM

- Founded by Abraham more than 5,000 years ago.

- The major areas of practice are Israel, the U.S., and the U.S.S.R.

- The holy book is the *Torah* (the first five books of the Old Testament).

- Followers believe in one God, Jehovah, who is the creator and ruler of the Universe.

- Jews believe their souls will live forever.

## TAOISM

- Founded in 600 B.C. by Lao-Tze in China.

- Practiced mainly in China.

- The sacred book is the *Tao-te-Ching.*

- Tao means a way or a road.

- Followers believe in the yin and yang of the Universe. *Yin* represents the earth; *yang* represents heaven. The balance of yin and yang give order to the world. People are encouraged to work in harmony with nature.

# Sports

"The important thing in the Olympic Games is not to win, but to take part; the important thing in life is not the triumph but the struggle; the essential thing is not having conquered but to have fought well."

—BARON PIERRE DE COUBERTIN,
*father of the modern Olympic Games*

# Olympic Sports

The Olympic Games are the ultimate competition for the amateur athlete. They are held every four years in various countries throughout the world.

## OLYMPIC FACTS

**Olympic Symbol:** The five circles represent the following continents: Africa, the Americas (North and South), Asia, Australia, and Europe. They are interlocking to show friendship among the people of the world. The colors of the rings—blue, yellow, black, green, and red—were chosen because they are commonly found among the flags of all the countries of the world.

**Olympic Motto:** "Citius, Altius, Fortius" (Faster, Higher, Stronger).

**Olympic Creed:** "The most important thing in the Olympic games is not to win but to take part, just as the most important thing in life is not the triumph but the struggle. The essential thing is not to have conquered but to have fought well."

**Olympic Hymn:** "The Hymn Olympique" (composed in 1896 by Spyro Samaras of Greece).

**Olympic Prizes:**
    Ancient
        —First Prize—Laurel wreath
          Second Prize—Wild olive wreath
          Third Prize—Palm wreath
    Modern
        —First Prize—Gold medal
          Second Prize—Silver medal
          Third Prize—Bronze medal

**Olympic Athletes:** Each athlete represents a country; however he or she competes and wins as an individual. The only restrictive requirement for competitors is that they must be amateur (unpaid) athletes.

**Countries Represented in the Olympics:** Ancient Olympics—one country (Greece).

First Modern Olympics—Thirteen countries.

Present-Day Olympics—more than 120 countries.

# THE OFFICIAL OLYMPIC SPORTS

Track and Field—Men, Women
Team Handball—Men, Women
Volleyball—Men, Women
Water Polo—Men
Weightlifting—Men
Wrestling (freestyle and Greco-Roman)—Men
Yachting—Men, Women

## Summer Sports

Archery—Men, Women
Basketball—Men, Women
Boxing—Men
Canoeing—Men, Women
Cycling—Men, Women
Equestrain Games (horse riding) —Men, Women
Fencing—Men, Women
Field Hockey—Men, Women
Gymnastics—Men, Women
Judo—Men
Modern Pentathlon (cross-country running, fencing, riding, shooting, and swimming)—Men
Rowing—Men, Women
Shooting—Men, Women
Soccer—Men
Swimming and Diving—Men, Women

## Winter Sports

Biathlon (skiing and shooting)—Men
Bobsledding—Men
Figure Skating—Men, Women
Ice Dancing—Men, Women
Ice Hockey—Men
Luge (sledding)—Men, Women
Skiing (Nordic and Alpine)—Men, Women
Speed Skating—Men, Women

# OLYMPIC SYMBOLS

*Olympic sports pictograms © 1981, Los Angeles Olympic Organizing Committee*

## OLYMPIC GAMES TIMELINE

**B.C.**

**776** The first recorded Olympics were held in Olympia, Greece. There was only one sporting event. It was a race of 200 yards. These Olympics were held for 1,168 years—a total of 242 Olympiads.

**A.D.**

**394** The ancient Olympic Games were banned by the Romans.

**1896** The first modern Olympic Games were held in Athens, Greece. Baron Pierre de Coubertin, a Frenchman, founded the Games to foster sportsmanship among athletes and to create good will among people of all countries.

**1900** Women were allowed to compete in the Games. Six women participated in lawn tennis.

1920    The Flight of Doves was officially introduced to the opening ceremony of the Olympics.

1924    The winter Games were held for the first time. They were contested at Chamonix, France.

1928    The Olympic torch was lit for the first time at the Amsterdam Games.

1936    These were the first televised games and included the first lighted torch relay—from Olympia, Greece, to Berlin, the site of the Games.

1969    Athletes who participated in women's events were required to take a femininity control exam, to be sure they were women.

1984    The summer Games became the most televised in history when ABC (the American Broadcasting Company) bought the rights to show 200 hours of sports over a 2-week period.

# Memorable Olympic Athletes

**Vasili Alexeyev, U.S.S.R.** This 345-lb. superweight set a world record when he lifted 562 lbs. to become the world's strongest man. He won gold medals in the 1972 and 1976 summer Games.

**Robert Beamon, U.S.A.** His 29-foot, 2 ½-inch long jump at the 1968 Olympics was hailed as one of the greatest athletic achievements. It was 21¾ inches longer than the world record.

**Joan Benoit, U.S.A.** She won the first Olympic women's marathon at the 1984 Los Angeles Summer Games.

**Abebe Bikila, Ethiopia.** He was the first to win the marathon twice, in 1960 and 1964. He was also the first gold medalist from black Africa. In 1960, he ran the entire 26.7-mile marathon barefoot.

**Francine Blankers, Holland.** This 30-year-old mother was known as "Marvelous Mama" at the 1948 London Olympics where she won four gold medals in track and field events.

**Ethelda Bleibtrey, U.S.A.** She was the first woman to win three Olympic gold medals in any sport. She took the honors in swimming at the 1920 Olympics in Antwerp.

**Nadia Comaneci, Romania.** At the age of 14 she became the first gymnast to score a perfect 10. Altogether she won three gold medals, a silver, and a bronze at the Montreal Olympics in 1976. In Moscow, 1980 she won two more gold medals.

**James B. Connolly, U.S.A.** He was the first person to win a gold medal in the modern Olympic Games. He won the gold in the triple jump in Athens, Greece in 1896.

**Mildred "Babe" Didrikson, U.S.A.** She was one of the first females to be an Olympic star. An all-around athlete, she won a gold medal in the javelin and the hurdles, and a silver medal in the high jump at the 1932 Olympics in Los Angeles.

**Eddie Eagan, U.S.A.** He is the only athlete to win gold medals in both the winter and summer Games. He won the first in boxing at the 1920 summer Games and a second in bobsledding at the 1932 winter Games.

**Kornelia Ender, East Germany.** She is one of the greatest female swimmers of all time. She won 4 gold medals at the 1976 Montreal Games.

**Ray Ewry, U.S.A.** Known as "the rubber man," this track and field star won an all-time record string of ten consecutive Olympic championships from 1900–1908. His wins were in the standing high jump, standing long jump, and standing triple jump.

**Dick Fosbury, U.S.A.** He was the first Olympic high jumper to go over the pole head first, landing on his back. This style known as the "Fosbury Flop" earned him a gold medal in Mexico in 1968 and set a new trend in high jumping.

**Shane Gould, Australia.** This great swimmer won three gold medals, a silver, and bronze in the 1972 Olympics. She also broke world records in 3 swimming events in the same Olympics.

**Eric Heiden, U.S.A.** Considered the greatest men's speed skater in history, he won five gold medals in the 1980 Winter Olympics in Lake Placid. He was the only athlete to win five individual golds in the history of the Winter Olympics.

**Sonja Henie, Norway.** A world champion figure skater, she first competed at the age of 10 in 1924. She did not win that year but went on to win gold medals in the 1928, 1932, and 1936 Olympics.

**Ivan Johansson, Sweden.** The top Swedish wrestler, he won three gold medals in wrestling; two in 1932 and one in 1936.

**Olga Korbut, U.S.S.R.** This great Olympic gymnast won three gold medals at the age of 17 in 1972. At the following Olympics in 1976 she won another gold and two silver medals. She is famous for inspiring many youngsters to take up the sport of gymnastics.

**Alvin Kraenzlein, U.S.A.** He won four individual championships in 1900. He won the 60-meter spring, 110-meter high hurdles, 200-meter low hurdles, and the long jump.

**Carl Lewis, U.S.A.** He won four gold medals for track and field events at the 1984 Summer Games in Los Angeles. He excelled in the long jump, the 100 meter, 200 meter and the relay.

**Bob Mathias, U.S.A.** At the age of 17 he upset the field in the 1948 decathlon by winning the gold. He won again in 1952 and became the only athlete to win the decathlon twice.

**Paavo Nurmi, Finland.** The "Flying Finn" as he was called, set 22 world records, and won nine golds and three silvers in middle and long distance races. He participated in the 1924 and 1928 Winter Olympics.

**Alfred Oerter, U.S.A.** His record wins as a discus thrower have never been matched. From 1956 to 1968 he won 4 consecutive gold medals.

**James "Jesse" Owens, U.S.A.** The hero of the 1936 Berlin, Olympic Games, Owens won four gold medals in track and field. He is also remembered for Adolf Hitler's refusal to shake hands with him because he was black.

**Tamara Press, U.S.S.R.** She is one of the top field-event women in the world. Weighing in at 220 pounds, she won the shot put title in 1960 and 1964. In 1964 she also won the discus.

**Peter Snell, New Zealand.** He is remembered as the only athlete to win three Olympic gold medals in mid-distance races. He won two in 1960 and one in 1964.

**Mark Spitz, U.S.A.** He dominated the 1972 Olympics in swimming. He entered seven events and won seven gold medals in individual and team events. No athlete before him had ever won as many as seven golds in one Olympiad.

**Oscar Swahn, Sweden.** At age 72 he was the oldest person to win an Olympic medal. A legendary target shooter, he won three gold, one silver and two bronze medals in the 1908 and 1912 Olympics.

**James "Jim" Thorpe, U.S.A.** This native American was one of the greatest athletes of all time and the only one to win both the decathlon and pentathlon (1912). In 1913 his medals were taken away because it was learned that he played semiprofessional baseball in 1909 (all Olympic participants must be amateurs). In 1982, twenty years after his death, Thorpe's medals were returned to his family. His wins were once again recorded in Olympic history.

**Johnny Weissmuller, U.S.A.** Considered the greatest swimmer of the first half of the 20th century, he won five gold medals in the 1924 and 1928 Olympics. Later, he became famous as "Tarzan" in the movies.

# The Junior Olympics

This is the largest amateur sports program in the United States. It was designed to interest the nation's youth in Olympic sports. Competitions take place in towns and cities in every state. Youngsters 8 to 18 years old can compete only if they have never participated in competitive athletics before. There are competitions on local, state, regional, and national levels.

## THE OFFICIAL JUNIOR OLYMPIC SPORTS

Baseball
Basketball
Bobsled-Luge
Boxing
Cross Country Running
Decathlon
Diving
Field Hockey
Gymnastics
Judo
Soccer
Swimming
Synchronized Swimming
Table Tennis
Tae kwon Do
Track and Field
Trampoline and Tumbling
Volleyball
Water Polo
Weight Lifting
Wrestling

## FAMOUS ATHLETES WHO WERE FORMER JUNIOR OLYMPIANS

**Basketball Players:**
William Bradley, Jr.
Earvin "Magic" Johnson

**Boxers:**
Sugar Ray Leonard
Ken Norton

**Decathlon Competitors:**
Rafer Johnson
Bill Toomey

**Gymnast:**
Kurt Thomas

**Runners:**
Wilma Rudolph
Frank Shorter

**Swimmers:**
Donna DeVarona
Mark Spitz

For more information contact:
Junior Olympics
AAV House
3400 West 86th Street
Indianapolis, Indiana 46268

# The Special Olympics

This is an international program of physical fitness, sports training, and athletic competition for mentally retarded people 8 years old and up. Participants are often active in year-round training programs. There are local and national games each year. The international games are held every four years at selected sites in the U.S.

## THE SPECIAL OLYMPICS SPORTS

| | |
|---|---|
| Basketball | Soccer |
| Bowling | Softball |
| Diving | Swimming |
| Floor Hockey | Track and Field |
| Frisbee-Disc | Volleyball |
| Gymnastics | Wheel Chair Events |
| Poly Hockey | |

## THE SPECIAL OLYMPICS WINTER GAMES

Alpine Skiing
Cross Country Skiing
Ice Skating

For more information contact:
Special Olympics
1701 K Street NW, Suite 203
Washington, D.C. 20006

# Transportation

In this chapter you can read about nearly every vehicle made to move people around this world and out of this world. Here you'll find the first, the fastest, and other interesting facts about transportation.

U.S. FRIGATE CONSTITUTION

THE MAYFLOWER

# Transportation on Water

## FIRSTS ON WATER

• The ancient Sumerians built the first known oar-powered ships to carry them on the Tigris and Euphrates rivers in 3500 B.C.

• The first submarine was a leather-covered boat built in 1620 by a Dutchman, Cornelis Drebbel.

• The American inventor, John Fitch, was the first to demonstrate the steamboat as a means of transportation. In 1787 he launched it on the Delaware River. Four years later he patented his invention.

• In 1906, Enrico Forlanini of Italy invented the hydrofoil, a vessel which moved over water. Three sets of stilts or foils lift it above the water to reduce drag. Commercial use of the hydrofoil began in the 1930s.

• The hovercraft, which moves over the surface of the water supported by a cushion of air, was invented in 1955 by Christopher Cockerell. Hovercrafts are also used to travel over swamps, snow, and sand.

• The first nuclear-powered vessel was launched in 1954 by the U.S. This submarine, the USS Nautilus needed no air for its motors and could make long underwater journeys without refueling.

# FAMOUS SEACRAFT

### H.M.S. BOUNTY
This ship was the scene of one of the most famous mutinies in history. In 1701 the *Bounty* sailed under the English flag to the South Pacific. Its mission was to gather breadfruit trees to transplant in English colonies in the West Indies. First mate, Fletcher Christian, led a mutiny against Captain William Bligh. Bligh was cast adrift with 18 others in an open boat. They sailed nearly 4,000 miles in the small boat to reach safety in the East Indies. Some of the mutineers, including Christian, sailed to Pitcairn Island in the South Pacific. They founded a colony where their descendents continue to live.

### CLERMONT
Dubbed "Fulton's Folly" by nonbelievers, this boat achieved fame as the first commercially successful steamboat. In 1807, Robert Fulton navigated it 240 miles on the Hudson river from New York City to Albany and back. The entire journey took 63 hours.

### CONNECTICUT TURTLE
This was the first submarine used in warfare. Built by 34-year-old American, David Bushnell, it was used by the Americans against British ships in 1776.

### U.S.S. CONSTITUTION
This American warship was used in the War of 1812. It was nicknamed "Old Ironsides" because cannonballs seemed to bounce right off her. After 100 years of service it was retired. It can still be visited at dock in Boston.

### GOLDEN HIND
The flagship of the renowned British seaman Sir Francis Drake, the *Golden Hind* was the only one of his five ships to complete a voyage around the world (1577–1580). Drake was knighted on board and the ship was put on display in Deptford dockyard in England where it remained for over a century.

**KON-TIKI**

In 1947 Norwegian Thor Heyerdahl built a replica of the balsam rafts used by the natives of the South Pacific. He traveled in this raft, from South America to the Polynesian Islands by drifting 4,300 miles with the wind. Heyerdahl made the journey to prove his theory that the people of Polynesia originated in South America.

**LUSITANIA**

A British passenger ship, the *Lusitania* was torpedoed by German submarines on May 7, 1915. The boat sank in 20 minutes, and 1,195 lives were lost; among them 128 Americans. The U.S. was not involved in World War I at the time and protested the sinking to the German government.

**MAYFLOWER**

In 1620 this small ship (90 feet long) set sail with 130 passengers and crew from Southhampton, England. The ship was heading across the Atlantic to Virginia in America. Tossed about by a storm, it was thrown off course, and landed in Plymouth, Massachusetts on November 21. One hundred and two passengers, who were Pilgrims seeking religious freedom in America, disembarked. The *Mayflower* returned to England the following April.

**U.S.S. NAUTILUS**

The world's first nuclear-powered submarine, the *Nautilus,* was also the first sea vessel to reach the North Pole. Able to dive 750 feet, it traveled under ice to reach the northernmost point on the Earth in 1958.

### NINA, PINTA, AND SANTA MARIA

Christopher Columbus sailed from Spain on August 3, 1492 on the flagship the *Santa Maria*. The three ships of the expedition carried a total of 88 men. They sighted San Salvador in the New World on October 12, 1492. On Christmas day of the same year, the *Santa Maria* was wrecked off the shore of Haiti. The wood from the ship was used to build a fort on the island. Columbus and his men returned to Spain on the *Nina* and the *Pinta*.

### QUEEN ELIZABETH

The largest passenger liner ever built, the *Queen Elizabeth* was launched in 1938. This British ship was built as a luxury liner for 2,000 passengers. During World War II it was used to transfer entire divisions of the British army.

### TITANIC

This British transatlantic passenger ship was thought to be extremely safe and unsinkable. In 1912, on its maiden voyage to New York, it struck an iceberg. The ship sank and 1,589 passengers and crew drowned. Although the ship's capacity was more than 2,000, there were lifeboats for only 1,178 people. After this tragedy, safety drills and sufficient lifeboats became mandatory on all ships.

### TRITON

In 1960 this submarine became the first to circumnavigate the world. It covered 36,014 miles in 76 days.

# Transportation on Land

## FIRSTS ON LAND

B.C.

**3500** The first wheeled vehicles were drawn by animals and used in Mesopotamia.

**1675** The Egyptians used the first horse-drawn chariots for battle.

**170** The world's first paved streets, which were passable in all weather, were built by the Romans.

A.D.

**44** The Chinese invented the wheel barrow.

**1638** The first English stagecoaches began service. Roads and inns were built to accommodate travelers.

**1662** The first city bus service was inaugurated in Paris. The horse-drawn buses could accommodate eight people. They were called "Carrosses a Cinq Sous" because for five sous a passenger could travel any distance on the bus line.

**1769** The first self-driven carriage was propelled by steam. It was invented by Nicolas Cugnot of France. It was a three-wheeled vehicle with an "engine" on the front wheel. The first motor vehicle accident in history took place when Cugnot ran into a wall driving this machine.

**1791** The first bicycle was built by the Comte de Sirvac of France. It was a two-wheeled wooden machine with a seat. The rider sat on the seat and "walked" the bike, as there were no pedals.

**1804** The first commercial locomotive was built by Englishman Richard Trevithick.

**1869** American George Westinghouse patented a pneumatic (air-filled) brake for trains. It is still the most widely-used train brake.

**1869** The first known motorcycle was built in France. It was a pedal bicycle fitted with a small steam engine.

**1873** The first cable streetcar in the world was built in San Francisco.

**1886** Gottlieb Daimler of Germany built the first four-wheeled, gasoline-driven vehicle. The same year, another German, Karl Benz, built a gasoline-driven automobile with three wheels.

**1888** The pneumatic (air-filled) bicycle tire was invented by John Dunlop of Belfast, Ireland. By using rubber sheeting and strips of fabric he made a tire that would cushion his son's bike rides on the cobblestone streets of Belfast. He was awarded a patent for his invention.

**1889** American Nellie Bly gained international acclaim by traveling around the world in 72 days, 6 hours, and 11 minutes. The journalist traveled by train, ship, horse, sampan, and rickshaw to outdo the fictitious Phineas Fogg of the Jules Verne story, *Around the World in 80 Days.*

**1897** The first subway line in the U.S. was opened in Boston.

# LEGENDARY TRAINS

### THE B & O

This was the first U.S. train to carry (Baltimore and Ohio Railroad) passengers and freight. It was built in 1827 and extended 380 miles. It was the first train to carry a U.S. president, Andrew Jackson, the first to print a timetable, and the first to have an air-conditioned car.

### THE BLUE TRAIN

Considered the most luxurious train in the world, it was built in 1972 to run from Pretoria to Capetown, South Africa. It accommodates 108 passengers in its 16 coaches. Everyone has a private room. It has been called a five-star hotel on wheels.

### ORIENT EXPRESS

This is the most famous train in history. It began service in 1883 taking passengers from Paris to Constantinople (now Istanbul). Spies frequented this "train of Kings" and thieves stole from its rich passengers. It was the setting for three famous novels; *From Russia With Love, Murder on the Orient Express,* and *Stamboul Train.*

### PIONEER

In 1853 this Chicago train was equipped with the first practical sleeping car. George Pullman, a New York cabinetmaker, devised the convertible berths that pulled down for sleeping. These cars became known as Pullman cars.

### TOM THUMB

This was the first locomotive built in the U.S. New Yorker, Peter Cooper, used scraps of iron to make the locomotive for the B & O railroad.

## SHINKANSEN

Also known as the Bullet trains, these Japanese trains were designed in 1964 to provide the fastest passenger service in the world. The trains run from Tokyo to Osaka at an average speed of 103 mph. They can reach a top speed of 159 mph. The recently-built French Electric trains (TGVs) can now match the speed of "The Bullets."

## TRANS-SIBERIAN RAILROAD

This Russian railroad is the longest railroad line in the world. It has 5,799 miles of track that extend from Moscow to Vladivostok. There are 97 stops and the complete journey takes 7 days and 2 hours to complete.

## NOTABLE AUTOMOBILES

### CITROEN (1934)

This European car was the first front-wheel drive car in the world. It was made for twenty years without a change in design or engineering.

### MERCEDES

The oldest car in commercial automotive history, it was first built in 1901 by auto inventor, Gottlieb Daimler of Germany. It was the first automobile to look like a car, not a horseless carriage. Daimler named this car after his daughter, Mercedes.

### MOONCAR

The Apollo 15 mission to the moon introduced the moon car, also known as the lunar rover. It is an electric-powered four-wheel drive vehicle, which was developed at the cost of $60 million.

**OLDSMOBILE**

This was the first successful American-made car. Developed by Ranson Eli Olds in 1901, it still survives today.

**MODEL T—"TIN LIZZIE"**

Henry Ford's first car made history when it rolled off his assembly line in 1913. More than 10,000 of these noisy, hand-cranked cars were sold to the American public. It was the first car to be made on an assembly line.

**VOLKSWAGEN "BEETLE"**

This German-made car is the best-selling car, ever. It was designed by Ferdinand Porsche in 1934 for the German dictator, Adolf Hitler. Hitler wanted a "car for the people," which is what the word *volkswagen* means.

# MEMORABLE BICYCLES

**THE PENNY FARTHING**

Also known as the ordinary bike, it was invented by Englishman James Starley in the 1870s. It had a large front wheel and a small back wheel. The rider pedaled cranks on the front wheel, turning the cranks in order to steer the bike.

**THE ROVER SAFETY**

This was one of the first bicycles with wheels of equal size and chain driven. It was mass-produced in 1885.

**THE SWIFT LADIES**

Made in 1926, this bike was unique because it was made without a crossbar so a woman wearing a skirt could easily get off and on the bike.

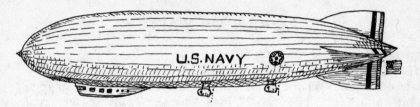

# Air Travel

## FIRST IN FLIGHT

**1783**  The first hot-air balloon took flight over France. The Montgolfier brothers, Jacques and Joseph, invented the balloon, which rose 6,000 feet and stayed aloft for 10 minutes.

**1785**  The parachute was invented by Jean Pierre Blanchard of France.

**1852**  The first dirigible, a steam-powered balloon, was flown by Henri Giffard. The balloon traveled at a speed of 6.7 mph from Paris, France to Trappe, France.

**1853**  The first manned glider to succeed in flight soared 500 yards. The glider was built by Englishman Sir George Cyley who was 80 years old at the time. He sent his coachman aloft for the first flight.

**1900**  The first zeppelin (rigid-frame airship) took flight. Count Ferdinand von Zeppelin of Germany flew at a speed of 18 mph for 3½ miles.

**1903**  The first airplane flight took place in a biplane built by the American brothers Orville and Wilbur Wright. Because he won the toss of a coin, Orville was the first to make the flight. He traveled 120 feet in 12 seconds.

**1911**  The hydroplane (seaplane) was invented by Glenn Curtis of the U.S. The plane is designed to take off and to land on water.

**1923**  The first flight in a rotary-wing aircraft was made by Juan de la Cierva in Madrid, Spain.

**1930**  Jet-propelled aircraft was invented by Sir Frank Whittie of England.

# FAMOUS AIRCRAFT

**BOEING B-50A SUPERFORTRESS**
This aircraft was the first to make a round-the-world nonstop flight. Captained by James Gallagher of the United States Air Force, it took off from Fort Worth, Texas on February 27, 1949. After 23,452 miles and four aerial refuelings, it landed in Fort Worth on March 2, 1949.

**BOEING 747**
The largest jumbo jet, this plane has a passenger capacity of 490. It is also notable for setting a speed record for around-the-world flight. From October 28 to October 31, 1977, it flew 26,382 miles over both the Earth's poles in 54 hours.

**CONCORDE SST**
This British-French aircraft was the first supersonic (faster than the speed of sound) transporter in commercial service. It carries 104 passengers at the speed of 1,300 mph. Its flight from Paris to New York takes 3 hours instead of the 6½ hours it takes an ordinary jet to travel the distance.

**ENOLA GAY**
This U.S. plane dropped the atom bomb on Hiroshima, Japan during World War II.

**DE HAVILAND COMET**
Jetliner service began when this plane was flown by BOAC from London to Johannesburg, South Africa in 1952.

**EXPLORER I**
The largest balloon to take flight, the *Explorer I*, had over 3 million cubic feet of surface area. In 1934, three men ascended in the balloon over the Black Hills of South Dakota. At 60,613 feet it exploded. The crew and equipment safely parachuted to earth.

**FLYER**
This biplane was flown by the Wright Brothers in their history-making flights over Kitty Hawk, North Carolina. In 1904 they made the first airplane maneuvers; a turn and a complete circle, in the *Flyer*.

**HINDENBERG**

At 803-feet long, this was the largest dirigible ever built. It was made in Germany for transatlantic flight. After 35 successful trips across the ocean, it was destroyed by fire while trying to land in Lakehurst, New Jersey, in 1937. Thirty-six people died in the accident. No more of these aircraft were ever manufactured.

**SPIRIT OF ST. LOUIS**

When American Charles Lindbergh made the first solo transatlantic flight in this monoplane, it became one of the most famous planes ever. In 1927 Lindbergh took off from Roosevelt Field, Long Island, New York. Thirty-three hours, 39 minutes later, he safely landed 3,600 miles away in Le Bourget Field outside Paris, France.

THE
WINNIE MAE

**WINNIE MAE**

This Lockheed Vega was piloted by Wiley Post in the first round-the-world-solo flight. In 1933 Post traveled 15,596 miles around the world in 7 days, 18 hours, 49½ minutes.

**SPRUCE GOOSE**

This, the largest plane ever built, was designed and made by American millionaire, Howard Hughes. Made of wood, its wingspan is 320 feet. The only flight of this plane took place on November 2, 1947 when Hughes piloted it to a height of 70 feet for one mile. Today the plane is on exhibition in Long Beach, California.

# Space Travel

## FIRSTS

**1961**  The first person to travel in space was Yuri Gagarin, a Soviet cosmonaut. He traveled around the Earth on April 12, in *Vostok I.*

The first American in space was Alan Shepard, who made a suborbital 15-minute flight on May 5.

**1962** The first American to orbit in space was John Glenn, who traveled around the Earth three times on February 20. His flight time was 4 hours, 55 minutes.

**1965** The first person to walk in space was Aleksei Leonov of the U.S.S.R., who spent 10 minutes outside his spacecraft on a tether.

**1969** The first person to walk on the moon was American astronaut Neil Armstrong. On July 20, he put his left foot on the surface on the moon. He and fellow astronaut, Edwin Aldrin spent two hours walking on the moon collecting samples of rocks and soil.

**1972** *Pioneer 10* was the first spacecraft to pass through the asteroid belt between Mars and Jupiter. This proved that spacecraft could safely travel to the outer solar system. It was launched on March 3.

**1975** The first time space crews from two different countries met and exchanged visits in space was July, 1975. The U.S. *Apollo 18* and the U.S.S.R. *Soyuz 19* met 145 miles above the Earth and docked in space. The U.S. astronauts were Thomas Stafford, Vance Brand, and Donald Slayton. The Soviet cosmonauts were Aleksei Leonov and Valentin Kubason.

**1981** The first reusable spacecraft was the *Columbia* space shuttle launched by the U.S. on April 12. After orbiting the Earth 36 times, astronauts Robert Crippen and John Young successfully landed at Edwards Air Force Base in California on April 14.

**1984** This space shuttle *Challenger* mission was one of firsts. It had the first seven-person crew. It was the first time two women were aboard the same spacecraft (Sally Ride and Kathy Sullivan). It was the first time a U.S. woman (Ms. Sullivan) walked in space. It was the first demonstration of a satellite refueling technique in space.

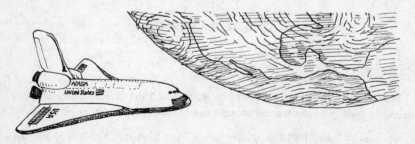

# U.S. SPACE MISSIONS

## Manned Missions

**MERCURY**
The first manned space program in the U.S. was called Project Mercury. It was designed to see if people could withstand the shock of launch, reentry, and weightlessness in space. In 1963, astronaut Gordon Cooper spent more than 34 hours orbiting the earth in his spacecraft *Faith 7*. In doing so, he successfully proved people were capable of living and working in space.

**GEMINI**
This project was named from the Greek word *Gemini*, meaning "twin." These spacecraft were twice as large as those of the Mercury project and could accommodate two astronauts. The goal of this project was to see if people could live in space for long periods of time—two weeks or more. Walks in space and walks on the moon were part of the Gemini mission.

**APOLLO**
The goal of this project was to land a person on the moon and return the person safely to Earth. The last three Apollo flights landed lunar rover vehicles. The astronauts used these to explore the surface of the moon.

**SKYLAB**
This project successfully put a space station in orbit around the Earth. The working crew members proved that people could live in space for at least three months. Thousands of pictures were taken of the Earth and the sun. Experimental animals spent time on board. They were studied to see how well they adapted to life in space.

**SPACE SHUTTLE**
The space shuttle *Columbia* was launched in 1981. It was a reusable space transport designed to replace other U.S. launch vehicles as a cost-saving device. It can be used again for space transport, scientific exploration, and defense needs.

## U.S. Planetary Unmanned Spacecraft

**MARINER**
*Mariner 9* orbited Mars and sent back photographs of the planet in 1971. *Mariner 10* orbited Venus and Mercury in 1973.

**PIONEER**

In 1973 and 1974 *Pioneer 10* and *Pioneer 11* explored Saturn and Jupiter. *Pioneer Venus 1* and *Pioneer Venus 2* explored Venus in 1978. *Pioneer 10* will be the first spacecraft to escape the solar system. By the 1990s, it will be 9 billion kilometers from the sun.

**VIKING**

*Viking 1* and *Viking 2* landed on the planet Mars in 1976 and sent back pictures of the red planet.

# LITTLE KNOWN FACTS ABOUT SPACE TRAVEL

• An interesting note about manned spacecraft landings: Soyuz cosmonauts always land on the ground; Americans always land at sea. (One exception is the American space shuttle which landed on the ground.)

• America's *Skylab* was a "space house" which resembled a small two-story house in the suburbs. The first floor contained a workshop, a sleeping area, a kitchen, and a bathroom. The second floor was an experiment chamber where scientific tests were conducted.

• The L5 Society is a worldwide group of people who have dedicated themselves to being the first settlers in space.

• Twelve Americans have walked on the moon.

• Three women have been in space: Soviet cosmonaut Valentina Tereshkova and U.S. astronauts Sally Ride and Kathryn Sullivan.

• The footprint left on the moon by Neil Armstrong will stay there a very long time as there is no wind or water to disturb it.

• Astronauts have brought back to Earth 843 pounds of common rock.

• The space shuttle can go from the U.S. to Europe in less than 20 minutes.

• The U.S. space shuttle *Columbia* is 52 stories high and is the world's largest (not tallest) "building." It covers 8 acres of space.

• There is a space camp in Huntsville, Alabama for future astronauts. Campers must be in the 6th, 7th, or 8th grade. Camp activities include working at Mission Control consoles, sitting in space shuttle seats for their lessons in astronautics and space flight, and operating equipment once used by Gemini and Apollo astronauts. The U.S. Space Camp is at the Alabama Space and Rocket Center, Huntsville, Alabama, 35807. Phone: 205-837-3400.

# Transportation Centers

- The premier bicycling center in the world is the city of Shanghai, China, where an estimated 2.5 million bike trips take place a day.
- Chicago International Airport at O'Hare Field is the world's busiest airport. Day and night, a landing or take-off occurs every 42 seconds.
- The world's largest railroad station is Grand Central Station in New York City. The station covers 248 acres—the size of 37 football fields. An average of 550 trains use the station's 67 tracks each day.
- The most extensive subway system in the world is in London. The Underground or "tube" has 252 miles of track and 279 stations.
- The busiest subway system in the world is in New York City. More than 2 million people use the subways each work day.
- Land speed records are set at Bonneville Salt Flats in Utah.
- Mission Control for the United States space program is in Houston, Texas.
- Hong Kong is known as the sampan center of the world.

# Around the World in Unique Vehicles

**THE GONDOLA** is a long, thin rowboat. It is used as a taxi in the canals of Venice, Italy. The gondolier uses a long, narrow pole to push the boat through the canals.

**AN ICEBOAT** can move very fast with the wind. It is a narrow, pointed sailboat that moves over ice on three runners. Iceboating is a favorite pastime in the northern European countries of Norway, Denmark, Finland, and Sweden where sea, river, and lake water is frozen most of the year.

**A JEEPNESS** is a jitney bus of Manila, the Philippines. A jeepness is a brightly-decorated, converted jeep which holds 12 passengers.

**A JUNK** is a wooden sailboat used in the Orient. These boats have flat bottoms and high backs with two or more sails. They are usually painted in bright colors.

**KAYAKS** are long, painted canoes covered with sealskin. They are built with a small opening to fit the person who paddles it. For several thousand years, Eskimos of North America have been making and using kayaks.

**PEDICABS** are the modern replacements for rickshaws. A rickshaw was a two-wheeled cart with two poles in front pulled by a person. Rickshaws were used in Asia in the late 1800s. There are three wheels on a pedicab, two on the back of the cart and one in the front. A driver sits on what looks like the back half of a bicycle and pedals the cart around. Pedicabs are found in the cities of Southeast Asia.

**SAMPANS** are small boats found in China and Japan. They are used as homes for families, or as places of business—stores, restaurants, or small poultry farms.

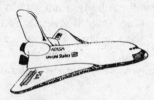

# Comparative Speeds of Selected Vehicles

| | |
|---|---|
| **Stagecoach** | 8 miles per hour |
| **Early steam locomotive** (Stephenson's Rocket) | 15 miles per hour |
| **Henry Ford's first car** (Model T) | 45 miles per hour |
| **Snowmobile** | 135 miles per hour |
| **Electric train** | 200 miles per hour |
| **Supersonic transport** (SST) | 1,450 miles per hour |
| **Rocketship** | 25,000 miles per hour (minimum to escape Earth's gravity) |

# Travel Talk

## HOW FIVE VEHICLES WERE NAMED

**BUS**
This word is short for the Latin word *omnibus* which means "for all."

**CLIPPER SHIP**
This long, slender sailing ship of the 19th century was named for its speed. It was said to "clip through the waves."

**HELICOPTER**
When Leonardo da Vinci, the 16th-century artist/inventor first drew a design for a rotating wing machine, he called it a helix pteron, meaning "spiral wing." These Greek words were later written as "helicopter."

**SCHOONER**
This large sailboat was named after an 18th-century game known as "schooning," whereby children skipped pebbles across the water.

**TAXICAB**
This word comes from a one-horse carriage called a cabriolet. This kind of carriage for hire had a tax-imeter inside which recorded the cost of the ride. Today, cars for hire are called taxicabs, cabs, or taxis.

# The Universe

Get ready for the *space age* with this chapter which defines and explains what every future astronaut should know; from asteroids to stars, and how you can name your own comet.

# A Guide to the Universe

## WHAT IS WHAT IN THE UNIVERSE

**Asteroid**—A small rocky or metal object that revolves around the sun. Most asteroids are found in the asteroid belt that lies between the planets Mars and Jupiter.

**Black Hole**—It is thought to be a collapsed object, maybe a large star, which has a surrounding field of gravity so strong that neither light nor matter can escape from it.

**Comet**—A "dirty snowball" of dust and ice which orbits the sun. Comets have two tails, one of white dust and one of blue gas.

**Cosmos**—Another word for the universe. All energy, matter, and space. Everything that exists.

**Eclipse**—A lunar eclipse occurs when the sun, the Earth, and the moon are in line and the moon enters the Earth's shadow. A solar eclipse occurs when the moon passes between the sun and the Earth causing a shadow to fall upon the Earth.

**Galaxy**—A collection of billions of stars held together by gravitational force. There are at least 100 billion galaxies in the universe. Three are visible to the naked eye. They are: Andromeda, the Magellanic Cloud, and the Milky Way.

**Interstellar Space**—The space between stars. Space outside our solar system is interstellar space.

**Light Year**—The distance light travels in one year, which is approximately 6 trillion miles. The universe is measured in light years.

**Meteoroid**—A small chunk of rock or metal made by small asteroids banging into large asteroids. When a meteoroid enters the Earth's atmosphere it is called a meteor. If it strikes the ground of the Earth it is known as a meteorite.

**Moon**—A satellite that revolves around a planet. With the exception of Mercury and Venus, all the planets have moons.

**Neutron Star**—The core of a star left over after a supernova explodes.

**Nova**—A star which suddenly explodes and is temporarily bright.

**Planet**—A large rotating (turning) body that moves in orbit (revolves) around the sun.

**Pulsar**—A rotating neutron star that emits beams of radiation.

**Quasar**—A starlike object which is extremely bright, small, and distant. A quasar is a source of strong radio energy.

**Star**—A celestial body which gives off heat and light. Our local star is the sun.

**Supernova**—The explosion of a dying star whereby the star becomes a thousand times brighter than a nova for that instant.

## OUR PLACE IN THE UNIVERSE

We live in the Milky Way galaxy. Our solar system and a spiral-shaped system of 120 billion stars are part of the Milky Way. It would take 100,000 light years to travel from one end of our galaxy to the other.

Our solar system is made up of one star, the sun, nine known planets, forty-four moons, more than 30,000 asteroids, an estimated 100 billion comets, and at least 1,500 quasars.

## FACTS ABOUT THE SUN

• The sun is a 5 billion-year-old star which, it is estimated, will continue to exist for another 5 billion years.
• The sun is an average-size star. There are much larger stars in the universe.
• 109 Earths would fit side by side across the diameter of the sun.
• The sun spins on its axis from left to right.
• The sun is not a ball of fire. It is more like a huge hydrogen bomb that is continuously exploding and giving off energy and light.

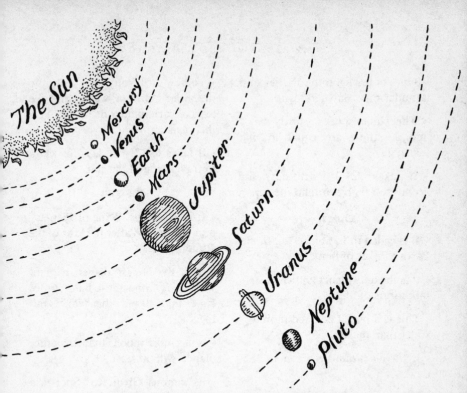

# FACTS ABOUT THE PLANETS

Mercury, Venus, Earth, and Mars all have solid surfaces. Jupiter, Saturn, Uranus, and Neptune all are fluid bodies made of gas or liquid.

### MERCURY

• It was named after Mercury, the speedy messenger of the Roman gods.

• It is the swiftest-moving planet.

• It is the planet closest to the sun.

• It travels around the sun in 88 Earth days.

• Mercury has no moons and no atmosphere (air).

• It has a rocky, cratered surface.

• It is one of the hottest and coldest planets with extreme temperatures ranging from 300 degrees below zero to 800 degrees above zero.

### VENUS

• This planet was once called the "Planet of Mystery" because of the cloud-like veil that covers it. The ancients thought a lush world was hidden underneath the veil and so named it after Venus, the goddess of springtime and flowers.

• It is bathed in red light because its atmosphere scatters red wavelengths of sunlight.

• On Venus, lightning flashes and thunder roars day and night.

• This planet spins so slowly that 4 months there are equal to one Earth day.

• It takes 224.7 Earth days for Venus to revolve around the sun.

### EARTH

• It is called in Latin, *Terra Mater,* Earth Mother of humans.

• It is the only planet known to sustain forms of life.

• This is a planet covered more by water than by land.

• It travels around the sun in 365 days.

• The same side of the moon always faces the Earth.

• The moon shines because it reflects the light of the sun.

• A full moon is when sunlight reflects against the side of the moon facing us on Earth.

• It takes 27 days for the moon to travel around the Earth.

### MARS

• Known as the angry red planet, Mars was named for the Roman god of war.

• It is red in color because of its rustlike soil which is coated with iron oxide.

• It is known for its severe dust storms.

• There are canyons, volcanic mountains, frozen water, and ice caps of carbon dioxide (dry ice) on this planet.

• It takes 687 Earth days for Mars to travel around the sun.

### JUPITER

• It is called the "King of Planets" and was named after the king of the Roman gods.

• It is the largest planet, a giant which is one-and-a-half times larger than all the other planets put together.

• It has more moons than any other planet, with at least 17.

• Its famous Great Red Spot is a hurricane-like storm, larger than the Pacific Ocean, that has been raging for centuries.

• Jupiter travels around the sun in 11.86 Earth years.

### SATURN

• This planet was named for the Roman god of farming.

• It is famous for its 7 main rings made up of icy particles; some tiny, others as large as buildings.

• It is mostly yellow in color.

• It takes 29.46 Earth years to travel around the sun.

### URANUS

• Uranus was the Roman god who was the father of Saturn and the grandfather of Jupiter.

• It is bluish-green in color.

• It has black rings around it which are thought to be made of chunks of dark rock.

• This planet is unusual in that it lies almost on its side.

• It travels around the sun in 84 Earth years.

### NEPTUNE

• Because of its ocean color it was named for Neptune, the Roman god of water.

• It has two moons, one which orbits the planet in a year; the other completes its orbit in 6 days, moving backwards.

• It is pale blue in color.

• It radiates more heat than it receives from the sun.

• It travels around the sun every 16½ years.

### PLUTO

• It was named for Pluto, a Greek god who ruled the underworld.

• It has a large moon, Charon, which is very close in distance to Pluto, causing some to think it might be a double planet.

• It is the planet farthest from the sun; 3,658 million miles away.

• Its unusual orbit causes Pluto to come closer to the sun than its neighbor, Neptune, at certain points in time.

• One year on Pluto is equal to 248 Earth years.

# Have You Ever Wondered?

1. **What is a "blue moon"?** When there are two full moons in a month, the second one is called a blue moon. It is a rare occurrence.

2. **What is the brightest star?** Sirius, which is 50 billion miles away, is the brightest-appearing star.

3. **How often do meteors hit the Earth?** Meteors strike the Earth every day. They add a quarter of a ton to the Earth's mass.

4. **What is a shooting star?** It is another name for a meteor.

5. **How are comets named?** They are usually named after their discoverers. For example, Halley's comet, which appears every 76 years and will reappear in 1986, was named after Edmund Halley of England. Halley was the first to predict the reappearance of a comet.

6. **What is a constellation?** It is a nonscientific name for a group of stars. Some of the imaginary shapes of constellations are humans, real-life animals, and legendary beasts such as dragons and unicorns.

7. **How old is the moon?** It is as old as the Earth, which is at least 4.6 million years old.

8. **Which planet was the only one discovered in the 20th century?** Pluto, by Clyde Tombaugh in 1930 at the Lowell Observatory in Arizona.

9. **What was the first planet visited by a spacecraft from Earth?** Venus, by the U.S. spacecraft *Mariner 10* in 1974.

10. **What is the distance of the moon from the Earth?** The moon is 239,000 miles away. Its distance is equal to 9 times around the Earth's equator.

11. **How many stars are in the known universe?** About 100 sextillion. (Counting all known stars at a rate of 10 stars per second, it would take 100,000 times longer than the universe has been known to exist.)

# The World and Weather

Here are hundreds of odd and fascinating facts about the entire world—from the largest continent to the smallest, from the coldest place to the driest—cities, mountains, rivers, countries, oceans—you name it.

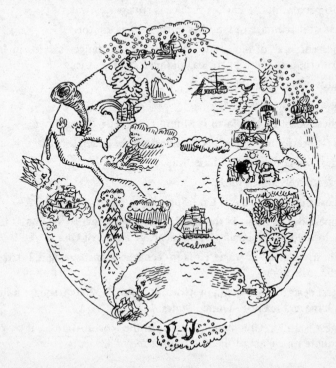

becalmed

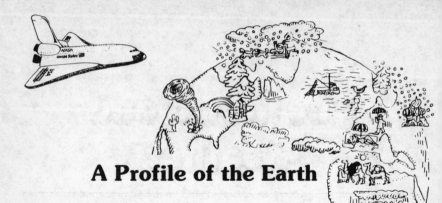

# A Profile of the Earth

- The Earth is the fifth largest planet in the solar system.

- It is approximately 93 million miles from the sun. It would take a jet plane a little over 21 years to reach the sun at 500 mph.

- It is pear shaped and "fattest" just below the equator.

- A jet plane can fly around the Earth in less than a day.

- An astronaut can circle the Earth in a rocket ship in 90 minutes.

- About 70 percent of the Earth's surface is covered by water.

- The greatest percentage of land lies north of the equator.

- The "four corners" of the Earth are made by four bulges located in Ireland, near Peru, just south of Africa, and near New Guinea.

- The largest ocean is the Pacific.

- The largest continent is Asia.

- The highest point on the Earth is Mount Everest in Nepal-Tibet.

- The lowest point on the Earth is the Dead Sea in Israel/Jordan.

- The largest sea is the South China Sea.

- The longest river is the Nile.

- The largest freshwater lake is Lake Superior in North America.

- The deepest ocean point is the Mariana's Trench, which is 35,810 feet deep. It is located in the Pacific Ocean near the island of Guam.

- The highest waterfall is Angel Falls in Venezuela, measuring 3,281 feet, about ⅗ of a mile high.

- The largest desert is the Sahara in Africa. It covers 3,320,000 square miles, almost as large as the entire United States.

- The largest island is Greenland. Located in the North Atlantic, it covers 839,999 square miles, about the size of the state of Texas.

# Continents

## NORTH AMERICA

North America is the third largest continent.

The world's largest group of fresh water lakes are located in North America. They are the Great Lakes.

North America has the longest coastline of any continent. It is 96,000 miles long.

**Population:** 390 million
**Size:** 9,366,000 square miles
**Highest Point:** Mt. McKinley, Alaska; 20,320 feet above sea level, almost 4 miles high
**Lowest Point:** Death Valley, California; 282 feet below sea level
**Largest Country:** Canada; 3,851,787 square miles
**Most Populous Country:** United States; 232 million

## SOUTH AMERICA

South America is the fourth largest continent.

The world's longest mountain range, the Andes, are in South America. The Andes mountains are 15,000 miles long.

Most of the people of South America live along the coastline of the continent.

The southernmost city in the world, Punta Arenas, Chile, is located in South America.

**Population:** 259 million (approximately)
**Size:** 6,881,000 square miles
**Highest Point:** Mt. Aconcagua, Argentina; 22,834 feet above sea level, about 4⅓ miles high
**Lowest Point:** Salinas Grande, Argentina; 131 feet below sea level
**Largest Country:** Brazil; 3,286,470 square miles
**Most Populous Country:** Brazil; 127,700,000

# EUROPE

Europe is the second smallest continent.

The largest ice cave in the world is located in Europe. It is the Eisriesenwelt Cave in Austria.

**Population:** 692,879,000
**Size:** 4,017,000 square miles
**Highest Point:** Mt. El, Brus, Russia; 18,510 feet above sea level, about 3½ miles high
**Lowest Point:** Caspian Sea; 92 feet below sea level
**Largest Country:** U.S.S.R.; 8,649,490 square miles
**Most Populous Country:** U.S.S.R.; 268,800,000

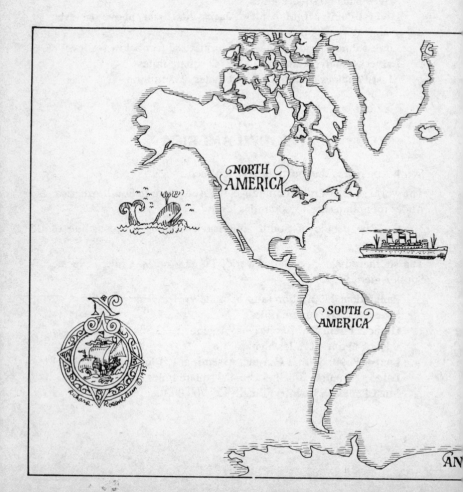

# AFRICA

It is the second largest continent.

Africa is the warmest continent in the world.

There are 48 countries on the continent of Africa; which makes it the continent with the most countries.

**Population:** 513 million
**Size:** 11,688,000 square miles
**Highest Point:** Mt. Kibo, Kilimanjaro in Tanzania; 19,340 feet above sea level, about 3½ miles high
**Lowest Point:** Lake Assal, Djibouti; 510 feet below sea level
**Largest Country:** Sudan; 967,000 square miles
**Most Populous Country:** Nigeria; 82,300,000

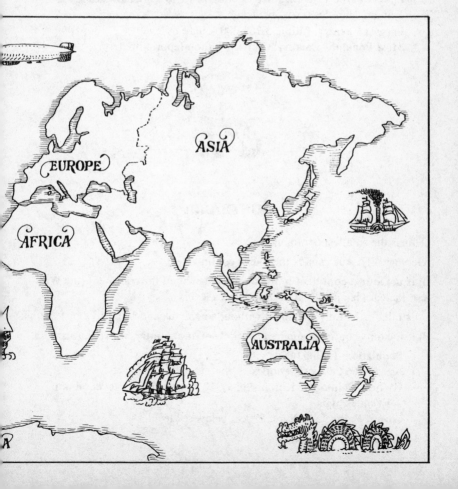

# ASIA

Asia covers one-third of the Earth's land surface.

It is the world's largest continent.

More than one half of the people in the world live in Asia.

Five of the longest rivers in the world are located in Asia. They are the Yangtse, Yensei, Yellow, Ob-Irtysh and Amur rivers.

The highest point and the lowest point in the world are in Asia.

**Population:** 2 billion (approximately)
**Size:** 17,139,455 square miles
**Highest Point:** Mt. Everest, Nepal-Tibet; 29,028 feet above sea level, about 5½ miles high
**Lowest Point:** Dead Sea, Israel/Jordan; 1,296 feet below sea level, about 1½ miles below sea level
**Largest Country:** China, 3,769,000 square miles
**Most Populous Country:** China; 1 billion (approximately)

# AUSTRALIA

This is the smallest continent.

Geologically, Australia is the oldest continent.

It is the lowest continent in the world. One half of the continent (the Western Plateau) is only 1,000 feet above sea level.

Australia is the only continent without active volcanoes.

It is the only continent made up entirely of one country, which is Australia.

**Population:** 15,300,000
**Size:** 2,966,000 square miles
**Highest Point:** Mt. Kosciusko; 7,310 feet above sea level, about 1⅓ miles high
**Lowest Point:** Lake Eyre; 52 feet below sea level

## ANTARCTICA

The fifth largest continent is Antarctica.

Antarctica is the world's highest continent. It is covered by an ice sheet which averages a height of one mile above sea level.

Antarctica is the coldest, emptiest, and most remote continent.

The purest, driest air in the world surrounds this continent. There is no mold or mildew in Antarctica.

Nine-tenths of the ice in the world can be found in Antarctica.

**Size:** 5.1 million square miles
**Highest Point:** Vinson, Massif; 16,864 feet above sea level, about 3 miles high
**Lowest Point:** Not known

# Countries of the World
### (There are a total of 215 countries in the world.)

## The Five Largest Countries Ranked by Size

1. U.S.S.R.
2. Canada
3. China
4. United States
5. Brazil

## The Country with the Longest Coastline

Canada boasts the world's longest coastline with 56,453 miles of waterfront.

## The Highest Country

Tibet is called the "rooftop" of the world. It is located on a mountain plateau 15,000 feet above sea level, which is about 3 miles high.

## The Smallest Country in Size and Population

Vatican City (also known as State of Vatican City) in Europe covers 3.17 square miles (about 110 football fields). It has a population of approximately 738.

## The Five Most Populous Countries

1. China
2. India
3. U.S.S.R.
4. United States
5. Indonesia

## The Country with the Most Lakes and Rivers

Canada—8.29 percent is covered by water, of which 755,165 sq. kilometers are lakes and rivers.

## The Poorest Country in the World

Bangladesh, where more people live in poverty than anywhere else.

## The Countries with the Highest Literacy Rates

These 8 countries claim that 99.5 percent of their people over the age of 12 can read a simple sentence and write basic information about themselves.

| | |
|---|---|
| Bermuda | Nauru |
| Czechoslovakia | South Africa |
| Macao | United States |
| Monaco | Vatican City |

## Countries and Communications

The following is a list of countries with the greatest number of items, per person. They are ranked in order.

| Daily Newspapers | Radios | Telephones | Televisions |
|---|---|---|---|
| U.S. | U.S. | U.S. | U.S. |
| India | Canada | Sweden | Kuwait |
| U.S.S.R. | Australia | Switzerland | Denmark |

# How Many Kids Are in the World

The total world population increases by 2 percent each year. It is estimated that in 1986 there will be 5 billion people living in the world. The number of children under the age of 15 will total 1 billion, 700 million. The breakdown of percentages of kids in selected countries of the world is as follows.

| Country | % of Population 15 and Under* | Country | % of Population 15 and Under* |
|---|---|---|---|
| Australia | 26 | India | 41 |
| Bolivia | 44 | Kenya | 50 |
| Canada | 24 | Mexico | 44 |
| China | 52 | U.S.S.R. | 24 |
| Honduras | 49 | U.S. | 27 |

*UNICEF 1980 statistics

# A Profile of the U.S.

The United States is the fourth largest country in the world.
The U.S.:

- Owns one half of the world's wealth.
- Has the largest government budget in the world.
- Has the largest postal service in the world.
- Produces the greatest amount of meat and coal in the world.
- Uses more energy than any other country.
- Uses more cars than any other country.
- Sells more candy and soda pop than any other country.

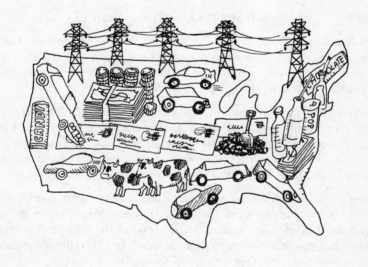

## The Geographic Extremes of the U.S. Are:

**Center**—Castle Rock, South Dakota
**Northern**—Point Barrow, Alaska
**Southern**—Ka Lae Island, Hawaii
**Eastern**—West Quoddy Head, Maine
**Western**—Cape Wrangell, Alaska

# Cities of the World

**Most Populous City:**   Shanghai, China has an estimated population of 11,000,000.

**Highest City:**   Lhasa, Tibet (12,087 feet above sea level, or about 2¼ miles).

**Highest Capital:**   La Paz, Bolivia (12,001 feet above sea level).

**Oldest Existing City:**   Damascus, Syria, inhabited since prehistoric times.

**Oldest City in the U.S.:**   St. Augustine, Florida, settled by the Spanish in 1565.

**Most Expensive City in Which to Live:**   Tokyo, Japan.

**A Divided City:**   Before WW II, Berlin was the capital of Germany. Today the city lies within the borders of East Germany but a wall divides it into East Berlin and West Berlin. East Berlin is part of East Germany; West Berlin is a city of West Germany.

**A Buried City:**   The ancient city of Pompeii, Italy, was buried under ash and rock when the volcano, Mt. Vesuvius, erupted in 79 A.D. For 1,600 years it was forgotten. Then, in 1789, an Italian farmer was digging a well and discovered the buried city. When archeologists uncovered the city, they found homes, public buildings, and shops still standing.

**A Lost City:**   Machu Picchu was once an important Inca city located high in the Andes mountains of Peru. The city was thought to be the last stronghold of the Incas against the invasion of the Spanish conquistadores. For generations it was a guarded secret. In 1911, Hiram Bingham, an archeologist from Yale University, found the once-lost city.

**A Winter City Without Furnaces:**   Reykjavik, Iceland, is a cold northern city. The people who live there do not have stoves or furnaces to heat their homes. Instead, they use the hot water which is heated by the earth and found in abundance in springs and geysers under their city.

**A City Within a City:**   The Kremlin is a wall-enclosed city of government buildings, palaces, churches, and museums within the city of Moscow, U.S.S.R.

**Holiday Cities:**   Loveland, Colorado is known as "America's Sweetheart City." On Valentine's Day of each year, millions of Americans mail their

love notes from this city so they will be postmarked "from Loveland."
Santa Claus, Indiana is a city where the spirit of Christmas is always
alive. A large statue of Santa stands in the center of the city.

**The Southernmost City in the World:** Punta Arenas at the tip of Chile in
South America is further south than any other city in the world.

**One City from Two:** Budapest is the capital city of Hungary. Before 1872,
Buda and Pest were separate cities. Buda was the original capital of Hungary (1371). By the early 1800s, Pest, the city across the Danube River
from Buda, had become a more important city. The people of Hungary
made the two cities one and called their capital Budapest.

## THE HOLY CITIES OF WORLD RELIGIONS

| | |
|---|---|
| Benares, India | Hinduism |
| Buddh Gaya, India | Buddhism |
| Jerusalem, Israel | Christianity and Judaism |
| Kiev, Russia | Russian Orthodox |
| Mecca, Saudi Arabia | Islam |

## CITIES AND THEIR NICKNAMES

| | | |
|---|---|---|
| **Chicago** | "The Windy City" | Located on Lake Michigan, it is subject to frequent stiff breezes. |
| **Los Angeles** | "The City of Angels" | Los Angeles is Spanish for "City of Angels." |
| **Minneapolis St. Paul** | "The Twin Cities" | These two cities were built next to each other. Only the Mississippi River, which flows between the two cities, separates them. |

| | | |
|---|---|---|
| **New York** | "The Big Apple" | Jazz musicians touring the country in the 1920s had a saying: "There are many apples on the tree but to play New York is to play the Big Time—'The Big Apple.'" |

| | | |
|---|---|---|
| **Paris** | "The City of Lights" | Paris was the first European city to have street lights. |
| **Philadelphia** | "City of Brotherly Love" | In Greek, philadelphia means "brotherly love." |
| **Rome** | "The Eternal City" | The ancient Romans thought their city was the center of an eternal universe. |
| **Venice** | "Bride of the Sea" | Venice, Italy, is built on 118 islands in the Adriatic Sea. |

# Oceans and Seas

## OCEANS

### Oceans Ranked By Size

| *Ocean* | *Size* |
|---|---|
| **Pacific** | 64,186,300 square miles, almost 20 times the size of the U.S. |
| **Atlantic** | 33,420,000 square miles, about half the size of the Pacific, or 10 times the size of the U.S. |
| **Indian** | 28,350,500 square miles, about 8 times the size of the U.S. |
| **Arctic** | 5,105,700 square miles, about 1½ times the size of the U.S. |

## Deepest Ocean

• The Pacific Ocean has an average depth of 12,925 feet, or 2½ miles.

## Shrinking and Growing Oceans

• Every year the Atlantic Ocean grows wider by an inch or so. Every year the Pacific shrinks by an inch or so. This is due to the movement of the Earth's surface.

## An Ocean to Walk Across

• In winter, the arctic Ocean forms a 10-foot ice cover linking the United States and Russia.

## Ocean of Commerce

• The Atlantic is the busiest ocean for commercial trade.

## Ocean of Monsoons

• The Indian Ocean is known for seasonal wind and rain storms which are called the monsoons.

## Ocean of Oil

• The Indian Ocean is the world's greatest source of offshore oil. More than 40 percent of all offshore oil comes from this ocean.

## Saltiest Ocean

• The Mediterranean Ocean has the greatest density of salt at an average salinity rate of 39 percent.

## Ocean Names

• The Pacific was named by the Spanish Explorer, Ferdinand Magellan. When Magellan sailed on the Pacific it was calm and peaceful. The Spanish word for peaceful is *pacifico*.

• The Atlantic was named by the ancient Romans. They thought the Atlas Mountains in Africa were the end of the earth's land. They named the ocean on the other side of the mountains Atlantic.

# SEAS

## The Four Largest Seas

| Sea | Size |
|---|---|
| South China Sea | 1,148,500 square miles, about twice the size of the state of Alaska |
| Caribbean Sea | 971,400 square miles, about 3½ times the size of the state of Texas |
| Mediterranean Sea | 969,100 square miles |
| Bering Sea | 873,000 square miles |

## How Five Seas Were Named

**The Black Sea** is landlocked between Europe and Asia. It has a high concentration of hydrogen sulfide, a deadly gas which colors the sea floor black.

**The Dead Sea** was given its name because no fish live in it and very few plants grow in it. This is because its water is extremely salty.

**The Red Sea** was so named because the coral reefs, seaweed, and tiny sea animals that live in this sea are red.

**The White Sea** is north of the U.S.S.R. Most of the year it is covered by ice and snow.

**The Yellow Sea** was named for the yellow mud carried by the rivers which empty into it.

# Mountains

## FAMOUS MOUNTAIN PEAKS

**ADAM'S PEAK** in Sri Lanka is a mountain considered to be sacred by three religious groups; Buddhists, Hindus, and Moslems.

**MAUNA KEA** in Hawaii is the tallest mountain peak measuring from its seabed to its peak. It is 33,476 feet high. Only 13,796 feet, or less than

half of the mountain, is above ground.

**MT. ARARAT** located near the Turkish-Iranian border is, according to the *Bible*, the place where Noah's ark rested after the rains subsided.

**MT. FUJI** in Japan is the most photographed and painted mountain in the world.

**MT. HUASCARAN** in Peru was the first major peak climbed by a woman, Annie Peck, of Providence, Rhode Island, in 1908.

**MT. OLYMPUS**, the highest mountain peak in Greece, was known as the "home of the gods" to the ancient Greeks.

**MT. RUSHMORE** in the Black Hills of South Dakota is noted for its gigantic sculpture of four U.S. presidents. The heads of George Washington, Thomas Jefferson, Abraham Lincoln, and Teddy Roosevelt have been carved in 70-foot-high likenesses. It took John Borglum and his son, Lincoln, fourteen years to carve the sculpture.

**MT. SINAI** located in Egypt is, according to the *Bible*, the mountaintop where Moses received the 10 Commandments.

**MT. VESUVIUS** in Italy erupted and destroyed the City of Pompeii in 79 A.D. Today, it is the only active volcano on the continent of Europe.

## RECORD BOOK MOUNTAINS

**Tallest Mountain Range:** The Himalaya mountain range contains 96 of the world's 109 tallest peaks.

**Tallest Underwater Mountain Range:** The Cordillera, which is in the Indian and East Pacific Oceans. Its average height is 8,000 feet above the base ocean depth.

**Longest Mountain Range:** The Andes in South America. They are 15,000 miles long.

**Richest Mountain Range:** The Andes are the most abundant mountain source of gold, silver, copper, and other valuable minerals.

**Highest Mountain Peak:** Mt. Everest in the Himalayas, Tibet-Nepal. It is 29,028 feet above sea level or about 5½ miles high.

**Highest Island Mountain Peak:** Jaja Peak, West Irian, New Guinea; which is 16,503 feet above sea level or about 5 miles high.

**Largest Volcanic Mountain:** Mauna Loa in Hawaii is 13,680 feet high, with a crater 3 miles long and 1½ miles wide.

# Rivers

### THE WORLD'S LONGEST AND MOST FAMOUS RIVER
The Nile River in Africa starts in the tributaries of Lake Victoria, travels north for 4,145 miles, then empties into the Mediterranean Sea. It flows through the "cradle of civilization," past the world famous pyramids of Egypt. For centuries the Nile has given life to a rainless land. Although it passes through desert lands, its river valley is one of the most fertile farming areas in the world.

### THE MIGHTIEST RIVER
There is more water in the Amazon River of South America than in any other river in the world. It carries one-fifth of the world's running water; three billion gallons a day. The Amazon is so powerful that it pushes its fresh water 200 miles out to sea, where it empties into the Atlantic Ocean.

### "THE FATHER OF WATERS"
The Mississippi, the great American river, has earned its nickname. It begins as a tiny stream (only six steps across) in Lake Itasca, Minnesota, widens to a mile across where it joins the Ohio River, then ends its 2,348-mile journey at the Gulf of Mexico. The Mississippi with its tributaries passes through 31 states, providing America with 15,000 miles of transport waterways. It is America's river of music, folklore, history, and adventure.

### "CHINA'S MAIN STREET"
The Yangtze is the chief river of China. The people of China call it "The River" for it is their life stream. It is a trade river; half the commerce of all China travels on the Yangtze. It is also an agricultural river, irrigating millions of farms. One-tenth of mankind depends on the Yangtze as a means of transportation and as a source of food.

### "THE RIVER OF FAITH"

Millions of Hindus consider the Ganges River in India to be holy water. They bathe in it to wash away their sins. They have built temples near its headwaters, high in the Himalayan Mountains. They sprinkle the ashes of their dead into it to insure the dead's salvation.

### "THE RIVER THAT FLOWS TWO WAYS"

The American Indian called the Hudson River of New York "shatemuc," which means "the river that flows two ways." The name was later changed to the Hudson in honor of the European explorer, Henry Hudson. The Hudson river is known for the strong incoming ocean tides which push salt water 150 miles upstream. When the tides recede, the water flows back into the ocean. This gives the appearance of a river which flows both north and south.

### A RIVER OF INSPIRATION

The Thames River in England has been the setting and inspiration for two children's classics, *The Wind in the Willows* by Kenneth Grahame and *Alice's Adventures in Wonderland* by Lewis Carroll.

### THE RIVER OF DIAMONDS

The Orange River in South Africa might be considered the richest river in the world. It carries diamonds as it flows. The diamonds are deposited along the riverbanks where they can be picked by hand. Today, a mining company owns the valuable rights to the diamonds in this river.

### "BACKWARD"-FLOWING RIVER

The Chicago River in Illinois once emptied into Michigan. Because of industrial pollutants in the river, engineers rerouted it with a series of canals. It now flows the opposite way, into the Mississippi.

# Lakes

**World's Largest Salt Water Lake:** The Caspian Sea in the U.S.S.R., which is 760 miles long, with a total area of 143,244 square miles, about twice the size of the state of Texas.

**World's Largest Freshwater Lake:** Lake Superior in North America, which covers 31,700 square miles.

**World's Largest Underground Lake:**   The lost sea in the Craighead caverns in Sweetwater, Tennessee. It covers 4½ acres.

**World's Deepest Lake:**   Lake Baykal in Siberia, U.S.S.R. It is 5,315 feet deep.

**Deepest Lake in the U.S.:**   Crater Lake in Oregon is 1,932 feet deep.

**World's Highest Lake:**   Lake Titicaca in Peru/Bolivia, South America is 12,500 feet above sea level. It is the highest lake in the world that can be navigated by steam powered engines. An unnamed lake near Mt. Everest is 19,300 feet high but not navigable.

**World's Most Polluted Lake:**   Lake Erie, one of the Great Lakes of North America, has the greatest amount of oil-soaked debris and industrial pollution.

**Largest Manmade Lake in the U.S.:**   Lake Mead on the Arizona/Nevada border covers 28,700 acres. It is the result of the Hoover Dam.

# Deserts

- Approximately 1⅛ percent of the world's land is covered by desert.
- Every continent in the world has deserts except Europe.
- The largest desert in the world is the Sahara in northern Africa. It covers 3,320,000 square miles, almost as large as the U.S.
- The largest desert in the U.S. is the Mojave. It covers 15,000 square miles; twice the size of New Jersey.
- The sandiest desert in the world is the Arabian Desert in Africa.
- The highest desert in the world is the Atacama in northern Chile. It is 13,500 feet above sea level at its highest point.

# Caves

• Scientists who study caves are called speleologists.

• The sport of cave exploring is called "spelunking."

• The longest cave in the world is Mammoth Cave in Kentucky, U.S.A. It is 150 miles long.

• The deepest cave in the world is Goeffre de la Pierre in St. Martin, France. It is 48,360 feet deep.

• There are 11,791 known caves in the United States.

• Caves have been found in every state in the U.S. except for Rhode Island.

• The following are caves in U.S. National Parks and Monuments where guided tours are available.

1. Mammoth Cave, Kentucky
2. Mesa Verde, Colordao
3. Carlsbad Caverns, New Mexico
4. Wind Cave, South Dakota
5. Canyon de Chelly, Arizona
6. Craters of the Moon, Idaho
7. Gila Cliff Dwellings, New Mexico
8. Jewel Cave, South Dakota
9. Lehman Caves, Nevada
10. Oregon Caves, Oregon
11. Pinnacles, California
12. Timpanogos Cave, Utah
13. Walnut Canyon, Arizona

# Ten Earthquake Facts

1. The earth shakes when it releases energy. These tremors are called earthquakes.

2. About a half million earthquakes are detected by scientists each year.

3. Scientists who study earthquakes are called seismologists.

4. Seismologists have drawn two "earthquake belts" around the earth. These are the areas where earthquakes occur most frequently.

5. In 132 A.D., a Chinese mathematician devised the first instrument to measure earthquakes.

6. Today, earthquakes are measured on a scale of 1 to 9. The scale was devised by Dr. Charles Richter of the California Institute of Technology. It is called the Richter scale. This is a simple explanation of what the numbers on the Richter scale mean.

1—Felt by scientific instruments only.

2—Felt by very sensitive people and some animals.

3—Felt by most people.

4—Felt by all people.

5—Walls may crack, household objects fall.

6—Structures like smokestacks may tumble. Destructive in populated areas.

7—A major quake in which lives are lost and buildings destroyed.

8—A disaster.

9—No earthquake has yet measured 9 on this scale.

7. The worst earthquake in world history took place in China on January 23, 1556. The death toll was 830,000.

8. The worst earthquake in North America took place in Alaska on March 27, 1964. It measured 8.5 on the Richter scale.

9. The worst year for recorded earthquakes was 1976. Major tremors occurred in China, Guatemala, Indonesia, Italy, the Philippines, the U.S.S.R., and Turkey.

10. Giant waves caused by earthquakes are called tsunami, not tidal waves. Tsunami can travel at speeds of 500 mph. The largest recorded tsunami was 278 feet high. It appeared off southwest Alaska after a 1964 earthquake there.

# Legendary Creatures of the Earth

## THE ABOMINABLE SNOWMAN

The Abominable Snowman, also known as the Yeti, is said to live in the Himalayan Mountains of Asia. The natives of the Himalayas firmly believe that the Yeti is a magical creature who walks on two legs, moving about during the night and sleeping throughout the day. The Yeti has been described as a tall apelike figure covered with hair. Its head is pointed and its mouth and teeth extremely large. It is said to have a loud roar, an unusual odor, and eats other animals for food.

Only a handful of westerners have claimed sightings of this creature. However, in 1951, Eric Shipton, a mountain climber, took photographs of what was supposedly the Yeti's footprint. These photos have kept the mystery of the Abominable Snowman alive in the western world.

The people of the Himalayas consider the Yeti a real creature, not a mythical one. For example, in 1958 the country of Nepal placed the Yeti on a protected species list. In the country of Bhutan the Yeti is the national animal and stamps with pictures of this creature have been issued.

## BIGFOOT

Bigfoot is the legendary creature of North America. It's also known as the Sasquatch, a name given by the Salish Indians of Canada, which means "wild man of the woods." In 1811, mysterious footprints of this creature were found in the Canadian Rockies by an explorer, David Thompson. The footprints were 14 inches long and 8 inches wide. They did not resemble the prints of any known animal. There have been more than 750 alleged sightings of this creature. Bigfoot is said to look like a huge hairy ape, who walks upright on two feet, is over 8 feet tall, and weighs over 400 pounds. In 1967 a film was made of Bigfoot, but the film and other photographs have been dismissed by nonbelievers as those of big men dressed in ape suits.

## LOCH NESS MONSTER

"Nessie" is the nickname of this creature who is said to live in Loch Ness, a lake in northern Scotland. Nessie has been described as a 30-foot long water beast with a long thin neck, a small head, and humps on its back.

The first sighting of the Loch Ness Monster was 1,500 years ago by St. Columba. Since then more than 10,000 sightings have been reported. Photographs and films have been taken of Nessie, and the British Royal Air Force have verified the films stating that this creature does exist. Today, scientific instruments are being used to locate and catch the elusive Nessie who is now protected under British law.

# Weather

## TEN WEATHER LEGENDS

1. Rain before seven, clear for eleven.

2. Rainbow at night, sailor's delight, rainbow at morning, sailor's warning.

3. Wind in the west suits everyone best.

4. Rain is near when hair curls disappear.

5. When the dew is on the grass, rain will never come to pass.

6. A growing halo around the moon tells of the rain that's coming soon.

7. When the comb crackles through the hair look for weather clear and fair.

8. If the groundhog sees his shadow and runs right back to sleep (on February 2), then its sure for six weeks more the wintertime will keep. But if clouds block out his sight and he stays out for a fling, then by this token be assured there'll be an early spring.

9. Flies will swarm before a storm.

10. On hurricanes:

> June—too soon
> July—stand by
> August—look out
> September—you remember
> October—it's all over

## WORLD WEATHER EXTREMES

**Coldest Spot:** Plateau Station, Antarctica with an average yearly temperature of −70°F.

**Coldest Inhabited Spot:** Oymyakon, Siberia, −96°F. in 1964.

**Hottest Spot:** Dalol, Ethiopia has an average yearly temperature of 94°F.

**Sunniest Spot:** The Sahara Desert where the sun shines 97 percent of the time.

**Rainiest Spot:** Mt. Waialeale, Hawaii with an annual average rainfall of 460 inches.

**Driest Spot:** Atacama Desert, Chile; has less than 1½ inches of rain a year.

**Windiest Spot:** Mt. Washington, New Hampshire, U.S. (In 1934 a world record wind of 231 mph swirled around this mountain top.)

**Coldest Recorded Temperature:** −128.6°F. in Vostok, Antarctica on August 24, 1960.

**Hottest Recorded Temperature:** 136°F. in El Azizia, Libya on September 13, 1922.

**Greatest One Day Rainfall:** Cilaos, La Reunion, Indian Ocean, 72.62 inches, March 15–16, 1952.

**Longest Hot Spell:** 162 consecutive days of 100°F. temperatures in Marble Bar, Australia.

## U.S. WEATHER EXTREMES

**Lowest Recorded Temperature:** −79.8°F., at Prospect Creek Camp, Alaska on January 13, 1971.

**Highest Recorded Temperature:** 134°F. at Greenland Ranch, Death Valley, California on July 10, 1913.

**Greatest One Day Rainfall:** 43 inches in Alvin, Texas, from July 25–26, 1979.

**Greatest One Day Snowfall:** 75.8 inches in Silver Lake, Colordao, April 14–15, 1921.

**Longest Dry Spell:** 993 days without rain, Bagdad, California from August 18, 1909 to May 6, 1912.

**Rainiest Place:** Kukui, Hawaii averaged 704.83 inches of rain in 1982. Mount Waialele, Hawaii averages the most rainfall annually.

**Driest Place:** Death Valley, California averages 1.6 inches of rain a year.

**Rainiest U.S. State:** Louisiana averages 55 inches of rain per year.

**Driest U.S. State:** Nevada averages 9 inches of annual rainfall.

**Coldest City:** Barrow, Alaska has an average annual temperature of 9°F.

**Hottest City:** Key West, Florida has an average annual temperature of 77.4°F.

**Foggiest City:** Eureka, California with an average of 49 foggy days a year.

**Sunniest City:** Las Vegas, Nevada averages 215 clear days a year.

# WEATHER THERMOMETERS

The Fahrenheit thermometer scale was developed in 1714 by a German physicist named Gabriel Fahrenheit. The Fahrenheit scale fixes 32°F. as the freezing point, 212°F. as the boiling point of water. The Fahrenheit scale is used in the U.S.

The centigrade or Celsius scale was devised by the Swedish astronomer, Andes Celsius in 1742. Its freezing point is 0°C. Its boiling point is 100°C. The Celsius scale is used by the World Meteorological Organization.

## Temperature Conversion Chart

| Degrees Fahrenheit | Degrees Celsius |
|---|---|
| 212 | 100 (Water Boils) |
| 194 | 90 |
| 176 | 80 |
| 158 | 70 |
| 140 | 60 |
| 134 | 56.7 |
| 122 | 50 |
| 104 | 40 |
| 86 | 30 |
| 68 | 20 |
| 50 | 10 |
| 32 | 0 (Water Freezes) |
| 14 | −10 |
| −4 | −20 |
| −22 | −30 |
| −40 | −40 |
| −58 | −50 |
| −76 | −60 |
| −79.8 | −62.1 |
| −94 | −70 |
| −112 | −80 |
| −130 | −90 |
| −148 | −100 |

# WIND CHILL

In the winter there is a lot of talk about the wind chill factor. Wind chill occurs when the air temperature and wind combine to make the air feel colder than the temperature reading. It can be very dangerous. For example, when the outside temperature is zero degrees and the wind speed is 20 miles per hour, the wind chill makes it feel like the temperature is −40°F.

## WIND CHILL FACTOR CHART

| Wind Speed (mph) | Thermometer Reading (degrees Fahrenheit) | | | | | | | | | | | | | | | |
|---|---|---|---|---|---|---|---|---|---|---|---|---|---|---|---|---|
| | 35 | 30 | 25 | 20 | 15 | 10 | 5 | 0 | −5 | −10 | −15 | −20 | −25 | −30 | −35 | −40 |
| 5 | 33 | 27 | 21 | 19 | 12 | 7 | 0 | −5 | −10 | −15 | −21 | −26 | −31 | −36 | −42 | −47 |
| 10 | 22 | 16 | 10 | 3 | −3 | −9 | −15 | −22 | −27 | −34 | −40 | −46 | −52 | −58 | −64 | −71 |
| 15 | 16 | 9 | 2 | −5 | −11 | −18 | −25 | −31 | −38 | −45 | −51 | −58 | −65 | −72 | −78 | −85 |
| 20 | 12 | 4 | −3 | −10 | −17 | −24 | −31 | −39 | −46 | −53 | −60 | −67 | −74 | −81 | −88 | −95 |
| 25 | 8 | 1 | −7 | −15 | −22 | −29 | −36 | −44 | −51 | −59 | −66 | −74 | −81 | −88 | −96 | −103 |
| 30 | 6 | −2 | −10 | −18 | −25 | −33 | −41 | −49 | −56 | −64 | −71 | −79 | −86 | −93 | −101 | −109 |
| 35 | 4 | −4 | −12 | −20 | −27 | −35 | −43 | −52 | −58 | −67 | −74 | −82 | −89 | −97 | −105 | −113 |
| 40 | 3 | −5 | −13 | −21 | −29 | −37 | −45 | −53 | −60 | −69 | −76 | −84 | −92 | −100 | −107 | −115 |
| 45 | 2 | −6 | −14 | −22 | −30 | −38 | −46 | −54 | −62 | −70 | −78 | −85 | −93 | −102 | −109 | −117 |

# Hurricanes

Hurricanes are devastating tropical cyclones in which rotating winds move as fast as 75 mph and up. Each year the United States Hurricane Bureau selects 21 names for hurricanes. The names are in alphabetical order. The first storm of the year is given a name beginning with the letter A. Below is the list of names designated for the hurricanes of 1986.

## Atlantic Ocean Hurricane Names
(EAST COAST OF U.S.)

| | | |
|---|---|---|
| Andrew | Hermine | Otto |
| Bonnie | Ivan | Paula |
| Charley | Jeanne | Richard |
| Danielle | Karl | Shary |
| Earl | Lisa | Tomas |
| Frances | Mitch | Virginie |
| Georges | Nicole | Walter |

## Pacific Ocean Hurricane Names
(WEST COAST OF U.S.)

| | | |
|---|---|---|
| Agatha | Howard | Orlene |
| Blas | Isis | Paine |
| Celia | Javier | Roslyn |
| Darby | Kay | Seymore |
| Estelle | Lester | Tina |
| Frank | Marty | Virgil |
| Georgette | Newton | Winifred |

# Environment

## ENVIRONMENTAL WORD LIST

**Acid rain**—Rain tainted by chemical waste which burns and harms plant and animal life.

**Biodegradable**—Something that can be broken down into small molecules that fit into nature's cycle.

**Conservation**—Careful use and protection of nature.

**Ecology**—The study of the natural relationship of living things to their environment.

**Habitat**—The place where people, animals, and plants live and grow; the total environment of air, water, and soil.

**Oil spill**—Accidental discharge of petroleum into bodies of water which can damage water life.

**Pesticides**—Substances used to control pests; too much can poison the food supply and environment.

**Pollutant**—Anything that dirties the air, water, or ground—thereby harming living things.

**Recycle**—To collect and rework used items (such as empty cans) so that materials from which the items are made can be used again.

**Thermal pollution**—The discharge of heated water into nature's water system which can harm plants and animals.

## TEN THINGS YOU CAN DO TO
## HELP PROTECT OUR ENVIRONMENT

• Walk or ride a bike instead of asking for a ride.

• Don't litter, put your trash in cans.

• Save newspapers for recycling.

• Use both sides of your writing and drawing paper.

• Be sure to turn off all water faucets tightly.

• When you leave a room be sure to turn off the lights.

• Don't let the water run when you brush your teeth.

• Don't use the toilet as a waste basket.

• Use reusable cups and plates instead of paper ones.

• Plant trees.

## ENVIRONMENTAL SYMBOLS

Ecology

 Recycling

 Land

 Air

 Population

 Water

Noise

## ECOLOGY ORGANIZATIONS

**Defenders of Wildlife**
1346 Connecticut Avenue NW
Washington, DC 20036

**National Audubon Society**
950 Third Avenue
New York, NY 10022

**Friends of the Earth**
529 Commercial Street
San Francisco, CA 94111

**Sierra Club**
1050 Mills Tower
San Francisco, CA 94104

# Fifty Questions Kids Ask Most

1. How much does the earth weigh?
   ANSWER: Six sextillion, 588 quintillion short tons (a short ton equals
   2,000 pounds).
   SOURCE: *Van Nostrand's Scientific Encyclopedia.*

2. What is the highest city in the world?
   ANSWER: Lhasa, Tibet, which is 12,002 feet above sea level.
   SOURCE: Kurian, George Thomas; *The Book of World Rankings.*

3. Who was the real St. Nicholas?
   ANSWER: He is thought to be the Bishop of Myra, who lived in Asia
   Minor during the 4th century.
   SOURCE: Myers, Robert J., *Celebrations: The Complete Book of American Holidays.*

4. How many copies must be sold of a record for it to be awarded a gold
   record? a platinum record?
   ANSWER: In the U.S., Gold Records are awarded to single records that
   sell one million copies; Platinum Records are awarded to those selling two million copies.
   SOURCE: *The World Almanac and Book of Facts 1984*

5. Which first lady was cross-eyed?
   ANSWER: Julia Dent Grant, the wife of Ulysses S. Grant.
   SOURCE: Bassett, Margaret; *Profiles and Portraits of American Presi-
   dents and Their Wives.*

6. What does "Triskaidekaphobia" mean?
   ANSWER: Fear of the number 13.
   SOURCE: *Webster's Third New International Dictionary.*

7. What is the largest animal that is living today?
   ANSWER: The blue whale, which can weigh up to 209 tons.
   SOURCE: *Guinness Book of World Records;* 1984 edition.

8. What is the difference between "adsorption" and "absorption"?
   ANSWER: Adsorption is the assimiliation of gas, vapor, or dissolved matter by the surface of a solid or liquid. Absorption is the act or process
   of absorbing or the condition of being absorbed, e.g., soaking up.

9. What makes popcorn "pop"?
   ANSWER: Popcorn is different from other kinds of corn because its kernels have a hard, tough waterproof covering. When popcorn kernels
   are heated, this covering keeps the natural moisture inside the kernels from escaping. If the kernels are heated enough, this moisture
   turns to steam and actually explodes the kernels.
   SOURCE: *The New Book of Knowledge;* 1982, volume "C."

10. What does the word "pixilated" mean?
    ANSWER: Pixilated means somewhat unbalanced mentally; also be-
    mused or whimsical.
    SOURCE: *Webster's Ninth New Collegiate Dictionary;* 1983.

11. What is the relationship between George Washington and Robert E. Lee?

    ANSWER: Robert E. Lee was married to Martha Washington's great-granddaughter.

    SOURCE: *World Book Encyclopedia;* 1984, Vol. 12.

12. What song is known as the Black National Anthem?

    ANSWER: "Lift Every Voice and Sing" by James Weldon Johnson.

    SOURCE: *The Negro Almanac: A Reference Work on the Afro-American,* edited by Harry A. Ploski and James Williams, 4th edition, 1983.

13. Who invented the pencil?

    ANSWER: The ancient Greeks and Romans first used writing tools made of lead shortly before the birth of Christ. The first graphite pencils were made by the English in the mid-1500s. About 1650, the Germans enclosed the piece of graphite in a wooden case.

    SOURCE: *World Book Encyclopedia;* 1984, Vol. 15.

14. Who were the nine muses?

    ANSWER: In Greek mythology, the nine daughters of Zeus, king of the gods, and Mnemosyne, goddess of memory, were the nine goddesses of the arts and sciences. Calliope was the muse of epic poetry; Erato, of love poetry; Euterpe, of lyric poetry; Melpomene, of tragedy; Thalia, of comedy; Clio, of history; Urania, of astronomy; Polyhymnia, of sacred song; and Terpischore, of dance.

    SOURCE: *World Book Encyclopedia;* 1984, Vol. 13.

STATUE OF ZEUS

15. When was the first Mother's Day?

    ANSWER: The first Mother's Day was celebrated in Philadelphia on May 10, 1908. In 1914, President Woodrow Wilson issued a proclamation asking all citizens to give a public expression of reverence to mothers. In the U.S. it is celebrated on the second Sunday in May.

    SOURCE: Gregory, Ruth; *Anniversaries and Holidays.*

16. Who was the first woman doctor?

    ANSWER: Elizabeth Blackwell.

    SOURCE: Crook, Bette; *Famous Firsts in Medicine.*

17. What do you feed a crayfish?
    ANSWER: Snails, small fish, tadpoles, and young insects.
    SOURCE: *World Book Encyclopedia;* 1984, Vol. 4.

18. What is the history of the yo-yo?
    ANSWER: Yo-yos began as weapons in the hands of early inhabitants of
    the primeval jungles of the Philippines. The word comes from the
    Philippine word meaning "to return." Since then, the yo-yo has ap-
    peared in many cultures and the toy has been called many other
    names.
    SOURCE: Olney, Ross; *The Amazing Yo-Yo.*

19. Who was the first honorary United States citizen?
    ANSWER: British prime minister, Winston Churchill in 1963.
    SOURCE: *World Book Encyclopedia;* 1984, Vol. 3.

20. Who is the illustrator behind Marvel Comics?
    ANSWER: Stan Lee.
    SOURCE: *The World Encyclopedia of Comics.*

21. What are the statistics for the suicide rates of teenagers?
    ANSWER: The rates per 100,000 people between the ages of 15 and 24
    are 5.2% in 1960, 8.8% in 1970, 12.5% in 1980, and 13.0% in 1981.
    SOURCE: *U.S. News and World Report,* June 20, 1983.

22. What does the word "ginnel" mean?
    ANSWER: A narrow passage or entry between buildings; an alley.
    SOURCE: Wright, Joseph; *English Dialect Dictionary, Vol. 2.*

23. Where is the U.S. Space Camp for Children?
    ANSWER: Near the Alabama Space and Rocket Center, Huntsville,
    Alabama.
    SOURCE: *National Geographic World,* May 1983.

24. In what year did the modern Olympics begin?
    ANSWER: 1896.
    SOURCE: Giller, Norman; *The 1984 Olympics Handbook.*

25. What is the tallest building in the world?
    ANSWER: The Sears Tower in Chicago, Illinois (110 stories, 1,454 feet).
    SOURCE: *Childcraft—The How and Why Library.*

26. What was Dr. Seuss' first published children's book?
    ANSWER: *And to Think That I Saw It on Mulberry Street* (Vanguard, 1937).
    SOURCE: Commire, Anne; *Something About the Author.*

27. What was the first state to ratify the Constitution?
    ANSWER: Delaware, on December 7, 1787.
    SOURCE: *The Encyclopedia of American Facts and Dates;* edited by Gordire Carruth and Associates.

28. Which state was the first to abolish slavery?
    ANSWER: Vermont, on July 1, 1777.
    SOURCE: *The Encyclopedia of American Facts and Dates;* edited by Gordire Carruth and Associates.

29. What were the Marx Brothers' real names?
    ANSWER: Chico—Leonard; Harpo—Adolph; Groucho—Julius; Zeppo—Herbert; Gummo—Milton.
    SOURCE: *The Oxford Companion to Film;* edited by Liz-Anne Bawden.

30. What is Cinco de Mayo?
    ANSWER: A Mexican holiday recognizing the anniversary of the Battle of Puebla, May 5, 1862, in which Mexican troops, outnumbered three to one, defeated the invading French troops of Napoleon III.
    SOURCE: Chase, William D. and Helen; *Chase's Annual Events.*

31. Who discovered Cleveland?
    ANSWER: Moses Cleaveland, an agent of the Connecticut Land Company, laid out the town in 1796.
    SOURCE: *Dictionary of American History.*

32. Where is Swahili spoken?
    ANSWER: In the African countries of Kenya, Tanzania, Zaire, Uganda, Somalia, and Mozambique.
    SOURCE: *World Book Encyclopedia;* 1973, Vol. 18.

33. Who said "Don't Give Up the Ship"?
    ANSWER: Captain James Lawrence on board the U.S. frigate, *Chesapeake,* on June 1, 1813.
    SOURCE: *Bartlett's Familiar Quotations.*

34. What is the smallest mainland nation in the Western Hemisphere?
    ANSWER: El Salvador, which covers only 8,123 square miles.
    SOURCE: Wallechinsky, David and Irving Wallace; *The People's Almanac 2.*

35. When did The Today Show go on the air?
   ANSWER: January 16, 1952.
   SOURCE: Wallechinsky, David and Irving Wallace; *The People's Almanac 2.*

36. What was the Black Sox Scandal?
   ANSWER: In 1919 eight members of the Chicago White Sox baseball team accepted bribes to "fix" the World Series between the Cincinnati Reds and the White Sox. When the case went to trial in 1921, the eight were acquitted. However, Baseball Commissioner Kenesaw Mountain Landis barred the eight players from professional baseball for life.
   SOURCE: Wallechinsky, David and Irving Wallace; *The People's Almanac 2.*

37. What are the categories for the Nobel Prize?
   ANSWER: Awards have been given for Literature, Physics, Chemistry, Physiology and Medicine, and Peace since 1901. In 1969 the sixth award, for Economics, was first given.
   SOURCE: *The Concise Columbia Encyclopedia.*

38. When did people in America start paying income taxes?
   ANSWER: During the Civil War the U.S. imposed a temporary income tax; the system became permanent with the adoption of the Sixteenth Amendment to the Constitution in 1913.
   SOURCE: *The Concise Columbia Encyclopedia.*

39. What is a swastika?
   ANSWER: The swastika is an ancient symbol which was used as an ornament or a religious sign. It is in the form of a cross with the ends of the arms bent at right angles in a given direction, usually clockwise. Swastikas were widely-used symbols among the Indians of North and South America. It was adopted as the symbol of the National Socialist Party (NAZIS) in Germany in 1920 and came to stand for all evil associated with the Nazis during World War II.
   SOURCE: *World Book Encyclopedia;* 1984, Vol. 18.

40. What is the coldest temperature ever recorded in the continental United States? the hottest?
   ANSWER: The coldest recorded temperature was $-70°$ Fahrenheit ($-57°$ Celsius) recorded on January 13, 1971 at Prospect Creek Camp, Alaska. The hottest recorded temperature was 134°F. (57° Celsius) recorded on July 10, 1913 in Death Valley, California.
   SOURCE: *The American Weather Book.*

41. Is there really a Swan Lake?
    ANSWER: Even though the lake in Tchaikovsky's ballet is fictional, there are at least six small lakes named Swan Lake located in British Columbia, Manitoba, Montana, South Dakota, Utah, and New York.

42. What is Robert C. O'Brien's (author of *Mrs. Frisby and the Rats of NIMH*) real name?
    ANSWER: Robert Leslie Conly.
    SOURCE: *Twentieth Century Children's Writers;* edited by D. L. Kirkpatrick.

43. When is Bill Peet's birthday and is he still alive?
    ANSWER: January 29, and yes.
    SOURCE: *Twentieth Century Children's Writers;* edited by D. L. Kirkpatrick.

44. What causes hiccups?
    ANSWER: A sudden involuntary intake of air caused by a spasm of the diaphragm.
    SOURCE: *World Book Encyclopedia;* 1984, Vol. 9.

45. Who was the first non-native child born in America?
    ANSWER: The first child born of English parents in New England was Peregrine White, born on board the Mayflower as she lay at anchor at Cape Cod Bay on November 20, 1620.
    SOURCE: *Famous First Facts.*

46. What was the earliest animated 3-D cartoon?
    ANSWER: The first animated three-dimensional cartoon in Technicolor was Walt Disney's *Melody.* Its world premiere took place on May 28, 1953.
    SOURCE: *Famous First Facts.*

47. How often can Halley's Comet be sighted?
    ANSWER: Once every 77 years.
    SOURCE: *World Book Encyclopedia;* 1973, Vol. 9.

48. When is Diana Ross' birthday?

    ANSWER: She was born on March 26, 1944 in Detroit, Michigan.

    SOURCE: *Who's Who in Rock.*

49. Why are leaves green?

    ANSWER: Leaves are the main photosynthetic, or food manufacturing organs of plants. They are green because chlorophyll is green and chlorophyll is the major photosynthetic pigment.

    SOURCE: *Encyclopedia Americana;* 1973, Vol. 17.

50. What is the definition of "curd"?

    ANSWER: Curd is the solid product obtained by the coagulation (curdling) of milk.

    SOURCE: *Young People's Science Dictionary.*

# Index

# World Almanac Publications
# Order Form

| Quantity | ISBN | Title/Author | Unit Price | Total |
|---|---|---|---|---|
| | 31655-X | Abracadabra! Magic and Other Tricks/Lewis | $5.95/$7.95 in Canada | |
| | 32836-1 | Africa Review 1986/Green | $24.95/$33.95 in Canada | |
| | 32834-5 | Asia & Pacific Review 1986/Green | $24.95/$33.95 in Canada | |
| | 32632-6 | Ask Shagg™/Guren | $4.95/$6.50 in Canada | |
| | 32189-8 | Big Book of Kids' Lists, The/Choron | $8.95/$11.95 in Canada | |
| | 31033-0 | Civil War Almanac, The/Bowman | $10.95/$14.75 in Canada | |
| | 31503-0 | Collector's Guide to New England, The/Bowles and Bowles | $7.95/$10.95 in Canada | |
| | 31651-7 | Complete Dr. Salk: An A-to-Z Guide to Raising Your Child, The/Salk | $8.95/$11.50 in Canada | |
| | 32662-8 | Confidence Quotient: 10 Steps to Conquer Self-Doubt, The/ Gellman and Gage | $7.95/$10.75 in Canada | |
| | 32627-X | Cut Your Own Taxes and Save 1986/Metz and Kess | $3.95 | |
| | 31628-2 | Dieter's Almanac, The/Berland | $7.95/$10.25 in Canada | |
| | 32835-3 | Europe Review 1986/Green | $24.95/$33.95 in Canada | |
| | 32190-1 | Fire! Prevention: Protection: Escape/Cantor | $3.95/$4.95 in Canada | |
| | 32192-8 | For the Record: Women in Sports/Markel and Brooks | $8.95/$11.95 in Canada | |
| | 32624-5 | How I Photograph Wildlife and Nature/Rue | $9.95/$13.50 in Canada | |
| | 31709-2 | How to Talk Money/Crowe | $7.95/$10.25 in Canada | |
| | 32629-6 | I Do: How to Choose Your Mate and Have a Happy Marriage/ Eysenck and Kelly | $8.95 | |
| | 32660-1 | Kids' World Almanac of Records and Facts, The/ McLoone-Basta and Siegel | $4.95 | |
| | 32837-X | Latin America & Caribbean Review 1986/Green | $24.95/$33.95 in Canada | |
| | 32838-8 | Middle East Review 1986/Green | $24.95/$33.95 in Canada | |
| | 31652-5 | Moonlighting with Your Personal Computer/Waxman | $7.95/$10.75 in Canada | |
| | 32193-6 | National Directory of Addresses and Telephone Numbers ,The/Sites | $24.95/$33.95 in Canada | |
| | 31034-9 | Omni Future Almanac, The/Weil | $8.95/$11.95 in Canada | |
| | 32623-7 | Pop Sixties: A Personal and Irreverent Guide, The/Edelstein | $8.95/$11.95 in Canada | |
| | 32624-5 | Singles Almanac, The/Ullman | $8.95/$11.95 in Canada | |
| | 31492-1 | Social Security and You: What's New, What's True/Kingson | $2.95 | |
| | 0-915106-19-1 | Synopsis of the Law of Libel and the Right of Privacy/Sanford | $1.95 | |
| | | Twentieth Century: An Almanac, The/Ferrell | | |
| | 31708-4 | Hardcover | $24.95/$33.95 in Canada | |
| | 32630-X | Paperback | $12.95/$17.50 in Canada | |
| | 32631-8 | Vietnam War: An Almanac, The/Bowman | $24.95/$33.95 in Canada | |
| | 32188-X | Where to Sell Anything and Everything/Hyman | $8.95/$11.95 in Canada | |
| | 32659-8 | World Almanac & Book of Facts 1986, The/Lane | $5.95/$6.95 in Canada | |
| | 32661-X | World Almanac Book of Inventions , The/Giscard d'Estaing | $10.95/$14.75 in Canada | |
| | 29775-X | World Almanac Book of World War II, The/Young | $10.95/$14.75 in Canada | |
| | 0-911818-97-9 | World Almanac Consumer Information Kit 1986, The | $2.50 | |
| | 32187-1 | World Almanac Executive Appointment Book 1986, The | $17.95/$24.95 in Canada | |
| | 32628-8 | World Almanac Guide to Natural Foods, The/Ross | $8.95/$11.95 in Canada | |
| | 32194-4 | World Almanac's Puzzlink™/Considine | $2.95/$3.95 in Canada | |
| | 32626-1 | World Almanac's Puzzlink™ 2/Considine | $2.95/$3.95 in Canada | |
| | 31654-1 | World Almanac Real Puzzle™ Book, The/Rubin | $2.95/$3.95 in Canada | |
| | 32191-X | World Almanac Real Puzzle™ Book 2, The/Rubin | $2.95/$3.95 in Canada | |
| | 32625-3 | World Almanac Real Puzzle™ Book 3, The/Rubin | $2.95/$3.95 in Canada | |
| | | World of Information: see individual titles | | |

**Mail order form to:** **World Almanac Publications**
**P.O. Box 984**
**Cincinnati, Ohio 45201**

Orders must be prepaid by one of the following methods:
☐ Check or Money Order for _____ attached
☐ Bill my charge card (Add $5.00 processing charge for orders under $20.00)

Visa Account # _____ Exp. Date

Master Card Account # _____ Exp. Date

Interbank # _____ Exp. Date

Authorized Signature

Order Total_____

Ohio residents add 5.5% sales tax_____

Shipping and Handling:_____
(Add $2.50 for every purchase up to $50.00, and $1.00 for every $10.00 thereafter)

TOTAL PAYMENT_____

Ship to:
Name_____
Street address_____
City/State/Zip Code_____
Special Instructions:_____

All orders will be shipped UPS unless otherwise instructed.
We cannot ship C.O.D.